THE RAPE REFERENCE
A Resource For People At Risk

MAUREEN HARRISON & STEVE GILBERT
EDITORS

EXCELLENT BOOKS
SAN DIEGO, CALIFORNIA

EXCELLENT BOOKS
Post Office Box 927105
San Diego, CA 92192-7105

Publisher's Cataloging in Publication Data

The Rape Reference: A Resource For People At Risk/
 Maureen Harrison, Steve Gilbert, editors.
  p. cm. -
Bibliography: p.
1. Rape. 2. Rape - United States. 3. Rape - Law and Legislation - United States. 4. Rape - Bibliography. 5. Rape - Statistics. 6. Rape Victims. 7. Rape Victims - Services for. 8. Rape - Prevention. 9. Women - Crimes Against. 10. Wife rape. 11. Child sexual abuse. 12. Incest. 13. Sodomy. 14. Sodomy - United States. 15. Violent crime. 16. Sex Crimes 17. Murder
I. Title. II. Harrison, Maureen. III. Gilbert, Steve.
HV6558.R35 1995   LC 95-061243
364.1'53-dc20

ISBN 1-880780-07-0

The horror of rape entered our lives
when our cousin, Betty,
was raped and murdered.

The Rape Reference is dedicated to her memory.

She was somebody's daughter.

She was somebody's mother.

She was somebody's sister.

She was somebody's friend.

She was loved by all who knew her.

Warning - Disclaimer

The Rape Reference is designed to provide information in regard to the subject matter covered. It is sold with the understanding that the publisher and editors are not engaged in rendering legal or other professional services. If legal or other expert assistance is required, the services of a competent professional should be sought.

It is not the purpose of *The Rape Reference* to reprint all the information that is otherwise available to the editors and/or publisher, but to complement, amplify and supplement other texts. You are urged to read the complete and original texts of all the available material, learn as much as possible about rape and rape survival, and tailor the information to your individual needs.

Every effort has been made to make *The Rape Reference* as complete and accurate as possible. However, there may be mistakes, both typographical and in content. Therefore, this text should be used only as a general guide and not as the ultimate source. Furthermore, *The Rape Reference* contains information only up to the printing date.

The purpose of *The Rape Reference* is to educate and inform. The editors and publisher shall have neither liability nor responsibility to any person or entity with respect to any loss or damage caused, directly or indirectly, by the information contained in this book.

Some words and phrases contained in *The Rape Reference* may be offensive to certain individuals. These words and phrases are an integral part of the official texts of federal and state rape laws and are used only to define medical, anatomical, or legal terms. No appeal to prurient interest is in any way intended or to be inferred.

Introduction

From prehistoric times to the present, I believe, rape has played a critical function. It is nothing more or less than a conscious process of intimidation by which all men keep all women in a state of fear. Susan Brownmiller, **Against Our Will**[1]

Rape is any sexual penetration, however slight, of the oral, vaginal, or anal openings of a person, committed against their will and without their consent, by the use of force, fear, or violence. Rape is not sex - it is sexual violence.

No one is immune from rape: An average of over 105,000 rape attacks have been *reported* for each of the first five years of this decade.[2] As few as 520,000[3] to as many as 2,000,000[4] additional rape attacks may have gone *unreported* for these years. The latest national *reported* rape rate for females above the age of sexual consent (between 15 and 21 depending on their state of residence) is 78 for every 100,000.[5] The *unreported* national rape rate for every 100,000 females could be anywhere from five to twenty times higher, anywhere from 390 to 1,560.

No place is immune from rape: The latest regional *reported* rape rates for each 100,000 females are 53 the Northeast, 87 in the South, 86 in the Midwest, and 80 in the West.[6] These rape rates are also subject to multiplication by from five to twenty.

98.9% of rape victims are female.[7] 98.7% of rapists are male.[8]

This is the arithmetic of rape: An estimated minimum of 12,000 women are raped in America every week.[9] Of these rapes, an estimated minimum of 84 per cent will go unreported,[10] leaving the police about 2,000 reported rapes. Of these reported rapes, the police will fail to make an arrest in about 62 percent of cases,[11] leaving about 760 individuals accused of rape. Of these accused rapists, prosecutors will fail to obtain a conviction, either because of dismissal or acquittal, in about 54 percent of cases,[12] leaving only about 350 convicted rapists awaiting sentence. Of these convicted rapists, judges will fail to sentence about 44 percent to more than one year in jail,[13] leaving only 200 rapists, or slightly more than *1-1/2 percent,* of all rapes resulting in a jail sentence of more than one year. This is the justice system's "2 percent solution" to the crime of rape.

Few rape cases, only the gruesome or the scandalous, ever come to public attention: the "Pool Table Rape" in New Bedford, Massachusetts; the Tawana Brawley "Cry Rape!" case in Wappingers Falls, New York; the "Broom Stick Rape" in Glen Ridge, New Jersey; the "Central Park Jogger Rape" in New York City; the "Condom and Consent" rape in Austin, Texas; the "Coma Rape" in Rochester, New York, the "Halloween Horror Rape-Murder" in Boston, Massachusetts; the rape acquittal of William Kennedy Smith in Palm Beach, Florida; the rape conviction of Mike Tyson in Indianapolis, Indiana. Even Hollywood's depictions of rape - *The Accused; To Kill a Mockingbird; A Street Car Named Desire; Johnny Belinda* - are far more known to the public than most actual rapes.

The vast majority of rapes take place in obscurity. The personal tragedy, physical outrage, and private mental anguish of these rapes are hidden away from the public view, banished to the dark corners of the American mind.

The purpose of *The Rape Reference* is to throw the full blinding cleansing light of day onto the hidden subject of rape - to educate, inform, and assist the lay reader in all aspects of rape. *The Rape Reference* collects in one complete resource: the laws of rape; the "the who, what, when, where" statistics of sexual assault; the expert writings on sexual abuse; the plain meaning of medical-legal sex crimes jargon; and the places of refuge from sexual violence.

The information contained in *The Rape Reference* is drawn from the most current and authoritative sources available and is designed by the editors, a law librarian and a textbook editor, to be an easy-to-read, easy-to-use, all-in-one resource on all aspects of rape and other forms of sexual violence. *The Rape Reference* is made up of five complementary elements:

In Chapter I: *America's Rape Laws*, you will find selected excerpts from the current rape laws of all fifty states and the District of Columbia, edited into plain non-legal English. These selected edited excerpts of each state's rape laws are all based on the official "black letter" rape law in each state's criminal code, translated from esoteric legalese to plain English without altering either the original content or context of the law.

In Chapter II: *Rape Statistics For The 1990's*, you will find rape facts and figures drawn from the single most authoritative criminal justice source available. These rape statistics are broken down into: *Rape Statistics By Regions*, *Rape Statistics By States*, and *Rape Statistics By Cities*. In each section, and for each year, you will find both the total number of reported rapes and - so that different regions, states, and cities can be compared - the total reported rape rates. This is the most up-to-date, comprehensive collection of rape statistics available today.

In Chapter III: *Rape Readings*, you will find a reading list for those most at risk - hundreds of books on every aspect of rape written not in technical "expert-to-expert" jargon but in plain "person-to-person" English. *Rape Readings* is a reading list to make you think, and rethink, everything you thought you knew about the causes, prevention, treatment, and aftermath of rape.

In Chapter IV: *The Rape Glossary*, you will find complete, plain-English definitions of the many medical and legal words and phrases associated with rape. From A: *Acquaintance Rape* to W: *Wife Rape*, the purpose of *The Rape Glossary* is to clearly explain the technical-medical-legal language of rape to the lay reader.

In Chapter V: *America's Rape Hot Lines*, you will find a listing of the rape counseling and crisis intervention telephone hot lines serving nearly three hundred cities and towns - urban, suburban, and rural - in every state throughout the nation. Help is out there. *America's Rape Hot Lines* can help you find it.

The basic message of this book is an ugly truth:

Rape is a fact of life.

The Rape Reference is about the facts of rape.

M.H. & S.G.

Footnotes To The Introduction

[1]Brownmiller, Susan. *Against Our Will: Men, Women, and Rape.* New York, NY: Simon & Schuster, 1975.

[2] United States Justice Department. Federal Bureau of Investigation. *Crime in the United States.*

[3]United States Senate. Judiciary Committee. *Violence Against Women.*

University of South Carolina. National Victim Center. *Rape in America.*

[4]United States Senate. Judiciary Committee. *The Response to Rape.*

[5]United States Justice Department. Federal Bureau of Investigation. *Crime in the United States.*

[6]United States Justice Department. Federal Bureau of Investigation. *Crime in the United States.*

[7]United States Justice Department. Bureau of Justice Statistics. *Sourcebook of Criminal Justice Statistics.*

[8]United States Justice Department. Federal Bureau of Investigation. *Crime in the United States.*

[9]United States Senate. Judiciary Committee. *Violence Against Women.*

[10]University of South Carolina. National Victim Center. *Rape in America.*

[11]United States Justice Department. Federal Bureau of Investigation. *Crime in the United States.*

[12]United States Senate. Judiciary Committee. *The Response to Rape.*

[13]United States Justice Department. Bureau of Justice Statistics. *Felony Sentences in State Courts.*

Table of Contents

America's Rape Laws

The controversy between rule of law and rule of men was never relevant to women - because, along with juveniles, imbeciles, and other classes of legal nonpersons, they had no access to law except through men.

Freda Adler
Sisters In Crime[1]

An early twentieth century definition of rape might have once read:

> **Criminal Rape:** Unlawful carnal knowledge of a woman by force and without her consent.
>
> (1) The carnal knowledge must be unlawful; thus, forcible carnal knowledge by a man against his wife is not rape.
>
> (2) The carnal knowledge must be without the woman's consent or "against her will." Unless asleep or insensible or intimidated by threats, the woman must resist "to the uttermost," that is, to the point of physical inability to resist. Acquiescence to carnal knowledge, however late or reluctant, prevents the offence from being rape.

Times change. Laws evolve. A late twentieth century definition of rape is now likely to read:

> **Rape.** An act of sexual intercourse without legal consent.
>
> (1) Sexual intercourse is committed by any penetration, however slight, and includes vaginal intercourse, anal intercourse, fellatio, cunnilingus, or analingus between persons, regardless of their sex.
>
> (2) Legal consent means positive cooperation in a sexual act pursuant to free will. Neither a legal marital relationship, a non-marital live-in relationship, nor a current dating relationship constitutes legal consent.

In *America's Rape Laws* you will find selected edited excerpts from the current rape laws of all fifty states and the District of Columbia. These selected edited excerpts of rape laws are all drawn from the official "black letter" law as found in each state's criminal codes. These "black letter" laws have gone through a two-step selection/editing process before their inclusion in the *The Rape Reference*.

First, we have made "look and feel" selections from each jurisdiction's basic rape laws. Every state has written into its rape laws certain general rape provisions and we look at many of these basic rape laws to give the reader a feel for how each state protects the innocent, prosecutes the accused, and punishes the guilty. These basic rape provisions define the terms, describe the crimes, and prescribe the punishments for rape, forcible sodomy, sexual torture, sexual assault, object rape, and rape and murder. Also included in these basic provisions are the laws covering statutory, spousal, gang, and date rape and child molestation.

In addition to these basic rape law provisions, some states have begun to enact new rape laws to cover evolving rape crimes such as AIDS- , elder- , and condom rape. Other states have enacted unique rape laws in response to specific local crimes. (While this book was still in production New Jersey enacted a sexual predator community notification law in reaction to the rape and murder of 7-year-old Megan Kanka by a convicted rapist, who had been released without any forewarning into her neighborhood. "Megan's Law" notifies all persons of the presence in their community of paroled sex offenders. We "stopped the presses!" to include this important new law in *The Rape Reference*.)

We have made every effort to include representative samples of the basic, evolving and unique rape laws in *America's Rape Laws* in order to give the reader a real "look and feel" for the varying degrees of protection afforded them by their respective states.

Second, for all these selected "look" and "feel" provisions we have made every effort to carefully edit out and replace the esoteric legalese in which these laws were written with plain non-legal English. In this translation process we have been guided by Justice Joseph Story's common sense statement: "The law must not be foreign to the ears of those who are to obey it."

In American law, legal speak (the esoteric language of the law) is the rule, plain speak (everyday English) the exception. Justice Story's plain speak statement turned into legal speak might read:

> Rules of conduct prescribed by controlling authority shall not in any way whatsoever be communicated in any language that is in whole or part so obfuscated as to cause the citizens subject to the sanctions thereto or legal consequences thereof hereinbefore provided to be denied any right, expressed or implied, in the foregoing.

In *America's Rape Laws* we have made every effort to translate esoteric legal speak to easy-to-read plain speak English without altering either the original content or context of the law. If we have erred in editing out this legalese it was consciously on the side of caution. Where indicated by [brackets] we have added plain English definitions of esoteric legal terms and where indicated by ellipses (. . . .) we have deleted redundant "wherefore/therefore" sections.

These selected edited excerpts do not contain the complete rape laws for any one state. For each state we have provided at the end of the edited selection a citation to the original state criminal code sources of the "black letter" rape law provisions. These provisions can be found in your state's criminal code at either your local public library, law school library, or county law library. It is these official "black letter" rape law provisions, not our selected edited excerpts, that are the law of each jurisdiction.

[1]Adler, Freda. *Sisters in Crime.* New York, NY: McGraw-Hill, 1975.

ALABAMA'S RAPE LAWS

Definitions

Sexual Intercourse. Such term has its ordinary meaning and occurs upon any penetration, however slight; emission is not required.

Deviate Sexual Intercourse. Any act of sexual gratification between persons not married to each other involving the sex organs of one person and the mouth or anus of another.

Sexual Contact. Any touching of the sexual or other intimate parts of a person not married to the actor, done for the purpose of gratifying the sexual desire of either party.

Female. Any female person.

Mentally Defective. Such term means that a person suffers from a mental disease or defect which renders him incapable of appraising the nature of his conduct.

Mentally Incapacitated. Such term means that a person is rendered temporarily incapable of appraising or controlling his conduct owing to the influence of a narcotic or intoxicating substance administered to him without his consent, or to any other incapacitating act committed upon him without his consent.

Physically Helpless. Such term means that a person is unconscious or for any other reason is physically unable to communicate unwillingness to an act.

Forcible Compulsion. Physical force that overcomes earnest resistance or a threat, express or implied, that places a person in fear of immediate death or serious physical injury to himself or another person.

(Alabama Criminal Code 13A-6-60)

First Degree Rape

A male commits the crime of rape in the first degree if:

(1) he engages in sexual intercourse with a female by forcible compulsion; or

(2) he engages in sexual intercourse with a female who is incapable of consent by reason of being physically helpless or mentally incapacitated; or

(3) he, being sixteen years or older, engages in sexual intercourse with a female who is less than twelve years old.

Rape in the first degree is a Class A Felony.

(Alabama Criminal Code 13A-6-61)

Second Degree Rape

A male commits the crime of rape in the second degree if:

(1) being sixteen years old or older, he engages in sexual intercourse with a female less than sixteen and more than twelve years old; provided, the actor is at least two years older than the female.

(2) he engages in sexual intercourse with a female who is incapable of consent by reason of being mentally defective.

Rape in the second degree is a Class B Felony.

(Alabama Criminal Code 13A-6-62)

First Degree Sodomy

A person commits the crime of sodomy in the first degree if:

(1) he engages in deviate sexual intercourse with another person by forcible compulsion; or

(2) he engages in deviate sexual intercourse with a person who is incapable of consent by reason of being physically helpless or mentally incapacitated; or

(3) he, being sixteen years old or older, engages in deviate sexual intercourse with a person who is less than twelve years old.

Sodomy in the first degree is a Class A Felony.

(Alabama Criminal Code 13A-6-63)

Second Degree Sodomy

A person commits the crime of sodomy in the second degree if:

(1) he, being sixteen years old or older, engages in deviate sexual intercourse with another person less than sixteen and more than twelve years old; or

(2) he engages in deviate sexual intercourse with a person who is incapable of consent by reason of being mentally defective.

Sodomy in the second degree is a Class B Felony.
(Alabama Criminal Code 13A-6-64)

Sexual Misconduct

A person commits the crime of sexual misconduct if:

(1) being a male, he engages in sexual intercourse with a female without her consent, under circumstances other than those covered by [the above Rape provisions]; or with her consent where consent was obtained by the use of any fraud or artifice; or

(2) being a female, she engages in sexual intercourse with a male without his consent; or

(3) he or she engages in deviate sexual intercourse with another person under circumstances other than those covered by [the above Sodomy provisions]. Consent is no defense to a prosecution under this [provision].

Sexual misconduct is a Class A misdemeanor.
(Alabama Criminal Code 13A-6-65)

Sexual Torture

A person commits the crime of sexual torture:

(1) by penetrating the vagina or anus or mouth of another person with an inanimate object by forcible compulsion with the intent to sexually torture or to sexually abuse;

(2) by penetrating the vagina or anus or mouth of a person who is incapable of consent by reason of physical helplessness or mental incapacity with an inani-

mate object, with the intent to sexually torture or to sexually abuse; or

(3) by penetrating the vagina or anus or mouth of a person who is less than twelve years old with an inanimate object, by a person who is sixteen years old or older with the intent to sexually torture or to sexually abuse.

The crime of sexual torture is a Class A felony.
(Alabama Criminal Code 13A-6-65.1)

First Degree Sexual Abuse

A person commits the crime of sexual abuse in the first degree if:

(1) he subjects another person to sexual contact by forcible compulsion; or

(2) he subjects another person to sexual contact who is incapable of consent by reason of being physically helpless or mentally incapacitated; or

(3) he, being sixteen years old or older, subjects another person to sexual contact who is less than twelve years old.

Sexual abuse in the first degree is a Class C felony.
(Alabama Criminal Code 13A-6-66)

Second Degree Sexual Abuse

A person commits the crime of sexual abuse in the second degree if:

(1) he subjects another person to sexual contact who is incapable of consent by reason of some factor other than being less than sixteen years old; or

(2) he, being nineteen years old or older, subjects another person to sexual contact who is less than sixteen years old, but more than twelve years old.

Sexual abuse in the second degree is a Class A misdemeanor.
(Alabama Criminal Code 13A-6-67)

Rape and Murder

A person commits the crime of murder if he commits or attempts to commit first degree rape [or] first degree sodomy and, in the course of committing or attempting to commit the crime of rape or sodomy, or in immediate flight therefrom, he or another participant, if there be any, causes the death of any person. (Alabama Criminal Code 13A-6-2)

The complete and unedited text of Alabama's rape laws excerpted above can be found in the Criminal Code of the Acts of Alabama.

ALASKA'S RAPE LAWS

Definitions

Without consent means that a person with or without resisting, is coerced by the use of force against a person or property, or by the express or implied threat of death, imminent physical injury, or kidnapping to be inflicted on anyone; or is incapacitated as a result of an act of the defendant.

Incapacitated means temporarily incapable of appraising the nature of one's own conduct and physically unable to express unwillingness to act.

Mentally incapable means suffering from a mental disease or defect that renders the person incapable of understanding the nature or consequences of the person's conduct, including the potential for harm to that person.

Sexual penetration means genital intercourse, cunnilingus, fellatio, anal intercourse, or an intrusion, however slight, of an object or any part of a person's body into the genital or anal opening of another person's body.

Sexual contact means the defendant's knowingly touching, directly or through clothing, the victim's genitals, anus, or female breast.

Victim means the person alleged to have been subjected to sexual assault in any degree or sexual abuse of a minor in any degree.

(Alaska Criminal Law 11.41.470)

First Degree Sexual Assault

A person commits the crime of sexual assault in the first degree if:

(1) being any age, the defendant engages in sexual penetration with another person without consent of that person;

(2) being any age, the defendant attempts to engage in sexual penetration with another person without consent of that person and causes serious physical injury to that person;

(3) being over the age of eighteen, the defendant engages in sexual penetration with another person:

(a) who the defendant knows is mentally incapable; and

(b) who is entrusted to the defendant's care [either] by authority of law, or in a facility or program that is required by law to be licensed by the Department of Health and Social Services.

Sexual assault in the first degree is an unclassified felony and is punishable as provided [by law].

(Alaska Criminal Law 11.41.410)

Second Degree Sexual Assault

An offender commits the crime of sexual assault in the second degree if:

(1) the offender engages in sexual contact with another person without the consent of that person;

(2) being over the age of eighteen, the offender engages in sexual contact with a person:

(a) who the offender knows is mentally incapable; and

(b) who is entrusted to the offender's care [either] by authority of law, or in a facility or program that is required by law to be licensed by the [Alaska] Department of Health and Social Services; or

(3) being over the age of eighteen, the offender engages in sexual penetration with a person who the offender knows is:

(a) mentally incapable; or

(b) incapacitated.

Sexual assault in the second degree is a Class B felony.

(Alaska Criminal Law 11.41.420)

Third Degree Sexual Assault

An offender commits the crime of sexual assault in the third degree if, being over the age of eighteen, the offender engages in sexual contact with a person who the offender knows is:

(1) mentally incapable; or

(2) temporarily incapable of appraising the nature of the person's conduct and is physically unable to express unwillingness to act.

Sexual assault in the third degree is a Class C felony.
(Alaska Criminal Law 11.41.425)

First Degree Sexual Abuse of a Minor

An offender commits the crime of sexual abuse of a minor in the first degree if:

(1) being sixteen years of age or older, the offender engages in sexual penetration with a person who is under thirteen years of age or aids, induces, causes, or encourages a person who is under thirteen years of age to engage in sexual penetration with another person;

(2) being eighteen years of age or older, the offender engages in sexual penetration with a person who is under the age of eighteen years of age and who:

(a) is entrusted to the offender's care by authority of law; or

(b) is the offender's son or daughter, including an illegitimate or adopted child, or a stepchild; or

(3) being eighteen years of age or older, the offender engages in sexual penetration with a person who is under sixteen years of age, and the victim at the time of the offense is:

(a) residing as a member of the social unit in the same household as the offender and the offender is in a position of authority over the victim; or

(b) temporarily entrusted to the offender's care.

Sexual abuse of a minor in the first degree is an unclassified felony and is punishable as provided [by law].
(Alaska Criminal Law 11.41.434)

Second Degree Sexual Abuse of a Minor

An offender commits the crime of sexual abuse of a minor in the second degree if:

(1) being sixteen years of age or older, the offender engages in sexual penetration with a person who is thirteen, fourteen, or fifteen years of age and at least three years younger than the offender, or aids, induces, causes or encourages a person who is thirteen,

fourteen, or fifteen years of age and at least three years younger than the offender to engage in sexual penetration with another person;

(2) being sixteen years of age or older, the offender engages in sexual contact with a person who is under the age of thirteen years of age or aids, induces, causes, or encourages a person under thirteen years of age to engage in sexual contact with another person;

(3) being eighteen years of age or older, the offender engages in sexual contact with a person who is under eighteen years of age and who:

(a) is entrusted to the offender's care by authority of law; or

(b) is the offender's son or daughter, including an illegitimate or adopted child, or a stepchild;

(4) being sixteen years of age or older, the offender aids induces, causes, or encourages a person who is under sixteen years of age to engage in conduct described in [the section of the law dealing with unlawful exploitation of a minor]; or

(5) being eighteen years of age or older, the offender engages in sexual contact with a person who is under sixteen years of age, and the victim at the time of the offense is:

(a) residing as a member of the social unit in the same household as the offender and the offender is in a position of authority over the victim; or

(b) temporarily entrusted to the offender's care.

Sexual abuse of a minor in the second degree is a Class B felony. (Alaska Criminal Law 11.41.436/.455)

Third Degree Sexual Abuse of a Minor

An offender commits the crime of sexual abuse of a minor in the third degree if, being sixteen years of age, the offender engages in sexual contact with a person who is thirteen, fourteen, or fifteen years and at least three years younger than the offender.

Sexual abuse of a minor in the third degree is a Class C felony. (Alaska Criminal Law 11.41.438)

Fourth Degree Sexual Abuse of a Minor

An offender commits the crime of sexual abuse of a minor in the fourth degree if being sixteen years of age or older, the offender engages in sexual penetration or sexual contact with a person who is under thirteen years of age and at least three years younger than the offender.

Sexual abuse of a minor in the fourth degree is a Class A misdemeanor.

(Alaska Criminal Law 11.41.440)

Spousal Rape

It is a defense to first, second, and third degree sexual assault that the offender is married to the person and neither party has filed with the court for a separation, divorce, or dissolution of the marriage. (Alaska Criminal Law 11.41.432)

Rape and Murder

A person commits the crime of murder in the second degree if, acting alone or with one or more persons, the person commits or attempts to commit first or second degree sexual assault and, in the course of either crime, or in immediate flight from that crime, any person causes the death of a person other than one of the participants. (Alaska Criminal Law 11.41.110)

The complete and unedited text of Alaska's rape laws excerpted above can be found in the Criminal Law of the Alaska Session Laws or Alaska Statutes.

ARIZONA'S RAPE LAWS

Definitions

Oral sexual contact means oral contact with the penis, vulva, or anus.

Sexual contact means any direct or indirect fondling or manipulating of any part of the genitals, anus, or female breast.

Sexual intercourse means penetration into the penis, vulva, or anus by any part of the body or by any object or manual masturbatory contact with the penis or vulva.

Spouse means a person who is legally married and cohabiting.

Without consent includes any of the following:

(a) the victim is coerced by the immediate use or threatened use of force against a person or property;

(b) the victim is incapable of consent by reason of mental disorder, drugs, alcohol, sleep, or any other similar impairment of cognition and such condition is known or should have reasonably been known to the defendant;

(c) the victim is intentionally deceived as to the nature of the act;

(d) the victim is intentionally deceived to erroneously believe that the person is the victim's spouse.

(Arizona Criminal Code 13-1401)

Sexual Abuse

A person commits sexual abuse by intentionally or knowingly engaging in sexual contact with any person fifteen or more years of age without consent of that person or with any person who is under fifteen years of age if the sexual contact involves only the female breast.

Sexual abuse is a Class 5 felony unless the victim is under fifteen years of age, in which case sexual abuse is a Class 3 felony.

(Arizona Criminal Code 13-1404)

Sexual Conduct with a Minor

A person commits sexual conduct with a minor by intentionally or knowingly engaging in sexual intercourse or oral sexual contact with any person who is under eighteen years of age.

Sexual conduct with a minor under fifteen years of age is a Class 2 felony. Sexual conduct with a minor fifteen years of age or over is a Class 6 felony.

(Arizona Criminal Code 13-1405)

Sexual Assault

A person commits sexual assault by intentionally or knowingly engaging in sexual intercourse or oral sexual contact with any person without consent of such person.

Sexual assault is a Class 2 felony. The person convicted is not eligible for suspension or commutation of sentence, probation, pardon, parole, work furlough, or release from confinement on any other basis . . . until the sentence imposed by the court has been served. If the victim is under fifteen years of age, sexual assault is punishable pursuant to [the section of the law dealing with dangerous crimes against children].

[I]f the sexual assault involved the use or exhibition of a deadly weapon or dangerous instrument or involved the intentional or knowing infliction of serious physical injury and the person has previously been convicted of sexual assault, or any offense committed outside this state which if committed in this state would constitute sexual assault, the person shall be sentenced to life imprisonment and is not eligible for suspension or commutation of sentence, probation, pardon, parole, work furlough, or release from confinement on any other basis . . . until twenty-five years have been served.

(Arizona Criminal Code 13-1406/-604.01)

Sexual Assault of a Spouse

A person commits sexual assault of a spouse by intentionally or knowingly engaging in sexual intercourse or oral sexual contact

with a spouse without consent of the spouse by the immediate or threatened use of force against the spouse or another.
A first offense sexual assault of a spouse is a Class 6 felony. Any subsequent sexual assault of a spouse is a Class 2 felony and the person convicted is not eligible for suspension or commutation of sentence, probation, pardon, parole, work furlough, or release from confinement on any other basis . . . until the sentence imposed by the court has been served.
(Arizona Criminal Code 13-1406.01)

Child Molestation

A person who knowingly molests a child under the age of fifteen years by directly or indirectly touching the private parts of such child or who causes a child under the age of fifteen years to directly or indirectly touch the private parts of such person is guilty of a Class 2 felony [and the person convicted is not eligible for suspension or commutation of sentence, probation, pardon, parole, work furlough, or release from confinement on any other basis . . . until the sentence imposed by the court has been served.] (Arizona Criminal Code 13-1410)

Rape and Murder

A person commits first degree murder if, acting either alone or with one or more other persons, such person commits or attempts to commit sexual conduct with a minor, sexual assault, or child molestation, and, in the course of such offense or immediate flight from such offense, such person or another person causes the death of any person.
First degree murder is a Class 1 felony and is punishable by death or life imprisonment.
(Arizona Criminal Code 13-1105)

The complete and unedited text of Arizona's rape laws excerpted above can be found in the Criminal Code of the Arizona Session Laws *or the* Arizona Revised Statutes Annotated.

ARKANSAS' RAPE LAWS

Definitions

Deviate sexual activity means any act of sexual gratification involving:

   (a) the penetration, however slight, of the anus or mouth of one person by the penis of another person; or

   (b) the penetration, however slight, of the vagina or anus of one person by any body member or foreign instrument manipulated by another person.

Forcible compulsion means physical force or a threat, expressed or implied, of death or physical injury to or kidnapping of any person.

Mentally defective means that a person suffers from a mental disease or defect which renders him incapable of appreciating the nature of his conduct.

Mentally incapacitated means that a person is temporarily incapable of appreciating or controlling his conduct as a result of the influence of a controlled or intoxicating substance administered to him without his consent.

Physically helpless means that a person is unconscious or is physically unable to communicate lack of consent.

Public place means a publicly or privately owned place to which the public or substantial numbers of people have access.

Public view means observable or likely to be observed by a person in a public place.

Sexual contact means any act of sexual gratification involving the touching, directly or through clothing, of the sex organs, or buttocks, or anus of a person or the breast of a female.

Sexual intercourse means penetration, however slight, of a vagina by a penis.

Guardian means a parent, stepparent, legal guardian, legal custodian, foster parent, or anyone who, by virtue of a living arrangement, is placed in an apparent position of power or authority over a minor.

(Arkansas Sexual Offenses 5-14-101)

Rape

A person commits rape if he engages in sexual intercourse or deviate sexual activity with another person:

(1) by forcible compulsion; or

(2) who is incapable of consent because he is physically helpless;

(3) who is less than fourteen years of age; or

(4) not his spouse who is less than sixteen years of age and who is incapable of consent because he is mentally defective or mentally incapacitated.

Rape is a Class Y felony.

(Arkansas Sexual Offenses 5-14-103)

Carnal Abuse

A person commits carnal abuse in the first degree if, being under the age of eighteen, he engages in sexual intercourse or deviate sexual activity with another person not his spouse who is less than fourteen years old.

A person commits carnal abuse in the second degree if he engages in sexual intercourse or deviate sexual activity with another person not his spouse who is incapable of consent because he is mentally defective or mentally incapacitated.

A person commits carnal abuse in the third degree if, being twenty years old or older, he engages in sexual intercourse or deviate sexual activity with another person not his spouse who is less than sixteen years old.

Carnal abuse in the first degree is a Class B felony, in the second degree a Class D felony, in the third degree a Class A misdemeanor.

(Arkansas Sexual Offenses 5-14-104-6)

Sexual Misconduct

A person commits sexual misconduct if he engages in sexual intercourse or deviate sexual activity with another person not his spouse who is less than sixteen years old.

Sexual misconduct is a Class B misdemeanor.

(Arkansas Sexual Offenses 5-14-107)

Sexual Abuse

A person commits sexual abuse in the first degree if:

(1) he engages in sexual contact with another person by forcible compulsion;

(2) he engages in sexual contact with another person who is incapable of consent because he is physically helpless;

(3) being eighteen years old or older, he engages in sexual contact with a person not his spouse who is less than fourteen years old; or

(4) he engages in sexual contact with a person who is less than sixteen years of age and who is incapable of consent because he is mentally defective or mentally incapacitated.

A person commits sexual abuse in the second degree if:

(1) he engages in sexual contact with another person not his spouse who is incapable of consent because he is mentally defective or mentally incapacitated;

(2) being less than eighteen years old, he engages in sexual contact with a person not his spouse who is less than fourteen years old.

Sexual abuse in the first degree is a Class C felony, in the second degree a Class A misdemeanor.
(Arkansas Sexual Offenses 5-14-104-8/9)

Sexual Solicitation of a Child

A person commits sexual solicitation of a child if, being eighteen years old or older, he solicits any person not his spouse who is less than fourteen years old to engage in sexual intercourse, deviate sexual activity, or sexual contact.
Sexual solicitation of a child is a Class A misdemeanor.
(Arkansas Sexual Offenses 5-14-104-10)

Violation of a Minor

A person commits the offense of violation of a minor in the first degree if he engages in sexual intercourse or deviate sexual activity with another person not his spouse, who is more than thirteen years of age and less than eighteen years of age, and the actor is the minor's guardian, an employee in the minor's school or school district, a temporary caretaker, or a person in a position of trust or authority of the minor.

A person commits the offense of violation of a minor in the second degree if he engages in sexual contact with another person not his spouse, who is more than thirteen years of age and less than eighteen years of age, and the actor is the minor's guardian, an employee in the minor's school or school district, a temporary caretaker, or a person in a position of trust or authority of the minor. Violation of a minor in the first degree is a Class C felony, in the second degree a Class D felony. (Arkansas Sexual Offenses 5-14-120/121)

Exposing Another Person to the HIV Virus

A person with acquired immunodeficiency syndrome (AIDS) or who tests positive for the presence of human immunodeficiency virus (HIV) is infectious to others through the exchange of body fluids during sexual intercourse and . . . is a danger to the public.

A person commits the offense of exposing another to human immunodeficiency virus if the person knows he or she has tested positive for human immunodeficiency virus and engages in sexual penetration with another person without first having informed the other person of the presence of human immunodeficiency virus.

As used in this section, **sexual penetration** means sexual intercourse, cunnilingus, fellatio, anal intercourse, or any other intrusion, however slight, of any part of a person's body or of any object into the genital or anal openings of another person's body, but emission of semen is not required.

Exposing another to human immunodeficiency virus is a Class A felony.
(Arkansas Sexual Offenses 5-14-123)

Rape and Murder

A person commits capital murder if, acting alone or with one or more other persons, he commits or attempts to commit rape, and in the course of and in furtherance of the crime, or in immediate flight therefrom, he or an accomplice causes the death of any person under circumstances manifesting extreme indifference to the value of human life. Capital murder is punishable by death or life imprisonment without parole. (Arkansas Criminal Offenses 5-10-101)

The complete and unedited text of Arkansas' rape laws excerpted above can be found in The General Acts of Arkansas *or* Arkansas Statutes Annotated.

CALIFORNIA'S RAPE LAWS

Definitions

Threatening to retaliate means a threat to kidnap or falsely imprison, or to inflict extreme pain, serious bodily injury, or death.

Public official means a person employed by a governmental agency who has the authority, as part of that position, to incarcerate, arrest, or deport another. The perpetrator does not actually have to be a public official.

Duress means a direct or implied threat of force, violence, danger, or retribution sufficient to coerce a reasonable person of ordinary susceptibilities to perform an act which otherwise would not have been performed, or acquiesce in an act to which one otherwise would not have submitted. The total circumstances, including the age of the victim, and his or her relationship to the defendant, are factors to consider in appraising the existence of duress.

Menace means any threat, declaration, or act which shows an intention to inflict an injury upon another.

Unconscious of the nature of the act means incapable of resisting because the victim meets one of the following conditions:

(a) was unconscious or asleep;

(b) was not aware, knowing, perceiving, or cognizant that the act occurred; or

(c) was not aware, knowing, perceiving, or cognizant of the essential characteristics of the act due to the perpetrator's fraud in fact.

(California Penal Code 261)

Rape

Rape is an act of sexual intercourse accomplished with a person not the spouse of the perpetrator, under any of the following circumstances:

(1) where a person is incapable, because of a mental disorder or developmental disability, of giving legal consent, and this is known or reasonably should be known to the person committing the act;

(2) where it is accomplished against a person's will by means of force, violence, duress, menace, or fear of immediate and unlawful bodily injury on the person or another;

(3) where a person is prevented from resisting by any intoxicating or anesthetic substance, or any controlled substance, administered by or with the privity of the accused;

(4) where a person is at the time unconscious of the nature of the act, and this is known to the accused;

(5) where a person submits under the belief that the person committing the act is the victim's spouse, and this belief is induced by any artifice, pretense, or concealment practiced by the accused, with intent to induce the belief;

(6) where the act is accomplished against the victim's will by threatening to retaliate in the future against the victim or any other person, and there is a reasonable possibility that the perpetrator will execute the threat; or

(7) where the act is accomplished against the victim's will by threatening to use the authority of a public official to incarcerate, arrest, or deport the victim or another, and the victim has a reasonable belief that the perpetrator is a public official.

Rape is punishable by imprisonment for three, six, or eight years.

(California Penal Code 261/263)

Unlawful Sexual Intercourse With a Person Under 18 Years of Age

Unlawful sexual intercourse is an act of sexual intercourse accomplished with a person who is not the spouse of the perpetrator, if the person is a minor. A **minor** is a person under the age of eighteen years.

Any person who engages in an act of unlawful sexual intercourse with a minor who is not more than three years older or three years younger than the perpetrator is guilty of a misdemeanor.

Any person who engages in an act of unlawful sexual intercourse with a minor who is more than three years younger than the perpetrator, is guilty of either a misdemeanor or a felony.

Any person over the age of twenty-one years who engages in an act of unlawful sexual intercourse with a minor who is under sixteen years of age is guilty of either a misdemeanor or a felony.

Unlawful sexual intercourse with a person under eighteen years of age is punishable by imprisonment for one, two, three, or four years.

(California Penal Code 261.5)

Spousal Rape

Rape of a person who is the spouse of the perpetrator is an act of sexual intercourse accomplished under any of the following circumstances:

(1) where it is accomplished against a person's will by means of force, violence, duress, menace, or fear of immediate and unlawful bodily injury on the person or another;

(2) where a person is prevented from resisting by any intoxicating or anesthetic substance, or any controlled substance, administered by or with the knowledge of the accused;

(3) where a person is at the time unconscious of the nature of the act, and this is known to the accused;

(4) where the act is accomplished against the victim's will by threatening to retaliate in the future against the victim or any other person, and there is a reasonable possibility that the perpetrator will execute the threat; or

(5) where the act is accomplished against the victim's will by threatening to use the authority of a public official to incarcerate, arrest, or deport the victim or another, and the victim has a reasonable belief that

the perpetrator is a public official. The perpetrator does not actually have to be a public official.

[N]o prosecution shall be commenced under this section unless the violation was reported to medical personnel, a member of the clergy, an attorney, a shelter representative, a counselor, a judicial officer, a rape crisis agency, a prosecuting agency, a law enforcement officer, or a firefighter within one year after the date of the violation. This reporting requirement shall not apply if the victim's allegation of the offense is corroborated by independent evidence.

Conviction for spousal rape is punishable by imprisonment for three, six, or eight years.

(California Penal Code 262/263)

Sodomy

Sodomy is sexual conduct consisting of contact between the penis of one person and the anus of another person. Any sexual penetration, however slight, is sufficient to complete the crime of sodomy. . . . [A]ny person who participates in an act of sodomy with another person who is under fourteen years of age and more than ten years younger than he or she, or when the act is accomplished against the victim's will by means of force, violence, duress, menace, or fear of immediate and unlawful bodily injury on the victim or another person or where the act is accomplished against the victim's will by threatening to retaliate in the future against the victim or any other person, and there is a reasonable possibility that the perpetrator will execute the threat shall be punished by imprisonment.

Sodomy is punishable by imprisonment for three, six, or eight years.

(California Penal Code 286)

Lewd or Lascivious Acts With a Child

Any person who shall willfully and lewdly commit any lewd or lascivious act . . . upon or with the body . . . of a child under the age of fourteen years, with the intent of arousing, appealing to, or gratifying the lust or passions or sexual desires of that person or of the child shall be guilty of a felony.

Any person who commits an act described [above] by use of force, violence, duress, menace, or fear of immediate and unlawful bodily injury on the victim or another person, shall be guilty of a felony.

Lewd or lascivious acts with a child under fourteen years of age is punishable by imprisonment for three, six, or eight years. (California Penal Code 288)

Oral Copulation

Oral copulation is the act of copulating the mouth of one person with the sexual organ or anus of another person. [A]ny person who participates in an act of oral copulation with another person who is under fourteen years of age and more than ten years younger than he or she, or when the act is accomplished against the victim's will by means of force, violence, duress, menace, or fear of immediate and unlawful bodily injury on the victim or another person, or where the act is accomplished against the victim's will by threatening to retaliate in the future against the victim or any other person, and there is a reasonable possibility that the perpetrator will execute the threat shall be punished by imprisonment.

Oral copulation is punishable by imprisonment for three, six, or eight years. (California Penal Code 288a)

Sexual Penetration by a Foreign Object

Every person who causes the penetration, however slight, of the genital or anal openings of any person or causes another person to so penetrate the defendant's or another person's genital or anal openings for the purpose of sexual arousal, gratification, or abuse by any foreign object, substance, instrument, or device when the act is accomplished against the victim's will by means of force, violence, duress, menace, or fear of immediate and unlawful bodily injury on the victim or another person or where the act is accomplished against the victim's will by threatening to retaliate in the future against the victim or any other person, and there is a reasonable possibility that the perpetrator will execute the threat, shall be punished by imprisonment.

Sexual penetration by a foreign object is punishable by imprisonment for three, six, or eight years.
(California Penal Code 289)

Sexual Consent

In prosecutions under the [rape, sodomy, oral copulation, or sexual penetration sections above] in which consent is at issue, **consent** shall be defined to mean positive cooperation in act or attitude pursuant to an exercise of free will. The person must act freely and voluntarily and have knowledge of the nature of the act or transaction involved. A current dating relationship shall not be sufficient to constitute consent in a prosecution under [the rape, sodomy, oral copulation, or sexual penetration sections]. (California Penal Code 261.6)

Rape And Murder

All murder . . . which is committed in the perpetration of, or attempt to perpetrate . . . rape . . . or any act punishable under [the sodomy, lewd and lascivious acts, oral copulation, or sexual penetration sections above] . . . is murder of the first degree.
(California Penal Code 189)

The complete and unedited text of California's rape laws excerpted above can be found in the Penal Codes of either West's Annotated California Code *or* Deering's Annotated California Code.

COLORADO'S RAPE LAWS

Definitions

Actor means the person accused of criminal assault.

Intimate parts means the external genitalia or the perineum or the anus or the pubes or the breast of any person.

Pattern of sexual abuse means the commission of two or more incidents of sexual contact involving a child when such offenses are committed by an actor upon the same victim.

Physically helpless means unconscious, asleep, or otherwise unable to indicate willingness to act.

One in a **position of trust** includes, but is not limited to, any person who is a parent or acting in the place of a parent and charged with any of a parent's rights, duties, or responsibilities concerning a child, or a person who is charged with any duty or responsibility for the health, education, welfare, or supervision of a child, including foster care, child care, family care, or institutional care, either independently or through another, no matter how brief, at the time of an unlawful act.

Sexual contact means the knowingly touching of the victim's intimate parts by the actor, or of the actor's intimate parts by the victim, or the knowingly touching of the clothing covering the immediate area of the victim's or actor's intimate parts if that sexual contact can reasonably be construed as being for the purposes of sexual arousal, gratification, or abuse.

Sexual intrusion means any intrusion, however slight, by any object or any part of a person's body, except the mouth, tongue, or penis, into the genital or anal opening of another person's body if that sexual intrusion can reasonably be construed as being for the purposes of sexual arousal, gratification, or abuse.

Sexual penetration means sexual intercourse, cunnilingus, fellatio, analingus, or anal intercourse. Emission need not be proved as an element of any sexual penetration. Any penetration, however slight, is sufficient to complete the crime.

Victim means the person alleging to have been subjected to a criminal sexual assault.

(Colorado Criminal Code 18-3-401)

First Degree Sexual Assault

Any actor who knowingly inflicts sexual intrusion or sexual penetration on a victim commits a sexual assault in the first degree if:

(a) the actor causes submission of the victim through the actual application of physical force or physical violence;

(b) the actor causes submission of the victim by threats of imminent death, serious bodily injury, extreme pain, or kidnapping, to be inflicted on anyone, and the victim believes that the actor has the present ability to execute these threats;

(c) the actor causes submission of the victim by threatening to retaliate in the future against the victim, or any other person, and the victim reasonably believes the actor will execute this threat. **To retaliate** includes threats of kidnapping, death, serious bodily injury, or extreme pain;

(d) the actor has substantially impaired the victim's power to appraise or control the victim's conduct by employing, without the victim's consent, any drug, intoxicant, or other means for the purpose of causing submission; or

(e) the victim is physically helpless and the actor knows the victim is physically helpless and the victim has not consented.

Sexual assault in the first degree is a Class 3 felony.
(Colorado Criminal Code 18-3-402)

Second Degree Sexual Assault

Any actor who knowingly inflicts sexual penetration or sexual intrusion on a victim commits sexual assault in the second degree if:

(a) the actor causes submission of the victim to sexual penetration by any means other than those set forth [in the first degree sexual assault section above], but of sufficient consequence reasonably calculated to cause submission against the victim's will;

(b) the actor causes submission of the victim to sexual intrusion by any means other than those set forth [above], but of sufficient consequence reasonably calculated to cause submission against the victim's will;

(c) the actor knows that the victim is incapable of appraising the nature of the victim's conduct;

(d) the actor knows that the victim submits erroneously, believing the actor to be the victim's spouse;

(e) at the time of the commission of the act, the victim is less than fifteen years of age and the actor is at least four years older than the victim and is not the spouse of the victim;

(f) at the time of the commission of the act, the victim is less than eighteen years of age and the actor is the victim's guardian or is responsible for the general supervision of the victim's welfare;

(g) the victim is in custody of law or detained in a hospital or other institution and the actor has supervisory or disciplinary authority over the victim and uses this position of authority, unless the sexual intrusion is incident to a lawful search, to coerce the victim to submit; or

(h) the actor engages in treatment or examination of a victim for other than bona fide medical purposes or in a manner substantially inconsistent with reasonable medical practices.

Sexual assault in the second degree is a Class 4 felony. (Colorado Criminal Code 18-3-403)

Third Degree Sexual Assault

Any actor who knowingly subjects a victim to any sexual contact commits sexual assault in the third degree if:

(a) the actor knows that the victim does not consent;

(b) the actor knows that the victim is incapable of appraising the nature of the victim's conduct;

(c) the victim is physically helpless and the actor knows that the victim is physically helpless and the victim has not consented;

(d) the actor has substantially impaired the victim's power to appraise or control the victim's conduct by employing, without the victim's consent, any drug, intoxicant, or other means for the purpose of causing submission;

(e) at the time of the commission of the act, the victim is less than eighteen years of age and the actor is the victim's guardian or is otherwise responsible for the general supervision of the victim's welfare;

(f) the victim is in custody of law or detained in a hospital or other institution and the actor has supervisory or disciplinary authority over the victim and uses this position of authority, unless incident to a lawful search, to coerce the victim to submit; or

(g) the actor engages in treatment or examination of a victim for other than bona fide medical purposes or in a manner substantially inconsistent with reasonable medical practices.

Sexual assault in the third degree is a Class 1 misdemeanor. (Colorado Criminal Code 18-3-404)

Sexual Assault on a Child

Any actor who knowingly subjects another not his or her spouse to any sexual contact commits sexual assault on a child if the victim is less than fifteen years of age and the actor is at least four years older than the victim.

Sexual assault on a child is a Class 4 felony, but is a Class 3 felony if:

(a) the actor commits the offense on a victim by use of such force, intimidation, or threat [as defined in first degree sexual assault];

(b) the actor who commits the offense on a victim is one in a position of trust with respect to the victim; or

(c) the actor commits the offense as a part of a pattern of sexual abuse.

(Colorado Criminal Code 18-3-405)

Spousal Rape

Any marital relationship between an actor and a victim shall not be a defense to any [sexual] offense.
(Colorado Criminal Code 18-3-409)

Sexual Assault by a Psychotherapist

Any actor who knowingly inflicts sexual penetration or sexual intrusion on a victim commits aggravated sexual assault on a client if:

(1) the actor is a psychotherapist and the victim is a client of the psychotherapist; or

(2) the actor is a psychotherapist and the victim is a client and the sexual penetration or intrusion occurred by means of therapeutic deception.

(Colorado Criminal Code 18-3-405.5)

Rape and Murder

A person commits the crime of murder in the first degree if, acting either alone or with one or more persons, he commits or attempts to commit sexual assault in the first or second degree or sexual assault on a child and, in the course of or in furtherance of the crime that he is committing or attempting to commit, or in immediate flight therefrom, the death of a person, other than one of the participants, is caused by anyone.
Murder in the first degree is a Class 1 felony.
(Colorado Criminal Code 18-3-102)

The complete and unedited text of Colorado's rape laws excerpted above can be found in Session Laws of Colorado *or* Colorado Revised Statutes.

CONNECTICUT'S RAPE LAWS

Definitions

Actor means a person accused of sexual assault.

Sexual intercourse means vaginal intercourse, anal intercourse, fellatio, or cunnilingus between persons regardless of sex. Its meaning is limited to persons not married to each other. Penetration, however slight, is sufficient to complete vaginal intercourse, anal intercourse, or fellatio and does not require emission of semen. Penetration may be committed by an object manipulated by the actor into the genital or anal opening of the victim's body.

Sexual contact means any contact with the intimate parts of a person not married to the actor for the purpose of sexual gratification of the actor or for the purpose of degrading or humiliating such person or any contact of the intimate parts of the actor with a person not married to the actor for the purpose of sexual gratification of the actor or for the purpose of degrading or humiliating such person.

Mentally defective means that a person suffers from a mental disease or defect which renders such person incapable of appraising the nature of such person's conduct.

Mentally incapacitated means that a person is rendered temporarily incapable of appraising or controlling such person's conduct owing to the influence of a drug or intoxicating substance administered to such person without such person's consent, or owing to any other act committed upon such person without such person's consent.

Physically helpless means that a person is unconscious or for any other reason is physically unable to communicate unwillingness to act.

Use of force means:
(a) use of a dangerous instrument; or
(b) use of actual physical force or violence or superior physical strength against the victim.

Intimate parts means the genital area, groin, anus, inner thighs, buttocks or breasts.

(Connecticut Penal Code 53a-65)

First Degree Sexual Assault

A person is guilty of sexual assault in the first degree when such person:

(1) compels another person to engage in sexual intercourse by the use of force against such other person or a third person, or by the threat of use of force against such other person or against a third person which reasonably causes such person to fear physical injury to such person or a third person; or

(2) engages in sexual intercourse with another person and such other person is under thirteen years of age and the actor is more than two years older than such person.

Sexual assault in the first degree is a Class B felony. (Connecticut Penal Code 53a-70)

First Degree Aggravated Sexual Assault

A person is guilty of aggravated sexual assault in the first degree when such person commits sexual assault in the first degree [as provided above] and in the commission of such offense:

(1) he uses or is armed with and threatens the use of or displays or represents by his words or conduct that he possesses a deadly weapon;

(2) with intent to disfigure the victim seriously and permanently, or to destroy, amputate or disable permanently a member or organ of the victim's body, he causes such injury to such victim;

(3) under circumstances evincing an extreme indifference to human life he recklessly engages in conduct which creates a risk of death to the victim, and thereby causes serious physical injury to such victim; or

(4) he is aided by two or more other persons actually present.

Aggravated sexual assault in the first degree is a Class B felony. (Connecticut Penal Code 53a-70)

Sexual Assault in a Spousal or Live-in Relationship

For the purposes of this section:

(1) **Sexual intercourse** means vaginal intercourse, anal intercourse, fellatio, or cunnilingus between persons regardless of sex. Penetration, however slight, is sufficient to complete vaginal intercourse, anal intercourse, or fellatio and does not require emission of semen. Penetration may be committed by an object manipulated by the actor into the genital or anal opening of the victim's body; and

(2) **Use of force** means:

(a) use of a dangerous instrument; or

(b) use of actual physical force or violence or superior physical strength against the victim.

(3) No spouse or cohabitator shall compel the other spouse or cohabitator to engage in sexual intercourse by the use of force against such other spouse or cohabitator, or by the threat of the use of force against such other spouse or cohabitator which reasonably causes such other spouse or cohabitator to fear physical injury.

Any person who violates any provision of this section shall be guilty of a Class B felony.

(Connecticut Penal Code 53a-70b)

Rape and Murder

A person is guilty of a capital felony who is convicted of murder committed in the course of the commission of sexual assault in the first degree. (Connecticut Penal Code 53a-54b)

The complete and unedited text of Connecticut's rape laws excerpted above can be found in The General Statutes of Connecticut *or* Connecticut Public Acts.

DELAWARE'S RAPE LAWS
Definitions

Cunnilingus means any oral contact with the female genitalia.

Fellatio means any oral contact with the male genitalia.

Object means any item, device, instrument, substance, or part of the body other than a tongue or penis.

Sexual intercourse means:

(a) any act of physical union of the genitalia or anus of one person with the mouth, anus, or genitalia of another person. It occurs upon any penetration, however slight; or

(b) any act of cunnilingus or fellatio regardless of whether penetration occurs.

Ejaculation is not required.

Sexual contact means any intentional touching of the anus, breast, buttocks, or genitalia of another person and shall also include touching of those specified areas when covered by clothing.

Without consent means:

(a) the defendant compelled the victim to submit by force, by gesture, or by threat of death, physical injury, pain, or kidnapping to be inflicted upon the victim or a third party, or by any other means which would compel a reasonable person under the circumstances to submit. It is not required that the victim resist such force or threat to the utmost, or to resist if resistance would be futile or foolhardy, but the victim need resist only to the extent that it is reasonably necessary to make the victim's refusal to consent known to the defendant;

(b) the defendant knew that the victim was unconscious, asleep, or otherwise unaware that a sexual act was being performed;

(c) the defendant knew that the victim suffered from a mental illness or mental defect which rendered the victim incapable of appraising the nature of the sexual conduct; or

(d) the defendant had substantially impaired the victim's power to appraise or control his conduct by administering or employing without the other person's knowledge or against his will, drugs, intoxicants or other means for the purpose of preventing resistance. (Delaware Criminal Code 761)

First Degree Unlawful Sexual Intercourse

A person is guilty of unlawful sexual intercourse in the first degree when he intentionally engages in sexual intercourse with another person and any of the following circumstances exist:

(1) the intercourse occurs without the victim's consent and he inflicts physical, mental or emotional injury upon the victim:

(a) on the occasion of the crime;

(b) during the immediate flight from the crime; or

(c) during an attempt to prevent the reporting of the crime;

(2) the intercourse occurs without the victim's consent and the defendant was not the victim's voluntary social companion on the occasion of the crime and had not permitted the defendant sexual intercourse within the previous twelve months;

(3) in the course of committing unlawful sexual intercourse in the third degree or unlawful sexual intercourse in the second degree, the defendant displayed what appeared to be a deadly weapon or a dangerous instrument; or

(4) the victim is less than sixteen years of age and the defendant is not the victim's voluntary social companion on the occasion of the crime.

Unlawful sexual intercourse in the first degree is a Class A felony.

(Delaware Criminal Code 775)

Second Degree Unlawful Sexual Intercourse

A person is guilty of unlawful sexual intercourse in the second degree when he intentionally engages in sexual intercourse with another person and any of the following circumstances exist:

(1) the intercourse occurs without the victim's consent and he inflicts physical, mental, or emotional injury upon the victim:

    (a) on the occasion of the crime;

    (b) during the immediate flight from the crime; or

    (c) during an attempt to prevent the reporting of the crime; or

(2) the intercourse occurs without the victim's consent and the defendant was not the victim's voluntary social companion on the occasion of the crime.

Unlawful sexual intercourse in the second degree is a Class B felony.

(Delaware Criminal Code 774)

Third Degree Unlawful Sexual Intercourse

A person is guilty of unlawful sexual intercourse in the third degree when he intentionally engages in sexual intercourse with another person and any of the following circumstances exist:

    (1) the intercourse occurs without the victim's consent; or

    (2) the victim is less than sixteen years of age.

Unlawful sexual intercourse in the third degree is a Class C felony.

(Delaware Criminal Code 773)

First Degree Unlawful Sexual Penetration

A person is guilty of unlawful sexual penetration in the first degree when he intentionally places one or more fingers or thumbs or [an object] inside the vagina or anus of a person under any of the following circumstances:

    (1) the sexual penetration occurs without the victim's consent and during the commission of the crime, or during the immediate flight from the crime, or during an attempt to prevent the reporting of the crime, he causes serious physical injury to the victim;

    (2) the victim is less than sixteen years old and during the commission of the crime, or during the immediate flight from the crime, or during an attempt to prevent

the reporting of the crime, he causes serious physical injury to the victim;

(3) the sexual penetration occurs without the victim's consent and during the commission of the crime, or during the immediate flight from the crime, or during an attempt to prevent the reporting of the crime, he displays what appears to be a deadly weapon or dangerous instrument; or

(4) the victim is less than sixteen years old and during the commission of the crime, or during the immediate flight from the crime, or during an attempt to prevent the reporting of the crime, he displays what appears to be a deadly weapon or dangerous instrument.

This [law] does not apply to a licensed medical doctor or nurse who places one or more fingers or an object inside the vagina or anus for the purpose of diagnosis or treatment.

Unlawful sexual penetration in the first degree is a Class C felony.

(Delaware Criminal Code 772)

Second Degree Unlawful Sexual Penetration

A person is guilty of unlawful sexual penetration in the second degree when he intentionally places one or more fingers or thumbs or [an object] inside the vagina or anus of a person under any of the following circumstances:

(1) the sexual penetration occurs without the victim's consent and during the commission of a crime, or during the immediate flight from the crime, or during an attempt to prevent the reporting of the crime, he causes physical injury to the victim; or

(2) the victim is less than sixteen years old and during the commission of the crime, or during the immediate flight from the crime, or during an attempt to prevent the reporting of the crime, he causes physical injury to the victim.

This law does not apply to a licensed medical doctor or nurse who places one or more fingers or an object inside a vagina or anus for the purpose of diagnosis or treatment.

Unlawful sexual penetration in the second degree is a Class D felony.
(Delaware Criminal Code 771)

Third Degree Unlawful Sexual Penetration

A person is guilty of unlawful sexual penetration in the third degree when he intentionally places one or more fingers or thumbs or [an object] inside the vagina or anus of a person under any of the following circumstances:

(1) the sexual penetration occurs without the victim's consent; or

(2) the victim is less than sixteen years old.

This law does not apply to a licensed medical doctor or nurse who places one or more fingers or an object inside a vagina or anus for the purpose of diagnosis or treatment.

Unlawful sexual penetration in the third degree is a Class E felony.
(Delaware Criminal Code 770)

First Degree Unlawful Sexual Contact

A person is guilty of unlawful sexual contact in the first degree when, in the course of committing unlawful sexual contact in the third degree or in the course of committing unlawful sexual contact in the second degree, or during the immediate flight from the crime, or during an attempt to prevent the reporting of the crime, he causes physical injury to the victim or he displays what appears to be a deadly weapon or dangerous instrument.

Unlawful sexual contact in the first degree is a Class F felony.
(Delaware Criminal Code 769)

Second Degree Unlawful Sexual Contact

A person is guilty of unlawful sexual contact in the second degree when he intentionally has sexual contact with another person who is less than sixteen years of age or causes the victim to have sexual contact with him or a third person.

Unlawful sexual contact in the second degree is a Class G felony.
(Delaware Criminal Code 768)

Third Degree Unlawful Sexual Contact

A person is guilty of unlawful sexual contact in the third degree when he has sexual contact with another person or causes the victim to have sexual contact with him or a third person and he knows that the contact is either offensive to the victim or occurs without the victim's consent. Unlawful sexual contact in the third degree is a Class A misdemeanor.
(Delaware Criminal Code 767)

Rape and Murder

A person is guilty of murder in the first degree when he, with criminal negligence, causes the death of another person in the course of and in furtherance of the commission or attempted commission of rape, or unlawful sexual intercourse in the first or second degrees.
Murder in the first degree is a Class A felony.
(Delaware Criminal Code 636)

The complete and unedited text of Delaware's rape laws excerpted above can be found in The Delaware Code Annotated *or* The Laws of Delaware.

THE DISTRICT OF COLUMBIA'S RAPE LAWS

Rape

Whoever has carnal knowledge of a female forcibly and against her will or whoever carnally knows and abuses a female child under sixteen years of age, shall be imprisoned for any term of years or for life. (District of Columbia Criminal Code 22-2801)

Seduction

If any person shall seduce and carnally know any female of previously chaste character, between the ages of sixteen and twenty-one years, out of wedlock, such seduction and carnal knowledge shall be deemed a misdemeanor, and the offender, being convicted thereof, shall be imprisoned for a term not exceeding three years. (District of Columbia Criminal Code 22-3001)

Seduction by a Teacher

Any male person, over twenty-one years of age, who is superintendent, tutor, or teacher in any public or private school, seminary, or other institution, or instructor of any female in any branch of instruction, who has sexual intercourse with any female under twenty-one years of age and not under sixteen years of age, with her consent, while under his instruction during the term of his engagement as superintendent, tutor, or teacher, shall be imprisoned for not less than one year nor more than ten. (District of Columbia Criminal Code 22-3002)

Rape and Murder

Whoever, being of sound memory and discretion, . . . kills another person in perpetrating or in attempting to perpetrate rape is guilty of murder in the first degree.

The punishment for murder in the first degree shall be life imprisonment.

(District of Columbia Criminal Code 22-2401/2404)

The complete and unedited text of the District of Columbia's rape laws excerpted above can be found in The District of Columbia Code Annotated *and* The District of Columbia Statutes at Large.

FLORIDA'S RAPE LAWS

Definitions

Consent means intelligent, knowing, and voluntary consent and does not include coerced submission.

Mentally defective means a mental disease or defect which renders a person temporarily or permanently incapable of appraising the nature of his or her conduct.

Mentally incapacitated means temporarily incapable of appraising or controlling a person's own conduct due to the influence of a narcotic, anesthetic, or intoxicating substance administered without his or her consent or due to any other act committed upon that person without his or her consent.

Offender means a person accused of a sexual offense in violation of a provision of this chapter.

Physically helpless means unconscious, asleep, or for any other reason physically unable to communicate unwillingness to act.

Retaliation includes, but is not limited to, threats of future physical punishment, kidnapping, false imprisonment or forcible confinement, or extortion.

Serious personal injury means great bodily harm or pain, permanent disability, or permanent disfigurement.

Sexual battery means oral, anal, or vaginal penetration by, or union with, the sexual organ of another or the anal or vaginal penetration of another by any other object; however, sexual battery does not include an act done for a bona fide medical purpose.

Victim means a person who has been the object of a sexual offense.

Physically incapacitated means bodily impaired or handicapped and substantially limited in ability to resist or flee.
(Florida Criminal Code 794.011)

Sexual Battery

A person eighteen years of age or older who commits sexual battery upon, or in an attempt to commit sexual battery injures the sexual organs of, a person less than twelve years of age commits a capital felony.

A person less than eighteen years of age or older who commits sexual battery upon, or in an attempt to commit sexual battery injures the sexual organs of, a person less than twelve years of age commits a life felony.

A person who commits sexual battery upon a person twelve years of age or older, without that person's consent, and the process thereof uses or threatens to use a deadly weapon or uses actual physical force likely to cause serious personal injury commits a life felony.

A person who commits sexual battery upon a person twelve years of age or older without that person's consent, under any of the following circumstances, commits a felony of the first degree:

(1) when the victim is physically helpless to resist;

(2) when the offender coerces the victim to submit by threatening to use force or violence likely to cause serious personal injury on the victim, and the victim reasonably believes that the offender has the present ability to execute the threat;

(3) when the offender coerces the victim to submit by threatening to retaliate against the victim, or any other person, and the victim reasonably believes that the offender has the ability to execute the threat in the future;

(4) when the offender, without the prior knowledge or consent of the victim, administers or has knowledge of someone else administering to the victim any narcotic, anesthetic, or other intoxicating substance which mentally or physically incapacitates the victim;

(5) when the victim is mentally defective and the offender has reason to believe this or has actual knowledge of this fact;

(6) when the victim is physically incapacitated.

A person who commits sexual battery upon a person twelve years of age or older, without that person's consent, and in the process thereof does not use physical force or violence likely to cause serious personal injury commits a felony of the second degree.

(Florida Criminal Code 794.011)

Familial/Custodial Sexual Battery

Without regard to the willingness or consent of the victim, which is not a defense under this section, a person who is in a position of familial or custodial authority to a person less than eighteen years of age and who:

(1) solicits that person to engage in any act which would constitute sexual battery [as defined above] commits a felony of the third degree;

(2) engages in any act with that person while the person is twelve years of age or older but less than eighteen years of age which constitutes sexual battery [as defined above] commits a felony of the first degree; or

(3) engages in any act with that person while the person is less than twelve years of age which constitutes sexual battery [as defined above], or in an attempt to commit sexual battery injures the sexual organs of such person commits a capital or life felony.

(Florida Criminal Code 794.011)

Publicly Identifying the Victim

No person shall print, publish, or broadcast, or cause or allow to be printed, published, or broadcast, in any instrument of mass communication the name, address, or other identifying fact or information of the victim of any sexual offense within this chapter.

An offense under this section shall constitute a misdemeanor of the second degree.

(Florida Criminal Code 794.03)

Under-Age Rapists

The common law rule "that a boy under fourteen years of age is conclusively presumed to be incapable of committing the crime of rape" shall not be in force in this state. (Florida Criminal Code 794.02)

Under-Age Victims

When the criminality of the conduct depends upon the victim's being below a certain specified age, ignorance of the age is no defense. Neither shall misrepresentation of age by such person nor a bona fide belief that such person is over the specified age be a defense. (Florida Criminal Code 794.021)

Reporting Sexual Battery

A person who observes the commission of the crime of sexual battery and who:

(1) has reasonable grounds to believe that he observed the commission of a sexual battery;

(2) has the present ability to seek assistance for the victim or victims by immediately reporting such offense to a law enforcement officer;

(3) fails to seek such assistance;

(4) would not be exposed to any threat of physical violence for seeking such assistance;

(5) is not the husband, wife, parent, grandparent, child, grandchild, brother, or sister of the offender or victim, by consanguinity or affinity; and

(6) is not the victim of such sexual battery;

is guilty of a misdemeanor of the first degree.
(Florida Criminal Code 794.027)

Rape and Murder

The unlawful killing of a human being when committed by a person engaged in the perpetration of, or in the attempt to perpetrate, sexual battery is murder in the first degree. (Florida Criminal Code 782.04)

The complete and unedited text of Florida's rape laws excerpted above can be found in Florida Statutes, Florida Statutes Annotated *or* The Laws of Florida.

GEORGIA'S RAPE LAWS

Rape

A person commits the offense of rape when he has carnal knowledge of a female forcibly and against her will.

Carnal knowledge in rape occurs when there is any penetration of the female sex organ by the male sex organ.

A person convicted of the offense of rape shall be punished by death, by imprisonment for life, or by imprisonment for not less than one nor more than twenty years.

(Georgia Criminal Code 26-2001)

Statutory Rape

A person commits the offense of statutory rape when he engages in sexual intercourse with any female under the age of fourteen years and not his spouse, provided that no conviction shall be had for this offense on the unsupported testimony of the female.

A person convicted of the offense of statutory rape shall be punished by imprisonment for not less than one nor more than twenty years.

(Georgia Criminal Code 26-2018)

Sodomy

A person commits the offense of sodomy when he performs or submits to any sexual act involving the sex organs of one person and the mouth or anus of another.

A person commits the offense of aggravated sodomy when he commits sodomy with force and against the will of the other person.

A person convicted of the offense of sodomy shall be punished by imprisonment for not less than one nor more than twenty years.

A person convicted of the offense of aggravated sodomy shall be punished by imprisonment for life or by imprisonment for not less than ten nor more than twenty years.

(Georgia Criminal Code 26-2002)

Sexual Assault

As used in this section:

(1) **Actor** means a person accused of sexual assault.

(2) **Intimate parts** means the genital area, groin, inner thighs, buttocks, or breasts of a person.

(3) **Psychotherapy** means the professional treatment or counseling of a mental or emotional illness, symptom, or condition.

(4) **Sexual contact** means any contact for the purpose of sexual gratification of the actor with the intimate parts of a person not married to the actor.

A probation or parole officer or other custodian or supervisor of another person referred to in this section commits sexual assault when he engages in sexual contact with another person who is a probationer or parolee under the supervision of said probation or parole officer or who is in the custody of the law or who is enrolled in a school or who is detained in or is a patient in a hospital or other institution and such actor has supervisory or disciplinary authority over such other person.

A person commits sexual assault when such person has supervisory or disciplinary authority over another person and such person engages in sexual contact with that other person who is:

(1) in the custody of the law; or

(2) detained in or is a patient in a hospital or other institution.

A person commits sexual assault when, as an actual or purported practitioner of psychotherapy, he or she engages in sexual contact with another person who the actor knew or should have known is the subject of the actor's actual or purported treatment or counseling, or, if the treatment or counseling relationship was used to facilitate sexual contact between the actor and the said person.

Consent of the victim shall not be a defense to a prosecution under this [section].

A person convicted of sexual assault shall be punished by imprisonment for not less than one nor more than three years.

(Georgia Criminal Code 2020.1)

Sexual Battery

A person commits the offense of sexual battery when he intentionally makes physical contact with the intimate parts of the body of another person without the consent of that person.

Intimate parts, for the purpose of this [section], means the primary genital area, anus, groin, inner thighs, or buttocks of a male or female and the breasts of a female.

A person convicted of sexual battery shall be punished as for a misdemeanor of a high and aggravated nature.
(Georgia Criminal Code 2024)

Child Molestation

A person commits the offense of child molestation when he does any immoral or indecent act to or in the presence of or with any child under the age of fourteen years with the intent to arouse or satisfy the sexual desires of either the child or the person.

A person convicted of a first offense of child molestation shall be punished by imprisonment for not less than one nor more than twenty years.

A person commits the offense of aggravated child molestation when he commits an offense of child molestation which act physically injures the child or involves an act of sodomy.

A person convicted of the offense of aggravated child molestation shall be punished by imprisonment for not less than ten nor more than thirty years.
(Georgia Criminal Code 26-2019)

Incest

A person commits the offense of incest when he engages in sexual intercourse with a person to whom he knows he is related either by blood or marriage as follows:

(1) father and daughter or stepdaughter;
(2) mother and son or stepson;
(3) brother and sister of the whole blood or of the half blood;
(4) grandparent and grandchild;
(5) aunt and nephew; or

(6) uncle and niece.

A person convicted of the offense of incest shall be punished by imprisonment for not less than one nor more than twenty years.

(Georgia Criminal Code 26-2006)

Rape and Murder

A person commits the offense of murder when he unlawfully and with malice aforethought, either expressed or implied, causes the death of another human being.

A person also commits the offense of murder when, in the commission of a felony, he causes the death of another human being irrespective of malice.

A person convicted of the offense of murder shall be punished by death or by imprisonment for life.

(Georgia Criminal Code 26-1101)

The complete and unedited text of Georgia's rape laws excerpted above can be found in The Official Code of Georgia Annotated, The Code of Georgia Annotated *or* Georgia Laws.

HAWAII'S RAPE LAWS

Definitions

Sexual penetration means vaginal intercourse, anal intercourse, fellatio, cunnilingus, analingus, deviate sexual intercourse, or any intrusion of any part of a person's body or of any object into the genital or anal opening of another person's body; it occurs upon any penetration, however slight, but emission is not required.

Sexual contact means any touching of the sexual or other intimate parts of a person not married to the actor, or of the sexual or other intimate parts of the actor by the person, whether directly or through the clothing or other material intended to cover the sexual or other intimate parts.

Married includes persons legally married, and a male and female living together as husband and wife regardless of their legal status, but does not include spouses living apart.

Mentally defective means a person suffering from a disease, disorder, or defect which renders him incapable of appraising the nature of his conduct.

Mentally incapacitated means a person rendered temporarily incapable of appraising or controlling his conduct owing to the influence of a substance administered to him without his consent.

Physically helpless means a person who is unconscious or for any other reason physically unable to communicate unwillingness to an act.

Bodily injury means physical pain, illness, or any impairment of physical condition.

Serious bodily injury means bodily injury which creates a substantial risk of death or which causes serious, permanent disfigurement, or protracted loss or impairment of the function of any bodily member or organ.

Compulsion means the absence of consent, or a threat, expressed or implied, that places a person in fear of public humiliation, property damage, or financial loss.

(Hawaii Penal Code 707.700)

Rape in the First Degree

A person commits the offense of rape in the first degree if:

(1) the person intentionally engages in sexual intercourse, by forcible compulsion, with another person and:

(a) the other person is not, upon the occasion, his voluntary social companion who had within the previous thirty days permitted him sexual intercourse of the kind involved; or

(b) recklessly inflicts serious bodily injury upon the other person; or

(2) the person intentionally engages in sexual intercourse with another person who is less than fourteen years old and he recklessly inflicts serious bodily injury upon the other person.

Rape in the first degree is a Class A felony.
(Hawaii Penal Code 707.730)

Rape in the Second Degree

A person commits the offense of rape in the second degree if:

(1) the person intentionally engages in sexual intercourse by forcible compulsion with another person; or

(2) the person intentionally engages in sexual intercourse with another person who is less than fourteen years old.

Rape in the second degree is a Class B felony.
(Hawaii Penal Code 707.731)

Rape in the Third Degree

A person commits the offense of rape in the third degree if the person intentionally engages in sexual intercourse with another person who is mentally defective, mentally incapacitated, or physically helpless.

Rape in the third degree is a Class C felony.
(Hawaii Penal Code 707.732)

Sodomy in the First Degree

A person commits the offense of sodomy in the first degree if:
(1) the person intentionally, by forcible compulsion, engages in deviate sexual intercourse with another person or causes another person to engage in deviate sexual intercourse, and:
(a) the other person was not, upon the occasion, his voluntary social companion who had within the previous thirty days permitted him sexual contact of the kind involved; or
(b) recklessly inflicts serious bodily injury upon the other person; or
(2) the person intentionally engages in deviate sexual intercourse with another person who is less than fourteen years old, or causes such person to engage in deviate sexual intercourse, and he recklessly inflicts serious bodily injury upon the person.
Sodomy in the first degree is a Class A felony.
(Hawaii Penal Code 707.733)

Sodomy in the Second Degree

A person commits the offense of sodomy in the second degree if:
(1) the person intentionally, by forcible compulsion, engages in deviate sexual intercourse with another person or causes another person to engage in deviate sexual intercourse; or
(2) the person intentionally engages in deviate sexual intercourse with another person who is less than fourteen years old.
Sodomy in the second degree is a Class B felony.
(Hawaii Penal Code 707.734)

Sodomy in the Third Degree

A person commits the offense of sodomy in the third degree if the person intentionally engages in deviate sexual intercourse with another person, or causes another person to engage in de-

viate sexual intercourse, and the other person is mentally defective, mentally incapacitated, or physically helpless.
Sodomy in the third degree is a Class C felony.
(Hawaii Penal Code 707.735)

Sexual Abuse in the First Degree

A person commits the offense of sexual abuse in the first degree if:

(1) he intentionally, by forcible compulsion, has sexual contact with another or causes another to have sexual contact with him; or

(2) he intentionally has sexual contact with another person who is less than fourteen years old or causes such a person to have sexual contact with him.

Sexual abuse in the first degree is a Class C felony.
(Hawaii Penal Code 707.736)

Rape and Murder

A person commits the offense of murder in the first or second degree if the person intentionally or knowingly causes the death of another person.

Murder in the first or second degree is a felony for which the defendant shall be sentenced to imprisonment.
(Hawaii Penal Code 707.701/.701.5)

The complete and unedited text of Hawaii's rape laws excerpted above can be found in Hawaii Revised Statutes *or in the* Session Laws of Hawaii.

IDAHO'S RAPE LAWS

Rape of a Female

Rape is defined as the penetration, however slight, of the oral, anal or vaginal opening with the perpetrator's penis accomplished with a female under either of the following circumstances:

    (1) where the female is under the age of eighteen years;

    (2) where she is incapable, through any unsoundness of mind, whether temporary or permanent, of giving legal consent;

    (3) where she resists but her resistance is overcome by force or violence;

    (4) where she is prevented from resistance by threats of immediate and great bodily harm, accompanied by apparent power of execution; or by any intoxicating, narcotic, or anesthetic substance administered by or with the privity of the accused;

    (5) where she is at the time unconscious of the nature of the act, and this is known to the accused;

    (6) where she submits under the belief that the person committing the act is her husband, and the belief is induced by artifice, pretense or concealment practiced by the accused, with intent to induce such belief.

Rape is punishable by imprisonment in the state prison not less than one year, and the imprisonment may be extended to life. (Idaho Code 18-6101/6104)

Rape of a Male

Male rape is defined as the penetration, however slight, of the oral or anal opening of another male, with the perpetrator's penis, for the purpose of sexual arousal, gratification or abuse, under any of the following circumstances:

    (1) where the victim is incapable, through any unsoundness of mind, whether temporary or permanent, of giving consent;

    (2) where the victim resists but his resistance is overcome by force or violence;

(3) where the victim is prevented from resistance by threats of immediate and great bodily harm, accompanied by apparent power of execution; or by use of any intoxicating, narcotic, or anesthetic substance administered by or with the privity of the accused;

(4) where the victim is at the time unconscious of the nature of the act, and this is known to the accused.

Male rape is punishable by imprisonment in the state prison for not less than one year, and the imprisonment may be extended to life.

(Idaho Code 18-6108/6109)

Rape of a Spouse

No person shall be convicted of rape for any act with the person's spouse except:

(1) where she resists but her resistance is overcome by force or violence;

(2) where she is prevented from resistance by threats of immediate and great bodily harm, accompanied by apparent power of execution; or by any intoxicating, narcotic, or anesthetic substance administered by or with the privity of the accused.

(Idaho Code 18-6107)

Object Rape

Every person who causes the penetration, however slight, of the genital or anal opening of another person, by any object, instrument or device, against the victim's will by use of force or violence or by duress, or by threats of immediate and great bodily harm, accompanied by apparent power of execution, for the purpose of sexual arousal, gratification or abuse shall be guilty of a felony and shall be punished by imprisonment in the state prison for not more than life. (Idaho Code 18-6608)

Proof of Ability to Rape

No conviction for rape can be had against one who was under the age of fourteen years at the time of the act alleged, unless his physical ability to accomplish penetration is proved as an independent fact, and beyond a reasonable doubt. (Idaho Code 18-6102)

Sexual Penetration

The essential guilt of rape consists in the outrage to the person and feelings of the female. Any sexual penetration, however slight, is sufficient to complete the crime. (Idaho Code 18-6103)

The Rape Shield

In prosecutions for the crime of rape, evidence of the prosecuting witness' previous sexual conduct shall not be admitted nor reference made thereto in the presence of the jury. (Idaho Code 18-6105)

Rape and Murder

Any murder committed in the perpetration of, or attempt to perpetrate, rape is murder of the first degree. (Idaho Code 18-4003)

The complete and unedited text of Idaho's rape laws excerpted above can be found in The Idaho Code *or* The Session Laws of Idaho.

ILLINOIS' RAPE LAWS

Definitions

Accused means a person accused of an offense prohibited by the [criminal sexual assault, aggravated sexual assault, criminal sexual abuse, or aggravated sexual abuse] sections of this code.

Bodily harm means physical harm, and includes, but is not limited to, sexually transmitted disease, pregnancy and impotence.

Family member means a parent, grandparent, or child, whether by whole blood, half-blood, or adoption and includes a step-grandparent, step-parent, or step-child. **Family member** also means, where the victim is a child under eighteen years of age, an accused who has resided in the household with such child continuously for at least one year.

Force or threat of force means the use of force or violence, or the threat of force or violence, including but not limited to the following situations:

(1) when the accused threatens to use force or violence on the victim or on any other person, and the victim under the circumstances reasonably believed that the accused had the ability to execute that threat; or

(2) when the accused has overcome the victim by use of superior strength or size, physical restraint, or physical confinement.

Sexual conduct means any intentional or knowing touching or fondling by the victim of the accused, either directly or through clothing, of the sex organs, anus, or breast of the victim or the accused, or any part of the body of a child under thirteen years of age, for the purpose of sexual gratification or arousal of the victim or the accused.

Sexual penetration means any contact, however slight, between the sex organ or anus of one person by an object, the sex organ, mouth, or anus of another person, or any intrusion, however slight, of any part of the body of one person, or of any animal or object into the sex organ or anus of another person, including but not limited to cunnilingus, fellatio, or anal penetration. Evidence of emission of semen is not required to prove sexual penetration.

Victim means a person alleging to have been subjected to an offense prohibited by the [criminal sexual assault, aggravated sexual assault, criminal sexual abuse, or aggravated sexual abuse] sections of this code.
(Illinois Code 5/12-12)

Criminal Sexual Assault

The accused commits criminal sexual assault if he or she:

(1) commits an act of sexual penetration by the use of force or threat of force;

(2) commits an act of sexual penetration and the accused knew that the victim was unable to understand the nature of the act or was unable to give knowing consent;

(3) commits an act of sexual penetration with a victim who was under eighteen years of age when the act was committed and the accused was a family member; or

(4) commits an act of sexual penetration with a victim who was at least thirteen years of age but under eighteen years of age when the act was committed and the accused was seventeen years of age or over and held a position of trust, authority, or supervision in relation to the victim.

Criminal sexual assault is a Class 1 felony.
(Illinois Code 5/12-13)

Aggravated Criminal Sexual Assault

The accused commits aggravated criminal sexual assault if he or she commits criminal sexual assault and any of the following aggravating circumstances existed during the commission of the offense:

(1) the accused displayed, threatened to use, or used a dangerous weapon or any object fashioned or utilized in such a manner as to lead the victim under the circumstances reasonably to believe it to be a dangerous weapon;

(2) the accused caused bodily harm to the victim;

(3) the accused acted in such a manner as to threaten or endanger the life of the victim or any other person;

(4) the criminal sexual assault was perpetrated during the course of the commission or attempted commission of any other felony by the accused;

(5) the victim was sixty years of age or over when the offense was committed; or

(6) the victim was a physically handicapped person.

The accused commits aggravated criminal sexual assault if:

(1) the accused was seventeen years of age or over and commits an act of sexual penetration with a victim who was under thirteen years of age when the act was committed; or

(2) the accused was under seventeen years of age, and:

(i) commits an act of sexual penetration with a victim who was under nine years of age when the act was committed; or

(ii) commits an act of sexual penetration with a victim who was at least nine years of age but under thirteen years of age when the act was committed and the accused used force or threat of force to commit the act.

The accused commits aggravated sexual assault if he or she commits an act of sexual penetration with a victim who was an institutionalized severely or profoundly mentally retarded person at the time the act was committed.

Aggravated criminal sexual assault is a Class X felony. (Illinois Code 5/12-14)

Criminal Sexual Abuse

The accused commits criminal sexual abuse if he or she:

(1) commits an act of sexual conduct by the use of force or threat of force; or

(2) commits an act of sexual conduct and the accused knew that the victim was unable to understand the nature of the act or was unable to give knowing consent.

The accused commits criminal sexual abuse if the accused was under seventeen years of age and commits an act of sexual penetration or sexual conduct with a victim who was at least nine years of age but under seventeen years of age when the act was committed.

The accused commits criminal sexual abuse if he or she commits an act of sexual penetration or sexual conduct with a victim who was at least thirteen years of age but under seventeen years of age and the accused was less than five years older than the victim.
Criminal sexual abuse is a Class A misdemeanor.
(Illinois Code 5/12-15)

Aggravated Criminal Sexual Abuse

The accused commits aggravated criminal sexual abuse if he or she commits criminal sexual abuse [as defined above] and any of the following aggravating circumstances existed during the commission of the offense:

(1) the accused displayed, threatened to use, or used a dangerous weapon or any object fashioned or utilized in such a manner as to lead the victim under circumstances reasonably to believe it to be a dangerous weapon;

(2) the accused caused bodily harm to the victim;

(3) the victim was sixty years of age or over when the offense was committed; or

(4) the victim was a physically handicapped person.

The accused commits aggravated criminal sexual abuse if he or she commits an act of sexual conduct with a victim who was under eighteen years of age when the act was committed and the accused was a family member.

The accused commits aggravated criminal sexual abuse if:

(1) the accused was seventeen years of age or over, and:

(a) commits an act of sexual conduct with a victim who was under thirteen years of age when the act was committed; or

(b) commits an act of sexual conduct with a victim who was at least thirteen years of age but under seventeen years of age when the act was committed and the accused used force or threat of force to commit the act;

(2) the accused was under seventeen years of age and:

(a) commits an act of sexual conduct with a victim who was under nine years of age when the act was committed; or

(b) commits an act of sexual conduct with a victim who was at least nine years of age but under seventeen years of age when the act was committed and the accused used force or threat of force to commit the act.

The accused commits aggravated criminal sexual abuse if he or she commits an act of sexual penetration or sexual conduct with a victim who was at least thirteen years of age but under seventeen years of age and the accused was at least five years older than the victim.

The accused commits aggravated criminal sexual abuse if he or she commits an act of sexual conduct with a victim who was an institutionalized severely or profoundly mentally retarded person at the time the act was committed.

The accused commits aggravated criminal sexual abuse if he or she commits an act of sexual conduct with a victim who was at least thirteen years of age but under eighteen years of age when the act was committed and the accused was seventeen years of age or over and held a position of trust, authority, or supervision in relation to the victim.

Aggravated criminal sexual abuse is a Class 2 felony. (Illinois Code 5/12-16)

Spousal Rape

No person accused of violating these criminal sexual assault, aggravated criminal sexual assault, criminal sexual abuse, or aggravated criminal sexual abuse provisions shall be presumed to be incapable of committing these offenses because of relationship to the victim. (Illinois Code 5/12-18)

Criminal Transmission of HIV

A person commits criminal transmission of HIV when he or she, knowing that he or she is infected with HIV, engages in intimate sexual contact with another. **Intimate contact with another** means the exposure of the body of one person to a bodily fluid of another person in a manner that could result in the transmission of HIV. **HIV** means the human immunodeficiency virus or any other identified causative agent of acquired immunodeficiency syndrome [AIDS]. It shall be an affirmative defense that the person exposed knew that the infected person was infected with HIV, knew that the action could result in infection with HIV, and consented to the action with that knowledge. (Illinois Code 5/12-16.2)

Sexual Consent

Consent means a freely given agreement to the act of sexual penetration or sexual conduct in question. Lack of verbal or physical resistance or submission by the victim resulting from the use of force or threat of force by the accused shall not constitute consent. The manner of dress of the victim at the time of the offense shall not constitute consent. (Illinois Code 5/12-17)

Rape and Murder

A person who kills an individual without lawful justification commits first degree murder if, in performing the acts which cause the death:

(1) he either intends to kill or do great bodily harm to that individual or another, or knows that such acts will cause death to that individual or another;

(2) he knows that such acts create a strong probability of death or great bodily harm to that individual or another; or

(3) he is attempting or committing a forcible felony other than second degree murder.

(Illinois Code 5/9-1)

The complete and unedited text of Illinois' rape laws excerpted above can be found in Illinois Revised Statutes, Illinois Annotated Statutes, *or* Laws of Illinois.

INDIANA'S RAPE LAWS

Definitions

Sexual intercourse means an act that includes any penetration of the female sex organ by the male sex organ.

Deviate sexual conduct means an act involving:

(1) a sex organ of one person and the mouth or anus of another person; or

(2) the penetration of the sex organ or anus of a person by an object.

Deadly weapon means the following:

(1) a loaded or unloaded firearm; or

(2) a weapon, device, taser, or electronic stun weapon, equipment, chemical substance, or other material that in the manner it is used, or could ordinarily be used, or is intended to be used, is readily capable of causing serious bodily injury.

(Indiana Criminal Code 35-41-1-8/9/26)

Rape

A person who knowingly or intentionally has sexual intercourse with a member of the opposite sex commits the offense of rape, a Class B felony, when:

(1) the other person is compelled by force or imminent threat of force;

(2) the other person is unaware that the sexual intercourse is occurring; or

(3) the other person is so mentally disabled or deficient that consent to sexual intercourse cannot be given.

However, the rape is a Class A felony if:

(1) it is committed by using or threatening the use of deadly force;

(2) it is committed while armed with a deadly weapon; or

(3) it results in serious bodily injury to a person other than a defendant.

(Indiana Criminal Code 35-42-4-1)

Criminal Deviate Conduct

A person who knowingly or intentionally causes another person to perform or submit to deviate sexual conduct commits the offense of deviate sexual conduct, a Class B felony, when:

(a) the other person is compelled by force or imminent threat of force;

(b) the other person is unaware that the sexual intercourse is occurring; or

(c) the other person is so mentally disabled or deficient that consent to the conduct cannot be given.

However, the deviate sexual conduct is a Class A felony if:

(a) it is committed by using or threatening the use of deadly force;

(b) it is committed while armed with a deadly weapon; or

(c) it results in serious bodily injury to any person other than a defendant.

(Indiana Criminal Code 35-42-4-2)

Sexual Battery

A person who, with intent to arouse or to satisfy the person's own sexual desires or the sexual desires of another person, commits sexual battery, a Class D felony, by touching another person when that person is:

(1) compelled to submit to the touching by force or the imminent threat of force; or

(2) so mentally disabled or deficient that consent to the touching cannot be given.

However, the offense of sexual battery is a Class C felony if:

(1) it is committed by using or threatening the use of deadly force; or

(2) it is committed while armed with a deadly weapon.

(Indiana Criminal Code 35-42-4-8)

Child Molesting

A person who, with a child under fourteen years of age, performs or submits to sexual intercourse or deviate sexual conduct commits the offense of child molesting, a Class B felony. However, the offense of child molesting is a Class A felony if:

(1) it is committed by using or threatening the use of deadly force;

(2) it is committed while armed with a deadly weapon; or

(3) it results in serious bodily injury.

A person who, with a child under fourteen years of age, performs or submits to any fondling or touching, of either the child or the older person, with the intent to arouse or to satisfy the sexual desires of either the child or the older person, commits child molesting, a Class C felony.

However, the offense of child molesting is a Class A felony if:

(1) it is committed by using or threatening the use of deadly force; or

(2) it is committed while armed with a deadly weapon.

(Indiana Criminal Code 35-42-4-3)

Rape and Murder

A person who kills another human being while committing or attempting to commit rape or child molesting commits murder, a felony. (Indiana Criminal Code 35-42-1-1)

The complete and unedited text of Indiana rape laws excerpted above can be found in The Indiana Code, Indiana Statutes Annotated, Annotated Indiana Code *and* The Acts of Indiana.

IOWA'S RAPE LAWS

Definitions

The term **sex act** or **sexual activity** means any sexual contact between two or more persons, except in the course of examination or treatment by a person [professionally] licensed, by:

(1) penetration of the penis into the vagina or anus;

(2) contact between the mouth and genitalia;

(3) contact between the genitalia of one person and the genitalia or anus of another person;

(4) contact between the finger or hand of one person and the genitalia or anus of another person; or

(5) by use of artificial sexual organs or substitutes therefor in contact with the genitalia or anus.

Sexual abuse means any sex act between persons is sexual abuse of either of the participants when the act is performed with the other participant in any of the following circumstances:

(1) the act is done by force or against the will of the other. If the consent or acquiescence of the other is procured by threats of violence toward any person or if the act is done while the other is under the influence of a drug-inducing sleep or is otherwise in a state of unconsciousness, the act is done against the will of the other;

(2) such other participant is suffering from a mental defect or incapacity which precludes giving consent, or lacks the mental capacity to know the right and wrong of conduct in sexual matters; or

(3) such other participant is a child.

Serious injury means disabling mental illness or bodily injury which creates a substantial risk of death or which causes serious permanent disfigurement or protracted loss or impairment of the function of any bodily member or organ.

Dangerous weapon is any instrument or device designed primarily for use in inflicting death or injury upon a human being. Dangerous weapons include, but are not limited to, any offensive weapon, pistol, revolver, or other firearm, dagger, razor, stiletto, switchblade knife, or knife having a blade exceeding five inches in length.

(Iowa Criminal Code 702.7/.17/.18/709.1)

Sexual Abuse

A person commits sexual abuse in the first degree when in the course of committing sexual abuse, the person causes another serious injury.

Sexual abuse in the first degree is a Class A felony.

A person commits sexual abuse in the second degree when the person commits sexual abuse under any of the following circumstances:

(1) during the commission of sexual abuse the person displays in a threatening manner a dangerous weapon, or uses or threatens to use force creating a substantial risk of death or serious injury to any person;

(2) the other participant is under the age of twelve; or

(3) the person is aided or abetted by one or more persons and the sex act is committed by force or against the will of the other participant.

Sexual abuse in the second degree is a Class B felony.

A person commits sexual abuse in the third degree when the person performs a sex act under any of the following circumstances:

(1) the act is done by force or against the will of the other participant, whether or not the other participant is the person's spouse or is cohabiting with the person; or

(2) the act is between persons who are not at the time cohabiting as husband and wife and if any of the following are true:

(a) the other participant is suffering from a mental defect or incapacity which precludes giving consent;

(b) the other participant is twelve or thirteen years of age; or

(c) the other participant is fourteen or fifteen years of age and any of the following are true:

(i) the person is a member of the same household as the other participant;

(ii) the person is related to the other participant by blood or affinity to the fourth degree;

(iii) the person is in a position of authority over the other participant and uses that authority to coerce the other participant to submit; or
(iv) the person is six or more years older than the other participant.

Sexual abuse in the third degree is a Class C felony.

Under the provisions of this sexual abuse chapter it shall not be necessary to establish physical resistance by a participant in order to establish that an act of sexual abuse was committed by force or against the will of the participant. However, the circumstances surrounding the commission of the act may be considered in determining whether or not the act was done by force or against the will of the other.

Any person who commits an assault with the intent to commit sexual abuse is guilty of a Class C felony if the person thereby causes serious injury to any person and guilty of a Class D felony if the person thereby causes any person a bodily injury other than a serious injury. The person is guilty of an aggravated misdemeanor if no injury results.

(Iowa Criminal Code 709.2/.3/.4/.5/.11)

Rape and Murder

A person commits murder in the first degree when the person commits murder under any of the following circumstances:

(1) the person willfully, deliberately, and with premeditation kills another person;
(2) the person kills another person while participating in a forcible felony; or
(3) the person kills another person while escaping or attempting to escape from lawful custody.

Murder in the first degree is a Class A felony.

(Iowa Criminal Code 707.2)

The complete and unedited text of Iowa's rape laws excerpted above can be found in The Code of Iowa, The Iowa Code Annotated, *and* The Acts of Iowa.

KANSAS' RAPE LAWS

Definitions

Sexual intercourse means any penetration of the female sex organ by a finger, the male sex organ, or any object. Any penetration, however slight, is sufficient to constitute sexual intercourse. **Sexual intercourse** does not include penetration of the female sex organ by a finger or object in the course of the performance of:

(1) generally recognized health care practices; or
(2) a body cavity search conducted in accordance with the law.

Sodomy means oral contact or oral penetration of the female genitalia or oral contact of the male genitalia; or anal penetration, however slight, of a male or female by any body part or object. Sodomy does not include penetration of the anal opening by a finger or object in the course of the performance of:

(1) generally recognized health care practices; or
(2) a body cavity search conducted in accordance with the law.

Spouse means a lawful husband or wife, unless the couple is living apart in separate residences or either spouse has filed an action for annulment, separate maintenance or divorce, or for relief under the protection from abuse act.

Unlawful sexual act means any rape, indecent liberties with a child, aggravated indecent liberties with a child, criminal sodomy, aggravated criminal sodomy, lewd and lascivious behavior, sexual battery, or aggravated sexual battery.
(Kansas Criminal Code 21-3501)

Rape

Rape is:

(1) sexual intercourse with a person who does not consent to the sexual intercourse, under any of the following circumstances:

(a) when the victim is overcome by force or fear;
(b) when the victim is unconscious or physically powerless; or
(c) when the victim is incapable of giving consent because of mental deficiency or disease, or when the victim is incapable of giving consent because

of the effect of any alcoholic liquor, narcotic, drug, or other substance, which condition was known by the offender or was reasonably apparent to the offender; or

(2) sexual intercourse with a child who is under fourteen years of age.

Rape is a severity level 2, person felony.

(Kansas Criminal Code 21-3502)

Sodomy

Criminal sodomy is:

(1) sodomy between persons who are sixteen or more years of age and members of the same sex;

(2) sodomy with a child who is fourteen or more years of age but less than sixteen years of age; or

(3) causing a child fourteen or more years of age but less than sixteen years of age to engage in sodomy with any person.

Aggravated criminal sodomy is:

(1) sodomy with a child under fourteen years of age;

(2) causing a child under fourteen years of age to engage in sodomy with any person; or

(3) sodomy with a person who does not consent to the sodomy or causing a person, without the person's consent, to engage in sodomy with any person, under any of the following circumstances:

(a) when the victim is overcome by force or fear;

(b) when the victim is unconscious or physically powerless; or

(c) when the victim is incapable of giving consent because of mental deficiency or disease, or when the victim is incapable of giving consent because of the effect of any alcoholic liquor, narcotic, drug, or other substance, which condition was known by the offender or was reasonably apparent to the offender.

Criminal sodomy is a severity level 3, person felony. Aggravated criminal sodomy is a severity level 2, person felony. (Kansas Criminal Code 21-3505/6)

Indecent Liberties with a Child

Indecent liberties with a child is engaging in any of the following acts with a child who is fourteen years of age but less than sixteen years of age:

(1) any lewd fondling or touching of the person of either the child or the offender, done or submitted to with the intent to arouse or to satisfy the sexual desires of either the child or the offender, or both; or

(2) soliciting the child to engage in any lewd fondling or touching of the person of another with the intent to arouse or satisfy the sexual desires of the child, the offender, or another.

Aggravated indecent liberties with a child is:

(1) sexual intercourse with a child who is fourteen or more years of age but less than sixteen years of age; or

(2) engaging in any of the following acts with a child who is fourteen or more years of age but less than sixteen years of age and who does not consent thereto:

(a) any lewd fondling or touching of the person of either the child or the offender, done or submitted to with the intent to arouse or to satisfy the sexual desires of either the child or the offender, or both;

(b) causing the child to engage in any lewd fondling or touching of the person of another with the intent to arouse or satisfy the sexual desires of the child, the offender, or another; or

(c) engaging in any of the following acts with a child who is under fourteen years of age:

(i) any lewd fondling or touching of the person of either the child or the offender, done or submitted to with the intent to arouse or to satisfy the sexual desires of either the child or the offender, or both; or

(ii) soliciting the child to engage in any lewd
fondling or touching of the person of another
with the intent to arouse or satisfy the sexual
desires of the child, the offender, or another.

Indecent liberties with a child is a severity level 5, person felony. Aggravated indecent liberties with a child is a severity level
3 or 4, person felony.

(Kansas Criminal Code 21-3503/4)

Sexual Battery

Sexual battery is the intentional touching of the person of
another who is sixteen or more years of age, who is not the
spouse of the offender and who does not consent thereto, with
the intent to arouse or satisfy the sexual desires of the offender
or another.

Aggravated sexual battery is the intentional touching of the
person of another who is sixteen or more years of age, and who
does not consent thereto, with the intent to arouse or satisfy the
sexual desires of the offender or another under any of the following circumstances:

(1) when the victim is overcome by force or fear;
(2) when the victim is unconscious or physically powerless; or
(3) when the victim is incapable of giving consent because of mental deficiency or disease, or when the victim is incapable of giving consent because of the effect of any alcoholic liquor, narcotic, drug, or other
substance, which condition was known by the offender or was reasonably apparent to the offender.

Sexual battery is a Class A, person misdemeanor. Aggravated
sexual battery is a severity level 5, person felony.

(Kansas Criminal Code 21-3517/18)

Rape and Murder

Murder in the first degree is the killing of a human being committed in the commission of, attempt to commit, or flight from
an inherently dangerous felony.

Any of the following shall be deemed an inherently dangerous
felony:

(1) rape; or
(2) aggravated criminal sodomy.
(Kansas Criminal Code 21-3401/3436)

The complete and unedited text of Kansas' rape laws excerpted above can be found in The Kansas Statutes Annotated *and* The Laws of Kansas.

KENTUCKY'S RAPE LAWS
Definitions

Deviate sexual intercourse means any act of sexual gratification involving the sex organs of one person and the mouth or anus of another.

Forcible compulsion means physical force or threat of physical force, express or implied, which places a person in fear of immediate death or physical injury to himself or another person or in fear that he or another person will be immediately kidnapped.

Physically helpless means that a person is unconscious or for any other reason is physically unable to communicate unwillingness to an act.

Sexual contact means any touching of the sexual or other intimate parts of a person done for the purpose of gratifying the sexual desire of either party.

Sexual intercourse means sexual intercourse in its ordinary sense and includes penetration of the sex organs or anus of one person by a foreign object manipulated by another person. Sexual intercourse occurs upon any penetration, however slight; emission is not required. Sexual intercourse does not include penetration of the sex organ or anus by a foreign object in the course of the performance of generally recognized health care practices.

Foreign object means anything used in commission of a sexual act other than the person of the actor.

Mental illness means a diagnostic term that covers many clinical categories, typically including behavioral or psychological symptoms, or both, along with impairment of personal and social function.

Mentally retarded person means a person with significantly subaverage general intellectual functioning existing concurrently with deficits in adaptive behavior and manifested during the developmental period.

Mentally incapacitated means that a person is rendered temporarily incapable of appraising or controlling his conduct as a result of the influence of a controlled substance administered to him without his consent or as a result of any other act committed upon him without his consent.

(Kentucky Criminal Code 510.010)

Sexual Consent

Whether or not specifically stated, it is an element of all the following offenses that the sexual act was committed without the consent of the victim.

Lack of consent results from:

(1) forcible compulsion;

(2) incapacity to consent; or

(3) if the offense charged is sexual abuse, any circumstances in addition to forcible compulsion or incapacity to consent in which the victim does not expressly or impliedly acquiesce in the actor's conduct.

A person is deemed incapable of consent when he is:

(1) less than sixteen years old;

(2) mentally retarded or suffers from a mental illness;

(3) mentally incapacitated; or

(4) physically helpless.

(Kentucky Criminal Code 510.020)

Rape

A person is guilty of rape in the first degree when:

(1) he engages in sexual intercourse with another person by forcible compulsion; or

(2) he engages in sexual intercourse with another person who is incapable of consent because he:

(a) is physically helpless; or

(b) is less than twelve years old.

A person is guilty of rape in the second degree when, being eighteen years old or more, he engages in sexual intercourse with another person less than fourteen years old.

A person is guilty of rape in the third degree when:

(1) he engages in sexual intercourse with another person who is incapable of consent because he is mentally retarded or mentally incapacitated; or

(2) being twenty-one years old or more, he engages in sexual intercourse with another person less than sixteen years old.

Rape in the first degree is a Class B felony unless the victim is under twelve years old or receives a serious physical injury in which case it is a Class A felony. Rape in the second degree is a Class C felony. Rape in the third degree is a Class D felony. (Kentucky Criminal Code 510.040/.050/.060)

Sodomy

A person is guilty of sodomy in the first degree when:

(1) he engages in deviate sexual intercourse with another person by forcible compulsion; or

(2) he engages in deviate sexual intercourse with another person who is incapable of consent because he:

(a) is physically helpless; or

(b) is less than twelve years old.

A person is guilty of sodomy in the second degree when, being eighteen years old or more, he engages in deviate sexual intercourse with another person less than fourteen years old.

A person is guilty of sodomy in the third degree when:

(1) he engages in deviate sexual intercourse with another person who is incapable of consent because he is mentally retarded or mentally incapacitated; or

(2) being twenty-one years old or more, he engages in deviate sexual intercourse with another person less than sixteen years old.

Sodomy in the first degree is a Class B felony unless the victim is under twelve years old or receives a serious physical injury, in which case it is a Class A felony. Sodomy in the second degree is a Class C felony. Sodomy in the third degree is a Class D felony.

(Kentucky Criminal Code 510.070/.080/.090)

Sexual Abuse

A person is guilty of sexual abuse in the first degree when:

(1) he subjects another person to sexual contact by forcible compulsion; or

(2) he subjects another person to sexual contact who is incapable of consent because he:

(a) is physically helpless; or

(b) is less than twelve years old.

A person is guilty of sexual abuse in the second degree when:

(1) he subjects another person to sexual contact who is incapable of consent because he is mentally retarded or mentally incapacitated; or

(2) he subjects another person who is less than fourteen years old to sexual contact.

A person is guilty of sexual abuse in the third degree when he subjects another person to sexual contact without the latter's consent.

In any prosecution for sexual abuse, it is a defense that:

(1) the other person's lack of consent was due solely to incapacity to consent by reason of being less than sixteen years old;

(2) the other person was at least fourteen years old; and

(3) the actor was less than five years older than the other person.

Sexual abuse in the first degree is a Class D felony. Sexual abuse in the second degree is a Class A misdemeanor. Sexual abuse in the third degree is a Class B misdemeanor.

(Kentucky Criminal Code 510.110/.120/.130)

Sexual Misconduct

A person is guilty of sexual misconduct when he engages in sexual intercourse or deviate sexual intercourse with another person without the latter's consent.

Sexual misconduct is a Class A misdemeanor.

(Kentucky Criminal Code 510.140)

Rape and Murder

A person is guilty of manslaughter in the first degree when, with intent to cause serious physical injury to another person, he causes the death of such person or of a third person.

Manslaughter in the first degree is a Class B Felony.

(Kentucky Criminal Code 507.030)

The complete and unedited text of Kentucky's rape laws excerpted above can be found in Kentucky Revised Statutes Annotated and Kentucky Acts.

LOUISIANA'S RAPE LAWS

Definitions

Rape is the act of anal or vaginal sexual intercourse with a male or female person committed without the person's lawful consent. Emission is not necessary and any sexual penetration, vaginal or anal, however slight is sufficient to complete the crime. (Louisiana Criminal Code 14:41)

Aggravated Rape

Aggravated rape is a rape committed where the anal or vaginal sexual intercourse is deemed to be without lawful consent of the victim because it is committed under any one of the following circumstances:

(1) when the victim resists the act to the utmost, but whose resistance is overcome by force;

(2) when the victim is prevented from resisting the act by threats of great and immediate bodily harm, accompanied by apparent power of execution;

(3) when the victim is prevented from resisting the act because the offender is armed with a dangerous weapon;

(4) when the victim is under the age of twelve years; or

(5) when two or more offenders participated in the act.

Whoever commits the crime of aggravated rape shall be punished by life imprisonment at hard labor without benefit of parole, probation, or suspension of sentence.
(Louisiana Criminal Code 14:42)

Forcible Rape

Forcible rape is a rape committed where the anal or vaginal sexual intercourse is deemed to be without the lawful consent of the victim because the victim is prevented from resisting the act by force or threats of physical violence under circumstances where the victim reasonably believes that such resistance would not prevent the rape.

Whoever commits the crime of forcible rape shall be imprisoned at hard labor for not less than five nor more than forty years. At least two years of the sentence imposed shall be without benefit of parole, probation, or suspension of sentence. (Louisiana Criminal Code 14:42.1)

Simple Rape

Simple rape is a rape committed when the anal or vaginal sexual intercourse is deemed to be without the lawful consent of a victim who is not the spouse of the offender because it is committed under any one or more of the following circumstances:

(1) when the victim is incapable of resisting or of understanding the nature of the act by reason of stupor or abnormal condition of the mind produced by an intoxicating, narcotic, or anesthetic agent, administered by or with the privity of the offender; or when victim has such incapacity, by reason of a stupor or abnormal condition of mind from any cause, and the offender knew or should have known of the victim's incapacity;

(2) when the victim is incapable, through unsoundness of mind, whether temporary or permanent, of understanding the nature of the act and the offender knew or should have known of the victim's incapacity; or

(3) when the female victim submits under the belief that the person committing the act is her husband and such belief is intentionally induced by any artifice, pretense, or concealment practiced by the offender.

For the purposes of simple rape, a person shall not be considered to be a spouse if a judgment of separation from bed and board has been rendered, or if the person and the offender are not legally separated but are living separate and apart and the offender knows that a temporary restraining order, preliminary or permanent injunction, or other order or decree has been issued prohibiting or restraining the offender from sexually or physically abusing, intimidating, threatening violence against, or in any way physically interfering with the person.

Whoever commits the crime of simple rape shall be imprisoned, with or without hard labor, for not more than twenty-five years.
(Louisiana Criminal Code 14:43)

Sexual Battery

Sexual battery is the intentional engaging in any of the following acts with another person, who is not the spouse of the offender, where the offender acts without the consent of the victim, or where the other person has not yet attained fifteen years of age and is at least three years younger than the offender:

> (1) the touching of the anus or genitals of the victim by the offender using any instrumentality or any part of the body of the offender; or
>
> (2) the touching of the anus or genitals of the offender by the victim using any instrumentality or any part of the body of the victim.

Aggravated sexual battery is the intentional engaging in any of the following acts with another person when the offender intentionally inflicts serious bodily injury on the victim:

> (1) the touching of the anus or genitals of the victim by the offender using any instrumentality or any part of the body of the offender; or
>
> (2) the touching of the anus or genitals of the offender by the victim using any instrumentality or any part of the body of the victim.

Whoever commits the crime of sexual battery shall be imprisoned, with or without hard labor, for not more than ten years. Whoever commits the crime of aggravated sexual battery shall be imprisoned, with or without hard labor, for not more than fifteen years.
(Louisiana Criminal Code 14:43.1/.2)

Oral Sexual Battery

Sexual battery is the intentional engaging in any of the following acts with another person, who is not the spouse of the offender, when the offender compels the other person to submit by placing the person in fear of receiving bodily harm, or when the other person has not yet attained fifteen years of age and is at least three years younger than the offender:

(1) the touching of the anus or genitals of the victim by the offender using the mouth or tongue of the offender; or

(2) the touching of the anus or genitals of the offender by the victim using the mouth or tongue of the victim.

Aggravated oral sexual battery is an oral sexual battery committed when the intentional touching of the anus or genitals of one person and the mouth or tongue of another is deemed to be without the lawful consent of the victim because it is committed under any one or more of the following circumstances:

(1) when the victim resists the act to the utmost, but whose resistance is overcome by force;

(2) when the victim is prevented from resisting the act by threats of great and immediate bodily harm, accompanied by apparent power of execution;

(3) when the victim is prevented from resisting the act because the offender is armed with a dangerous weapon;

(4) when the victim is under the age of twelve years; or

(5) when two or more offenders participated in the act.

Whoever commits the crime of oral sexual battery shall be imprisoned, with or without hard labor, for not more than fifteen years. Whoever commits the crime of aggravated oral sexual battery shall be imprisoned, with or without hard labor, for not more than twenty years.

(Louisiana Criminal Code 14:43.3/.4)

Rape and Murder

First degree murder is the killing of a human being when the offender has specific intent to kill or inflict great bodily harm and is engaged in the perpetration or attempted perpetration of aggravated rape or forcible rape.

Whoever commits the crime of first degree murder shall be punished by death or by life imprisonment at hard labor without benefit of parole, probation, or suspension of sentence. (Louisiana Criminal Code 14:30)

The complete and unedited text of Louisiana's rape laws excerpted above can be found in Louisiana Revised Statutes Annotated *and* Acts of the State of Louisiana.

MAINE'S RAPE LAWS

Definitions

Spouse means a person legally married to the actor, but does not include a legally married person living apart from the actor under a separation.

Sexual act means:

(1) any act between two persons involving direct physical contact between the genitals of one and the mouth or anus of the other, or direct physical contact between the genitals of one and the genitals of the other;

(2) any act between a person and an animal being used by another person which act involves direct physical contact between the genitals of one and the mouth or anus of the other, or direct physical contact between the genitals of one and the genitals of the other; or

(3) any act involving direct physical contact between the genitals or anus of one and an instrument or device manipulated by another person when that act is done for the purpose of arousing or gratifying sexual desire or for the purpose of causing bodily injury or offensive physical contact.

A sexual act may be proved without allegation or proof of penetration.

Sexual contact means any touching of the genitals or anus, directly or through clothing, other than as would constitute a sexual act, for the purpose of arousing or gratifying sexual desire.

Compulsion means the use of physical force, a threat to use physical force or a combination thereof that makes a person unable to physically repel the actor or produces in that person a reasonable fear that death, serious bodily injury or kidnapping might be imminently inflicted upon that person or another human being.

Compulsion, as defined above, places no duty upon the victim to resist the actor.

(Maine Criminal Code 251)

Gross Sexual Assault

A person is guilty of gross sexual assault if that person engages in a sexual act with another person and:

(1) the other person submits as a result of compulsion; or

(2) the other person, not the actor's spouse, has not in fact attained the age of fourteen years.

Violation of this section is a Class A crime.

A person is guilty of gross sexual assault if that person engages in a sexual act with another person and:

(1) the actor has substantially impaired the other person's power to appraise or control the other person's sexual acts by administering or employing drugs, intoxicants or other similar means;

(2) the actor compels or induces the other person to engage in the sexual act by any threat;

(3) the other person suffers from a mental disability that is reasonably apparent or known to the actor, and which in fact renders the other person substantially incapable of appraising the nature of the contact involved or of understanding that the person has the right to deny or withdraw consent;

(4) the other person is unconscious or otherwise physically incapable of resisting and has not consented to the sexual act;

(5) the other person, not the actor's spouse, is in official custody as a probationer or a parolee, or is detained in a hospital, prison or other institution, and the actor has supervisory or disciplinary authority over the other person;

(6) the other person, not the actor's spouse, has not in fact attained the age of eighteen years and is a student enrolled in a private or public elementary, secondary, or special education school, facility or institution and the actor is a teacher, employee or other official having instructional, supervisory or disciplinary authority over the student;

(7) the other person, not the actor's spouse, has not attained the age of eighteen years and is a resident in or

attending a children's home, day care facility, residential child care facility or institution regularly providing care or services for children, and the actor is a teacher, employee or other person having instructional, supervisory or disciplinary authority over the other person;

(8) the other person has not in fact attained the age of eighteen years and the actor is a parent, stepparent, foster parent, guardian or other similar person responsible for the long-term care and welfare of that other person; or

(9) the actor is a psychiatrist, a psychologist or licensed social worker or purports to be a psychiatrist, psychologist or licensed social worker to the other person and the other person, not the actor's spouse, is a patient or client for mental health therapy of the actor.

Violations of these sections are Class B or Class C crimes. (Maine Criminal Code 253)

Unlawful Sexual Contact

A person is guilty of unlawful sexual contact if the person intentionally subjects another person to any sexual contact, and:

(1) the other person has not expressly or impliedly acquiesced in the sexual contact;

(2) the other person is unconscious or otherwise physically incapable of resisting, and has not consented to the sexual contact;

(3) the other person, not the actor's spouse, has not in fact attained the age of fourteen years and the actor is at least three years older;

(4) the other person suffers from a mental disability that is reasonably apparent or known to the actor, which in fact renders the other person substantially incapable of appraising the nature of the contact involved or of understanding that the person has the right to deny or withdraw consent;

(5) the other person, not the actor's spouse, is in official custody as a probationer or parolee or is detained

in a hospital, prison or other institution, and the actor has supervisory or disciplinary authority over the other person;

(6) the other person, not the actor's spouse, has not in fact attained the age of eighteen years and is a student enrolled in a private or public elementary, secondary, or special education school, facility or institution and the actor is a teacher, employee or other official having instructional, supervisory or disciplinary authority over the student;

(7) the other person has not in fact attained the age of eighteen years and the actor is a parent, stepparent, foster parent, guardian or other similar person responsible for the long-term care and welfare of that other person; or

(8) the other person submits as a result of compulsion.

Unlawful sexual contact is a Class D crime.
(Maine Criminal Code 255)

Sexual Abuse of a Minor

A person is guilty of sexual abuse of a minor if, having attained the age of nineteen years, the person engages in a sexual act with another person, not the actor's spouse, who has attained the age of fourteen years but has not attained the age of sixteen years, provided that the actor is at least five years older than the other person.

Sexual abuse of a minor is a Class D crime.
(Maine Criminal Code 254)

Rape and Murder

A person is guilty of felony murder if acting alone or with one or more persons in the commission of, or an attempt to commit, or immediate flight after committing or attempting to commit rape, he or another participant in fact causes the death of a human being. Felony murder is a Class A crime. (Maine Criminal Code 202)

The complete and unedited text of Maine's rape laws excerpted above can be found in Maine Revised Statutes *and* The Laws of Maine.

MARYLAND'S RAPE LAWS
Definitions

Sexual act means cunnilingus, fellatio, analingus, or anal intercourse, but does not include vaginal intercourse. Emission of semen is not required. Penetration, however slight, is evidence of anal intercourse. **Sexual act** also means the penetration, however slight, by any object into the genital or anal opening of another person's body if the penetration can be reasonably construed as being for the purposes of sexual arousal or gratification or for the abuse of either party and if the penetration is not for accepted medical purposes.

Sexual contact means the intentional touching of any part of the victim's or actor's anal or genital areas or other intimate parts for the purposes of sexual arousal or gratification or for the abuse of either party and includes the penetration, however slight, by any part of a person's body, other than the penis, mouth, or tongue, into the genital or anal opening of another person's body if that penetration can be reasonably construed as being for the purposes of sexual arousal or gratification or for the abuse of either party.

Vaginal intercourse has its ordinary meaning of genital copulation. Penetration, however slight, is evidence of vaginal intercourse. Emission of semen is not required.

Physically helpless means:

(1) a victim who is unconscious; or

(2) a victim who does not consent to an act of vaginal intercourse, a sexual act, or sexual contact, and is physically unable to resist or communicate unwillingness to submit.

Mentally defective means:

(1) a victim who suffers from mental retardation; or

(2) a victim who suffers from a mental disorder, either of which temporarily or permanently renders the victim incapable of appraising the nature of his or her conduct, or resisting the act of vaginal intercourse, a sexual act, or sexual contact, or of communicating unwillingness to submit.

Mentally incapacitated means a victim who, due to the influence of a drug, narcotic or intoxicating substance, or due to any act committed upon the victim without the victim's consent or

awareness, is rendered either incapable of appraising the nature of his or her conduct, or resisting the act of vaginal intercourse, a sexual act, or sexual contact.
(Maryland Criminal Code 27-461)

Rape

A person is guilty of rape in the first degree if the person engages in vaginal intercourse with another person by force or threat of force against the will and without the consent of the other person and:

(1) employs or displays a dangerous or deadly weapon or an article which the other person reasonably concludes is a dangerous or deadly weapon;

(2) inflicts suffocation, strangulation, disfigurement, or serious physical injury upon the other person or upon anyone else in the course of committing the offense;

(3) threatens or places the victim in fear that the victim or any person known to the victim will be imminently subjected to death, suffocation, strangulation, disfigurement, serious physical injury, or kidnapping;

(4) the person commits the offense aided and abetted by one or more other persons; or

(5) the person commits the offense in connection with the breaking and entering of a dwelling house.

A person is guilty of rape in the second degree if the person engages in vaginal intercourse with another person:

(1) by force or threat or force against the will and without the consent of the other person;

(2) who is mentally defective, mentally incapacitated, or physically helpless, and the person performing the act knows or should reasonably know the other person is mentally defective, mentally incapacitated, or physically helpless; or

(3) who is under fourteen years of age and the person performing the act is at least four years older than the victim.

Any person violating the provisions of the first degree rape section is guilty of a felony and upon conviction is subject to imprisonment for a period of no more than his natural life. Any person violating the provisions of the second degree rape section is guilty of a felony and upon conviction is subject to imprisonment for a period of not more than twenty years. (Maryland Criminal Code 27-462/463)

Sexual Offense

A person is guilty of sexual offense in the first degree if the person engages in a sexual act with another person by force or threat of force against the will and without the consent of the other person and:

(1) employs or displays a dangerous or deadly weapon or an article which the other person reasonably concludes is a dangerous or deadly weapon;

(2) inflicts suffocation, strangulation, disfigurement, or serious physical injury upon the other person or upon anyone else in the course of committing the offense;

(3) threatens or places the victim in fear that the victim or any person known to the victim will be imminently subjected to death, suffocation, strangulation, disfigurement, serious physical injury, or kidnapping;

(4) the person commits the offense aided and abetted by one or more other persons; or

(5) the person commits the offense in connection with burglary in the first, second, or third degree.

A person is guilty of sexual offense in the second degree if the person engages in a sexual act with another person:

(1) by force or threat of force against the will and without the consent of the other person;

(2) who is mentally defective, mentally incapacitated, or physically helpless, and the person performing the act knows or should reasonably know the other person is mentally defective, mentally incapacitated, or physically helpless; or

(3) who is under fourteen years of age and the person performing the act is at least four years older than the victim.

Any person violating the provisions of the first degree sexual offense section is guilty of a felony and upon conviction is subject to imprisonment for no more than the period of his natural life. Any person violating the provisions of the second degree sexual offense section is guilty of a felony and upon conviction is subject to imprisonment for a period of not more than twenty years. (Maryland Criminal Code 27-464/464A)

Spousal Rape

A person may be prosecuted for rape or a sexual offense against his legal spouse if the person uses force against the will and without the consent of the person's legal spouse.

A person may be prosecuted for rape or a sexual offense against his legal spouse if the person and the person's legal spouse have lived separate and apart without cohabitation and without interruption:

(1) pursuant to a written separation agreement executed by both the person and the person's legal spouse; or

(2) for at least six months immediately before the commission of the alleged rape or sexual offense. (Maryland Criminal Code 27-464D)

Rape and Murder

All murder which shall be committed in the perpetration of, or attempt to perpetrate any rape in any degree [or] sexual offense in the first or second degree shall be murder in the first degree. (Maryland Criminal Code 27-410)

The complete and unedited text of Maryland's rape laws excerpted above can be found in The Maryland Code Annotated *and* The Laws of Maryland.

MASSACHUSETTS' RAPE LAWS

Definitions

Rape means sexual intercourse or unnatural sexual intercourse by a person with another person who is compelled to submit by force and against his will or by threat of bodily injury, or sexual intercourse or unnatural sexual intercourse with a child under sixteen years of age.

Aggravated rape means sexual intercourse or unnatural sexual intercourse by a person with another person who is compelled to submit by force and against his will or by threat of bodily injury; and either such sexual intercourse or unnatural sexual intercourse results in or is committed with acts resulting in serious bodily injury, or is committed by a joint enterprise, or is committed during the commission or attempted commission of [another] offense.
(Massachusetts Criminal Code 277-39)

Rape

Whoever has sexual intercourse or unnatural sexual intercourse with a person, and compels such person to submit by force and against his will, or compels such person to submit by threat of bodily injury and if either such sexual intercourse or unnatural sexual intercourse results in or is committed with acts resulting in serious bodily injury, or is committed by a joint enterprise, or is committed during the commission or attempted commission of [another] offense shall be punished by imprisonment for life or for any term of years.

Whoever has sexual intercourse or unnatural sexual intercourse with a person and compels such person to submit by force and against his will, or compels such person to submit by threat of bodily injury, shall be punished by imprisonment for not more than twenty years; and whoever commits a second or subsequent such offense shall be punished by imprisonment for life or for any term of years.
(Massachusetts Criminal Code 265-22)

Attempted Rape

Whoever assaults a person with intent to commit a rape shall be punished by imprisonment for not more than twenty years.

Whoever commits a second or subsequent such offense shall be punished by imprisonment for life or for any term of years. (Massachusetts Criminal Code 265-24)

Child Rape

Whoever has sexual intercourse or unnatural sexual intercourse with a child under sixteen, and compels said child to submit by force and against his will or compels said child to submit by threat of bodily injury, shall be punished by imprisonment for life or for any term of years; and whoever over the age of eighteen commits a second or subsequent such offense he shall be [punished by imprisonment] for life or for any term of years, but not less than five years.

Whoever unlawfully has sexual intercourse or unnatural sexual intercourse and abuses a child under sixteen years shall, for the first offense, be punished by imprisonment for life or for any term of years, and for the second or subsequent offense by imprisonment for life or for any term of years, but not less than five years.
(Massachusetts Criminal Code 265-22A/23)

Attempted Child Rape

Whoever assaults a child under sixteen with intent to commit a rape shall be punished by imprisonment for life or for any term of years. Whoever over the age of eighteen commits a subsequent such offense shall be punished by imprisonment for life or for any term of years but not less than five years.
(Massachusetts Criminal Code 265-24B)

The Rape Shield

That portion of the records of a court or any police department of the commonwealth which contains the name of the victim in an arrest, investigation or complaint for rape or assault with intent to rape shall be withheld from public inspection, except with the consent of a justice of such court. (Massachusetts Criminal Code 265-24C)

Rape and Murder

Murder committed with deliberately premeditated malice aforethought, or with extreme atrocity or cruelty, or in the commission or attempted commission of a crime punishable with death or imprisonment for life, is murder in the first degree.

The death penalty may be authorized when the murder was committed by the defendant and occurred during the commission or attempted commission or flight after attempting to commit aggravated rape, rape, rape of a child, assault with intent to rape, or assault with intent to rape a child under sixteen. (Massachusetts Criminal Code 265-1/279-69)

The complete and unedited text of Massachusetts' rape laws excerpted above can be found in General Laws of the Commonwealth of Massachusetts, Massachusetts General Laws Annotated, Annotated Laws of Massachusetts, *and* Acts and Resolves of Massachusetts.

MICHIGAN'S RAPE LAWS
Definitions

Actor means a person accused of criminal sexual conduct.

Developmental disability means an impairment of general intellectual functioning or adaptive behavior.

Intimate parts includes the primary genital area, groin, inner thigh, buttock, or breast of a human being.

Mental illness means a substantial disorder of thought or mood which significantly impairs judgment, behavior, capacity to recognize reality, or ability to cope with the ordinary demands of life.

Mentally disabled means that a person has a mental illness, is mentally retarded, or has a developmental disability.

Mentally incapable means that a person suffers from a mental disease or defect which renders that person temporarily or permanently incapable of appraising the nature of his or her conduct.

Mentally incapacitated means that a person is rendered temporarily incapable of appraising or controlling his or her conduct due to the influence of a narcotic, anesthetic, or other substance administered to that person without his or her consent.

Mentally retarded means significantly subaverage general intellectual functioning which originates during the developmental period and is associated with impairment in adaptive behavior.

Physically helpless means that a person is unconscious, asleep or for any any other reason is physically unable to communicate unwillingness to an act.

Personal injury means bodily injury, disfigurement, mental anguish, chronic pain, pregnancy, disease, or loss or impairment of a sexual or reproductive organ.

Sexual contact includes the intentional touching of the victim's or actor's intimate parts or the intentional touching of the clothing covering the immediate area of the victim's or actor's intimate parts, if that intentional touching can reasonably be construed as being for the purpose of sexual arousal or gratification.

Sexual penetration means sexual intercourse, cunnilingus, fellatio, anal intercourse, or of any other intrusion, however slight, of any part of a person's body or of any object into the genital or anal openings of another person's body, but emission of semen is not required.

Victim means the person alleging to have been subjected to criminal sexual conduct.

(Michigan Criminal Code 750.520a)

First and Second Degree Criminal Sexual Conduct

A person is guilty of criminal sexual conduct in the first degree if he or she engages in sexual penetration or is guilty of criminal sexual conduct in the second degree if he or she engages in sexual contact with another person and if any of the following circumstances exist:

(1) that other person is under thirteen years of age;

(2) that other person is at least thirteen but less than sixteen years of age and any of the following:

(a) the actor is a member of the same household as the victim;

(b) the actor is related to the victim by blood or affinity to the fourth degree; or

(c) the actor is in a position of authority over the victim and uses this authority to coerce the victim to submit;

(3) sexual penetration or sexual contact occurs under circumstances involving the commission of any other felony;

(4) the actor is aided or abetted by one or more other persons and either of the following circumstances exists:

(a) the actor knows or has reason to know that the victim is mentally incapable, mentally incapacitated, or physically helpless; or

(b) the actor uses force or coercion to accomplish the sexual penetration or contact;

(5) the actor is armed with a weapon or any article used or fashioned in a manner to lead the victim to reasonably believe it to be a weapon;

(6) the actor causes personal injury to the victim and force or coercion is used to accomplish sexual penetration or sexual contact. Force or coercion includes but is not limited to any of the following circumstances:

(a) when the actor overcomes the victim through the actual application of physical force or physical violence;

(b) when the actor coerces the victim to submit by threatening to use force or violence on the victim, and the victim believes that the actor has the present ability to execute these threats;

(c) when the actor coerces the victim to submit by threatening to retaliate in the future against the victim, or any other person, and the victim believes that the actor has the ability to execute this threat. **To retaliate** includes threats of physical punishment, kidnapping, or extortion;

(d) when the actor engages in the medical treatment or examination of the victim in a manner or for purposes which are medically recognized as unethical or unacceptable;

(e) when the actor, through concealment or by the element of surprise, is able to overcome the victim;

(7) the actor causes personal injury to the victim and the actor knows or has reason to know that the victim is mentally incapable, mentally incapacitated, or physically helpless; or

(8) that other person is mentally incapable, mentally disabled, mentally incapacitated, or physically helpless, and any of the following:

(a) the actor is related to the victim by blood or affinity to the fourth degree; or

(b) the actor is in a position of authority over the victim and used this authority to coerce the victim to submit.

Criminal sexual conduct in the first degree is a felony punishable by imprisonment for life or for any term of years. Criminal sexual conduct in the second degree is a felony punishable by

imprisonment for not more than fifteen years.
(Michigan Criminal Code 750.520b/c)

Third and Fourth Degree Criminal Sexual Conduct

A person is guilty of criminal sexual conduct in the third degree if the person engages in sexual penetration with another person and if any of the following circumstances exists:

(1) that other person is at least thirteen years of age and under sixteen years of age;

(2) force or coercion is used to accomplish the sexual penetration; or

(3) the actor knows or has reason to know that the victim is mentally incapable, mentally incapacitated, or physically helpless.

A person is guilty of criminal sexual conduct in the fourth degree if he or she engages in sexual contact with another person and if any of the following circumstances exist:

(1) force or coercion is used to accomplish the sexual contact; or

(2) the actor knows or has reason to know that the victim is mentally incapable, mentally incapacitated, or physically helpless.

Criminal sexual conduct in the third degree is a felony punishable by imprisonment for not more than fifteen years. Criminal sexual conduct in the fourth degree is a misdemeanor punishable by imprisonment for not more than two years, or by a fine of not more than $500, or both.
(Michigan Criminal Code 750.520d/e)

DNA Identification

A person convicted of a violation or an attempted violation of the above criminal sexual conduct provisions shall provide samples of his or her blood for chemical testing for DNA identification profiling or a determination of the blood's genetic markers. (Michigan Criminal Code 750.520m)

Spousal Rape

A person may be charged and convicted under the above criminal sexual conduct provisions even though the victim is his or her legal spouse. (Michigan Criminal Code 750.520l)

Rape and Murder

Murder which is committed in the perpetration, or attempt to perpetrate criminal sexual conduct in the first or third degree is murder of the first degree. (Michigan Criminal Code 750.316)

The complete and unedited text of Michigan's rape laws excerpted above can be found in Michigan Compiled Laws, Michigan Compiled Laws Annotated, Michigan Statutes Annotated, *and* Public Acts of the State of Michigan.

MINNESOTA'S RAPE LAWS

Definitions

Actor means a person accused of criminal sexual conduct.

Complainant means a person alleged to have been subjected to criminal sexual conduct.

Force means the infliction, attempted infliction, or threatened infliction by the actor of bodily harm or commission or threat of any other crime by the actor against the complainant or another, which:

(1) causes the complainant to reasonably believe that the actor has the present ability to execute the threat; and

(2) if the actor does not have a significant relationship to the complainant, also causes the complainant to submit.

Coercion means words or circumstances that cause the complainant reasonably to fear that the actor will inflict bodily harm upon, or hold in confinement, the complainant or another, or force the complainant to submit to sexual penetration or contact.

Consent means words or overt actions by a person indicating a freely given present agreement to perform a particular sexual act with the actor. Consent does not mean the existence of a prior or current social relationship between the actor and the complainant or that the complainant failed to resist a particular sexual act. A person who is mentally incapacitated or physically helpless [as defined below] cannot consent to a sexual act. Corroboration of the victim's testimony is not required to show lack of consent.

Intimate parts means the primary genital area, groin, inner thigh, buttocks, or breast of a human being.

Mentally impaired means that a person, as a result of inadequately developed or impaired intelligence or a substantial psychiatric disorder of thought or mood, lacks the judgment to give a reasoned consent to sexual contact or sexual penetration.

Mentally incapacitated means that a person under the influence of alcohol, a narcotic, anesthetic, or any other substance, administered to that person without the person's agreement, lacks the judgment to give a reasoned consent to sexual contact or sexual penetration.

Physically helpless means that a person is:
(1) asleep or not conscious;
(2) unable to withhold consent or to withdraw consent because of a physical condition; or
(3) unable to communicate non-consent and the condition is known or reasonably should have been known to the actor.

Position of authority includes but is not limited to any person who is a parent or acting in the place of a parent and charged with any of a parent's rights, duties or responsibility for the health, welfare, or supervision of a child.

Domestic abuse means criminal sexual conduct within the meaning of the sexual conduct provisions.
(Minnesota Criminal Code 609.341/518B.01)

Sexual Contact

Sexual contact includes any of the following acts committed without the complainant's consent:
(1) the intentional touching by the actor of the complainant's intimate parts;
(2) the touching by the complainant of the actor's, the complainant's, or another's intimate parts effected by coercion or the use of a position of authority, or by inducement if the complainant is under thirteen years of age or mentally impaired;
(3) the touching by another of the complainant's intimate parts effected by coercion or the use of a position of authority; or
(4) in any of the cases above, the touching of the clothing covering the immediate area of the intimate parts.
(Minnesota Criminal Code 609.341)

Sexual Penetration

Sexual penetration means any of the following acts committed without the complainant's consent:
(1) sexual intercourse, cunnilingus, fellatio, or anal intercourse; or

(2) any intrusion however slight into the genital or anal openings:

(a) of the complainant's body by any part of the actor's body or any object used by the actor for this purpose;

(b) of the complainant's body by any part of the body of the complainant, by any part of the body of another person, or by any object used by the complainant or another person for this purpose, when effected by coercion or the use of a position of authority, or by inducement if the child is under thirteen years of age or mentally impaired; or

(c) of the body of the actor or another person by any part of the body of the complainant or by any object used by the complainant for this purpose, when effected by coercion or the use of a position of authority, or by inducement if the child is under thirteen years of age or mentally impaired.

(Minnesota Criminal Code 609.341)

First Degree Criminal Sexual Conduct

A person who engages in sexual penetration with another person, or in sexual contact with a person under thirteen [as defined above] is guilty of criminal sexual conduct in the first degree if:

(1) the complainant is under thirteen years of age and the actor is more than thirty-six months older than the complainant. Neither mistake as to the complainant's age nor consent to the act by the complainant is a defense;

(2) the complainant is at least thirteen but less than sixteen years of age and the actor is more than forty-eight months older than the complainant and in a position of authority over the complainant, and uses this authority to cause the complainant to submit. Neither mistake as to the complainant's age nor consent to the act by the complainant is a defense;

(3) circumstances existing at the time of the act cause the complainant to have a reasonable fear of imminent great bodily harm to the complainant or another;

(4) the actor is armed with a dangerous weapon or any article used or fashioned in a manner to lead the complainant to reasonably believe it to be a dangerous weapon and uses or threatens to use the weapon or article to cause the complainant to submit; or

(5) the actor causes personal injury to the complainant.

[A] person convicted of criminal sexual conduct in the first degree may be sentenced to imprisonment for not more than thirty years or to the payment of a fine of not more than $40,000, or both.

(Minnesota Criminal Code 609.342)

Second Degree Criminal Sexual Conduct

A person who engages in sexual contact with another person is guilty of criminal sexual conduct in the second degree if:

(1) the complainant is under thirteen years of age and the actor is more than thirty-six months older than the complainant. Neither mistake as to the complainant's age nor consent to the act by the complainant is a defense. The State is not required to prove that the sexual contact was coerced;

(2) the complainant is at least thirteen but less than sixteen years of age and the actor is more than forty-eight months older than the complainant and in a position of authority over the complainant, and uses this authority to cause the complainant to submit. Neither mistake as to the complainant's age nor consent to the act by the complainant is a defense;

(3) circumstances existing at the time of the act cause the complainant to have a reasonable fear of imminent great bodily harm to the complainant or another;

(4) the actor is armed with a dangerous weapon or any article used or fashioned in a manner to lead the complainant to reasonably believe it to be a dangerous

weapon and uses or threatens to use the weapon or article to cause the complainant to submit; or

(5) the actor causes personal injury to the complainant.

[A] person convicted of criminal sexual conduct in the second degree may be sentenced to imprisonment for not more than twenty-five years or to a payment of a fine of not more than $35,000, or both.

(Minnesota Criminal Code 609.343)

Rape and Murder

Whoever does any of the following is guilty of murder in the first degree and shall be sentenced to imprisonment for life:

(1) causes the death of a human being while committing or attempting to commit criminal sexual conduct in the first or second degree with force or violence, either upon or affecting the person or another; or

(2) causes the death of a human being while committing domestic abuse, when the perpetrator has engaged in a past pattern of domestic abuse upon the victim and the death occurs under circumstances manifesting an extreme indifference to human life.

(Minnesota Criminal Code 609.185)

The complete and unedited text of Minnesota's rape laws excerpted above can be found in Minnesota Statutes, Minnesota Statutes Annotated, *or* The Laws of Minnesota.

MISSISSIPPI'S RAPE LAWS
Definitions

Sexual penetration includes cunnilingus, fellatio, buggery or pederasty, any penetration of the genital or anal openings of another person's body by any part of a person's body, and insertion of any object into the genital or anal openings of another person's body.

Mentally defective person is one who suffers from a mental disease, defect or condition which renders that person temporarily or permanently incapable of knowing the nature and quality of his or her conduct.

Mentally incapacitated person is one who is rendered incapable of knowing or controlling his or her conduct, or incapable of resisting an act due to the influence of any drug, narcotic, anesthetic, or other substance administered to that person without his or her consent.

Physically helpless person is one who is unconscious or one who for any reason is physically incapable of communicating an unwillingness to engage in an act.

(Mississippi Criminal Code 97-3-97)

Sexual Battery

A person is guilty of sexual battery if he or she engages in sexual penetration with:

(1) another person without his or her consent;

(2) a mentally defective, mentally incapacitated or physically helpless person; or

(3) a child under the age of fourteen years.

A person is guilty of sexual battery if he or she engages in sexual penetration with a child of fourteen but less than eighteen years if the person is in a position of trust or authority over the child including without limitation the child's teacher, counselor, physician, psychiatrist, psychologist, minister, priest, physical therapist, chiropractor, legal guardian, parent, stepparent, aunt, uncle, scout leader or coach.

Every person who shall be convicted of sexual battery shall be imprisoned for a period of not more than thirty years; however, any person convicted of a second or subsequent [sexual] offense shall be imprisoned for not more than forty years and

upon sentencing, the offender shall serve at least one-half of the sentence so imposed.
(Mississippi Criminal Code 97-3-95/101)

Assault with Intent to Forcibly Ravish

Every person who shall be convicted of an assault with intent to forcibly ravish any female of previous chaste character shall be punished by imprisonment for life, or for such shorter time as may be fixed by the jury, or by the [judge] upon the entry of a plea of guilty.
(Mississippi Criminal Code 97-3-71)

Carnal Knowledge of a Child Under Fourteen Years

Every person eighteen years of age or older who shall be convicted of rape by carnally knowing a child under the age of fourteen years, upon conviction, shall be sentenced to death or imprisonment for life.

However, any person thirteen years of age or over but under eighteen years of age convicted of [rape by carnally knowing a child under the age of fourteen years] shall be sentenced to such term of imprisonment as the court, in its discretion, may determine.

In all cases where the child is under the age of fourteen years it shall not be necessary to prove penetration of the child's private parts where it is shown the private parts have been lacerated or torn in the attempt to have carnal knowledge of the child.

Every person who shall forcibly ravish any person of the age of fourteen years or upward, or who shall have been convicted of having carnal knowledge of any person above the age of fourteen years without such person's consent, by administering to such person any substance or liquid which shall produce such stupor or such imbecility of mind or weakness of body as to prevent effectual resistance, upon conviction, shall be imprisoned for life.

This section shall apply whether the perpetrator is married to the victim or not.
(Mississippi Criminal Code 97-3-65)

Carnal Knowledge
of a Child Over Fourteen Years

Any person who shall have carnal knowledge of any unmarried person of previously chaste character younger than himself or herself and over fourteen and under eighteen years of age, upon conviction, shall be punished either by a fine not exceeding five hundred dollars, or by imprisonment not longer than six months, or by both such fine and imprisonment not exceeding five years; and such punishment shall be fixed by the jury trying each case, or by the [judge] upon the entry of a plea of guilty. (Mississippi Criminal Code 97-3-67)

Carnal Knowledge
of a Step- or Adopted Child

Any person who shall have carnal knowledge of his or her unmarried stepchild or adopted child younger than himself or herself and over fourteen and under eighteen years of age, upon conviction, shall be punished by imprisonment for a term not exceeding ten years. (Mississippi Criminal Code 97-5-41)

Spousal Rape

A person is not guilty of [the above rape provisions] if the alleged victim is that person's legal spouse and at the time of the alleged offense such person and the alleged victim are not separated and living apart; however, that the legal spouse of the alleged victim may be found guilty of sexual battery if the legal spouse engaged in forcible sexual penetration without the consent of the alleged victim. (Mississippi Criminal Code 97-3-99)

Rape and Murder

The killing of a human being without the authority of law by any means or in any manner shall be capital murder when done without any design to effect death by any person engaged in the commission of the crime of rape, sexual battery, unnatural intercourse with any child under the age of twelve, or nonconsensual unnatural intercourse with mankind, or in any attempt to commit such felonies.

Every person who shall be convicted of capital murder shall be sentenced to death or imprisonment for life without parole. (Mississippi Criminal Code 97-3-19/21)

The complete and unedited text of Mississippi's rape laws excerpted above can be found in The Mississippi Code Annotated or The General Laws of Mississippi.

MISSOURI'S RAPE LAWS

Definitions

Sexual intercourse means any penetration, however slight, of the female sex organ by the male sex organ, whether or not an emission results.

Deviate sexual intercourse means any act involving the genitals of one person and the mouth, tongue, or anus of another person or a sexual act involving the penetration, however slight, of the male or female sex organ or the anus by a finger, instrument or object done for the purpose of arousing or gratifying the sexual desire of any person.

Sexual contact means any touching of another person with the genitals or any touching of the genitals or anus of another person, or the breast of a female person, for the purpose of arousing or gratifying the sexual desire of any person.

Sexual conduct means sexual intercourse, deviate sexual intercourse or sexual contact.

(Missouri Criminal Code 566.010)

Rape

A person commits the crime of forcible rape if he has sexual intercourse with another person without that person's consent by the use of forcible compulsion.

A person commits the crime of rape if he has sexual intercourse with another person to whom he is not married who is less than fourteen years old.

Forcible rape or an attempt to commit forcible rape as described [above] or rape as described [above] is a felony for which the authorized term of imprisonment, including both prison and conditional terms, is life imprisonment or a term of years not less than five years and not greater than thirty years, unless in the course thereof the actor inflicts serious physical injury on any person, displays a deadly weapon or dangerous instrument in a threatening manner or subjects the victim to sexual intercourse or deviate sexual intercourse with more than one person or the victim of a rape as described [above] is less than twelve years of age, in which cases forcible rape or an attempt to commit forcible rape is a Class A felony.

(Missouri Criminal Code 566.030)

Sodomy

A person commits the crime of sodomy if he has deviate sexual intercourse with another person without that person's consent by the use of forcible compulsion.

A person commits the crime of sodomy if he has deviate sexual intercourse with another person to whom he is not married who is less than fourteen years old.

Forcible sodomy or an attempt to commit forcible sodomy as described [above] or sodomy as described [above] is a felony for which the authorized term of imprisonment, including both prison and conditional terms, is life imprisonment or a term of years not less than five years, unless in the course thereof the actor inflicts serious physical injury on any person, displays a deadly weapon or dangerous instrument in a threatening manner or subjects the victim to deviate sexual intercourse or sexual intercourse with more than one person, in which cases forcible sodomy or an attempt to commit forcible sodomy is a Class A felony.

(Missouri Criminal Code 566.060)

First Degree Sexual Abuse

A person commits the crime of sexual abuse in the first degree if:

(1) he subjects another person to sexual contact without that person's consent by the use of forcible compulsion; or

(2) he subjects another person who is less than twelve years old to sexual contact.

Sexual abuse in the first degree is a Class D felony unless in the course thereof the actor inflicts serious physical harm on any person, displays a deadly weapon in a threatening manner, or the offense is committed as part of a ritual or ceremony, in which cases the crime is a Class C felony.

(Missouri Criminal Code 566.100)

First Degree Sexual Assault

A person commits the crime of sexual assault in the first degree if he has sexual intercourse with another person to whom he is is not married and who is incapacitated or who is fourteen or fifteen years old.

Sexual assault in the first degree is a Class C felony unless in the course thereof the actor inflicts serious physical injury on any person, [or] displays a deadly weapon in a threatening manner, in which cases the crime is a Class B felony.
(Missouri Criminal Code 566.040)

First Degree Deviate Sexual Assault

A person commits the crime of deviate sexual assault in the first degree if he has deviate sexual intercourse with another person to whom he is not married and who is incapacitated or who is fourteen or fifteen years old.

Deviate sexual assault in the first degree is a Class C felony unless in the course thereof the actor inflicts serious physical injury on any person, [or] displays a deadly weapon in a threatening manner, in which cases the crime is a Class B felony.
(Missouri Criminal Code 566.070)

Sexual Misconduct

A person commits the crime of sexual misconduct if:

(1) being less than seventeen years old, he has sexual intercourse with another person to whom he is not married who is fourteen or fifteen years old;

(2) he engages in deviate sexual intercourse with another person to whom he is not married and who is under the age of seventeen years; or

(3) he has deviate sexual intercourse with another person of the same sex.
(Missouri Criminal Code 566.090)

The Rape Shield

In prosecutions under this section, opinion and reputation evidence of the [victim's] prior sexual conduct is inadmissible;

evidence of specific instances of the [victim's] prior sexual conduct or the absence of such instances is inadmissible, except where such specific instances are:

(1) evidence of the sexual conduct of the [victim] with the defendant to prove consent where consent is a defense to the alleged crime and the evidence is reasonably contemporaneous with the date of the alleged crime;

(2) evidence of specific instances of sexual activity showing alternative source or origin of semen, pregnancy or disease;

(3) evidence of immediate surrounding circumstances of the alleged crime; or

(4) evidence relating to the previous chastity of the [victim] in cases where previously chaste character is required to be proved by the prosecution.

(Missouri Criminal Code 491.015)

Spousal Rape

A person may be convicted of the crime of rape or sodomy or sexual abuse [as defined above] in the first degree even if at the time of the offense the defendant is married to the victim. Any provision of the common law to the contrary is hereby abrogated [annulled].

(Missouri Criminal Code 566.085)

Rape and Murder

In all cases of murder in the first degree for which the death penalty is authorized the [judge] shall consider whether aggravating circumstances are established beyond a reasonable doubt. Aggravating circumstances [include]: murder in the first degree committed while the defendant was engaged in the perpetration or was aiding or encouraging another person to perpetrate or attempt to perpetrate a felony of any degree of rape [or] sodomy. (Missouri Criminal Code 565.032)

The complete and unedited text of Missouri's rape laws excerpted above can be found in Missouri Revised Statutes, The Annotated Missouri Statutes, *and* The Laws of Missouri.

MONTANA'S RAPE LAWS
Definitions

Without consent means:
    (1) the victim is compelled to submit by force against himself or another; or
    (2) the victim is incapable of consent because he is:
        (a) mentally defective or incapacitated;
        (b) physically helpless; or
        (c) less than sixteen years old.

Force means:
    (1) the infliction, attempted infliction, or threatened infliction of bodily injury or the commission of a forcible felony by the offender; or
    (2) the threat of substantial retaliatory action that causes the victim to reasonably believe that the offender has the ability to execute the threat.

Sexual intercourse means:
    (1) the penetration of the vulva, anus, or mouth of one person by the penis of another person;
    (2) penetration of the vulva or anus of one person by any body member of another person; or
    (3) penetration of the vulva or anus of one person by any foreign instrument or object manipulated by another person for the purpose of arousing or gratifying the sexual desire of either party. Any penetration, however slight, is sufficient.

Sexual abuse means the commission of sexual assault, sexual intercourse without consent, [or] deviate sexual conduct.

Sexual contact means any touching of the sexual or other intimate parts of the person of another for the purpose of arousing or gratifying the sexual desire of either party.

Deviate sexual relations means sexual contact or sexual intercourse between two persons of the same sex or any form of sexual intercourse with an animal.

Serious bodily injury means bodily injury that:
    (1) creates a substantial risk of death;
    (2) causes serious permanent disfigurement or protracted loss or impairment of the function or process of any bodily member or organ; or

(3) at the time of injury, can reasonably be expected to result in serious permanent disfigurement or protracted loss or impairment of the function or process of any bodily member or organ.

The term includes serious mental illness or impairment.

Mentally defective means that a person suffers from a mental disease or defect that renders the person incapable of appreciating the nature of the person's own conduct.

Mentally incapacitated means that a person is rendered temporarily incapable of appreciating or controlling the person's own conduct as a result of the influence of an intoxicating substance.

Physically helpless means that a person is unconscious or is otherwise physically unable to communicate unwillingness to act.

(Montana Criminal Code 45-5-501/45-2-101)

Sex Crimes

When criminality depends on the victim being less than sixteen years old, it is a defense for the offender to prove that he reasonably believed the child to be above that age. Such belief shall not be deemed reasonable if the child is less than fourteen years old.

No evidence concerning the sexual conduct of the victim is admissible in prosecutions under this [section] except evidence of the victim's past sexual conduct with the offender or evidence of specific instances of the victim's sexual activity to show the origin or semen, pregnancy, or disease which is at issue in the prosecution.

Evidence of failure to make a timely complaint or immediate outcry does not raise any presumption as to the credibility of the victim.

Resistance by the victim is not required to show lack of consent. Force, fear, or threat is sufficient alone to show lack of consent.

(Montana Criminal Code 45-5-511)

Sexual Intercourse Without Consent

A person who knowingly has sexual intercourse with another person without consent commits the offense of sexual intercourse without consent.

A person convicted of sexual intercourse without consent shall be imprisoned for not less than two years or more than twenty years and may be fined not more than $50,000.

If the victim is less than sixteen years old and the offender is three or more years older than the victim or if the offender inflicts bodily injury upon anyone in the course of committing sexual intercourse without consent, the offender shall be imprisoned for not less than two years or more than forty years and may be fined not more than $50,000. If two or more persons are convicted of sexual intercourse without consent with the same victim in an incident in which each offender was present at the location where another offender's offense occurred during a time period in which each offender could have reasonably known of the other's offense, each offender shall be imprisoned for not less than five years or more than forty years and may be fined not more than $50,000. An act **in the course of committing sexual intercourse without consent** includes an attempt to commit the offense or flight after the attempt or commission.

In addition to any sentence imposed under [the above sections], after determining the financial resources and future ability of the offender to pay restitution, the court shall require the offender, if able, to pay the victim's reasonable medical and counseling costs that result from the offense.

(Montana Criminal Code 45-5-503)

Sexual Assault

A person who knowingly subjects another person to sexual contact without consent commits the offense of sexual assault.

A person convicted of sexual assault shall be fined not to exceed $500 or be imprisoned for any term not to exceed six months, or both.

If the victim is less than sixteen years old and the offender is three or more years older than the victim or if the offender inflicts bodily injury upon anyone in the course of committing sexual assault, he shall be imprisoned for any term not less than two years or more than twenty years and may be fined not more than $50,000.

An act **in the course of committing sexual assault** shall include an attempt to commit the offense or flight after the attempt or commission.

Consent is ineffective under this section if the victim is less than fourteen years old and the offender is three or more years older than the victim.

(Montana Criminal Code 45-5-502)

Deviate Sexual Conduct

A person who knowingly engages in deviate sexual relations or who causes another to engage in deviate sexual relations commits the offense of deviate sexual conduct.

A person convicted of the offense of deviate sexual conduct shall be imprisoned for any term not to exceed ten years or be fined an amount not to exceed $50,000 or both.

The fact that a person seeks testing or receives treatment for the HIV-related virus or another sexually transmitted disease (STD) may not be used as a basis for a prosecution under this section and is not admissible in evidence in a prosecution under this section.

(Montana Criminal Code 45-5-505)

Rape and Murder

A person commits the offense of deliberate homicide if he attempts to commit, commits, or is legally accountable for the attempt or commission of sexual intercourse without consent or any other forcible felony and in the course of the forcible felony or flight thereafter, he or any person legally accountable for the crime causes the death of another human being.

A person convicted of the offense of deliberate homicide shall be punished by death, by life imprisonment, or by imprisonment for a term of not less than ten years or more than one hundred years.

(Montana Criminal Code 45-5-102)

The complete and unedited text of Montana's rape laws excerpted above can be found in The Montana Code Annotated *and* The Laws of Montana.

NEBRASKA'S RAPE LAWS

Definitions

Actor shall mean a person accused of sexual assault.

Intimate parts shall mean the genital area, groin, inner thighs, buttocks, or breasts.

Past sexual behavior shall mean sexual behavior other than the sexual behavior upon which the sexual assault is alleged.

Serious personal injury shall mean great bodily injury or disfigurement, extreme mental anguish or mental trauma, pregnancy, disease, or loss or impairment of a sexual or reproductive organ.

Sexual contact shall mean the intentional touching of the victim's sexual or intimate parts or the intentional touching of the victim's clothing covering the immediate area of the victim's sexual or intimate parts. Sexual contact shall also mean the touching by the victim of the actor's sexual or intimate parts or the clothing covering the immediate area of the actor's sexual or intimate parts when such touching is intentionally caused by the actor. Sexual contact shall include only such conduct which can be reasonably construed as being for the purpose of sexual arousal or gratification of either party.

Sexual penetration shall mean sexual intercourse in its ordinary meaning, cunnilingus, fellatio, anal intercourse, or any intrusion, however slight, of any part of the actor's or victim's body or any object manipulated by the actor into the genital or anal openings of the victim's body which can be reasonably construed as being for nonmedical or nonhealth purposes. Sexual penetration shall not require emission of semen.

Victim shall mean the person alleging to have been sexually assaulted.

(Nebraska Criminal Code 28-318)

First Degree Sexual Assault

Any person who subjects another person to sexual penetration; and

> (1) overcomes the victim by force, threat of force, express or implied, coercion, or deception;

(2) knew or should have known that the victim was mentally or physically incapable of resisting or appraising the nature of his or her conduct; or

(3) the actor is nineteen years of age or older and the victim is less than sixteen years of age

is guilty of sexual assault in the first degree.

Sexual assault in the first degree is a Class II felony. The sentencing judge shall consider whether the actor caused serious personal injury to the victim in reaching a decision on the sentence.

Any person who is found guilty of sexual assault in the first degree for a second time when the first conviction was pursuant to this section or any other state or federal law with essentially the same elements as this section shall be sentenced to not less than twenty-five years and shall not be eligible for parole.
(Nebraska Criminal Code 28-319)

Second Degree Sexual Assault

Any person who subjects another person to sexual contact; and

(1) overcomes the victim by force, threat of force, express or implied, coercion, or deception; or

(2) knew or should have known that the victim was mentally or physically incapable of resisting or appraising the nature of his or her conduct

is guilty of sexual assault in the second degree.

Sexual assault shall be in the second degree and is a Class III felony if the actor shall have caused serious personal injury to the victim.
(Nebraska Criminal Code 28-320)

Third Degree Sexual Assault

Any person who subjects another person to sexual contact; and

(1) overcomes the victim by force, threat of force, express or implied, coercion, or deception; or

(2) knew or should have known that the victim was physically or mentally incapable of resisting or appraising the nature of his or her conduct

is guilty of sexual assault in the third degree.

Sexual assault shall be in the third degree and is a Class I misdemeanor if the actor shall not have caused serious personal injury to the victim.
(Nebraska Criminal Code 28-320)

Sexual Assault of a Child

A person commits sexual assault of a child if he or she subjects another person fourteen years of age or younger to sexual contact and the actor is at least nineteen years of age or older.

Sexual assault of a child is a Class IV felony for the first offense and a Class III felony for all subsequent offenses.
(Nebraska Criminal Code 28-320.1)

The Rape Shield

Evidence of a victim's past sexual behavior shall not be admissible unless such evidence is:

(1) evidence of past sexual behavior with persons other than the defendant, offered by the defendant upon the issue whether the defendant was or was not, with respect to the victim, the source of any physical evidence, including, but not limited to, semen, injury, blood, saliva, and hair; or

(2) evidence of past sexual behavior with the defendant when such evidence is offered by the defendant on the issue of whether the victim consented to the sexual behavior upon which the sexual assault is alleged if it is first established to the court that such activity shows such a relation to the conduct involved in the case and tends to establish a pattern of conduct or behavior on the part of the victim as to be relevant to the issue of consent.
(Nebraska Criminal Code 28-321)

Deadly Force and Self-Defense

[T]he use of force upon or toward another person is justifiable when the actor believes that such force is immediately necessary for the purpose of protecting himself against the use of unlawful force by such other person.

The use of deadly force shall not be justifiable under this section unless the actor believes that such force is necessary to protect himself against death, serious bodily harm, kidnapping or sexual intercourse compelled by force or threat. (Nebraska Criminal Code 28-1409)

Rape and Murder

A person commits murder in the first degree if he kills another person in the perpetration of or attempt to perpetrate any sexual assault in the first degree. (Nebraska Criminal Code 28-303)

The complete and unedited text of Nebraska's rape laws excerpted above can be found in Revised Statutes of Nebraska *and* The Laws of Nebraska.

NEVADA'S RAPE LAWS
Definitions

Perpetrator means a person who commits a sexual assault.

Sexual penetration means cunnilingus, fellatio, or any intrusion, however slight, of any part of a person's body or any object manipulated or inserted by a person into the genital or anal openings of the body of another, including sexual intercourse in its ordinary meaning.

Statutory sexual seduction means:

(1) ordinary sexual intercourse, anal intercourse, cunnilingus, or fellatio committed by a person eighteen years of age or older with a person under the age of sixteen years; or

(2) any other sexual penetration committed by a person eighteen years of age or older with a person under the age of sixteen years with the intent of arousing, appealing to, or gratifying the lust or passions or sexual desires of either of the persons.

Victim means a person who is subjected to a sexual assault.

Sexual molestation means any willful and lewd or lascivious act upon or with the body, or any part or member thereof, of a child under the age of fourteen years, with the intent of arousing, appealing to, or gratifying the lust, passions, or sexual desires of the perpetrator or of the child.

(Nevada Criminal Code 200.364/.030)

Sexual Assault

A person who subjects another person to sexual penetration, or who forces another person to make a sexual penetration on himself or another, against the victim's will or under conditions in which the perpetrator knows or should know that the victim is mentally or physically incapable of resisting or understanding the nature of his conduct, is guilty of sexual assault.

Any person who commits a sexual assault shall be punished:

(1) if substantial bodily harm to the victim results from the actions of the defendant committed in connection with or as part of the sexual assault:

(a) by imprisonment for life, without possibility of parole; or

(b) by imprisonment for life with possibility of parole, eligibility for which begins when a minimum of ten years has been served;

(2) if no substantial bodily harm to the victim results:

(a) by imprisonment for life, with possibility of parole which begins when a minimum of five years has been served; or

(b) by imprisonment for a definite term of five years or more, with eligibility for parole which begins when a minimum of five years has been served; [or]

(3) if the victim was a child under the age of fourteen years by imprisonment for life, with eligibility for parole, which begins when a minimum of ten years has been served.

(Nevada Criminal Code 200.366)

Statutory Sexual Seduction

A person who commits statutory sexual seduction shall be punished:

(1) if he is twenty-one years of age or older, by imprisonment for not less than one year nor more then ten years, and may be further punished by a fine of not more than $10,000; [or]

(2) if he is under the age of twenty-one years, for a gross misdemeanor.

(Nevada Criminal Code 200.368)

Spousal Sexual Assault

It is no defense to a charge of sexual assault that the perpetrator was, at the time of the assault, married to the victim, if the assault was committed by force or by the threat of force.

(Nevada Criminal Code 200.373)

Senior Sexual Assault

[A]ny person who commits the crime of sexual assault against any person who is sixty-five years of age or older shall be pun ished by imprisonment for a term equal to and in addition to the term of imprisonment prescribed by statute for the crime. (Nevada Criminal Code 193.167)

The Infamous Crime Against Nature

[E]very person of full age who commits the infamous crime against nature shall be punished by imprisonment for not less than one year nor more more than six years.

The "infamous crime against nature" means anal intercourse, cunnilingus, or fellatio between consenting adults of the same sex.

Any sexual penetration, however slight, is sufficient to complete the crime against nature.

Any person who incites, entices, or solicits a minor to engage in acts which would constitute the infamous crime against nature if performed by an adult:

(1) if the minor actually engaged in such acts as a result, shall be punished by imprisonment in the state prison for not less than one nor more than six years; [or]

(2) if the minor did not engage in such acts:

(a) for the first offense, is guilty of a gross misdemeanor;

(b) for any subsequent offense, is guilty of a felony and shall be punished by imprisonment in the state prison for not less than one nor more than six years.

(Nevada Criminal Code 193.190/.193/.195)

The Rape Shield

The purpose of [the rape shield law] is to protect the victims of sexual assault from harassment, intimidation, psychological trauma, and the unwarranted invasions of their privacy by prohibiting the disclosure of their identities to the public. [A]ny information which is contained in:

(1) court records, including testimony from witnesses;

(2) intelligence or investigative data, reports of crime, or incidents of criminal activity or other information;

(4) records in the central respository for Nevada records of criminal history, that reveals the identity of a victim of sexual assault is confidential, including but not limited to the victim's photograph, likeness, name, address or telephone number. The willful violation of any provision of this section or the willful neglect or refusal to obey any court order made pursuant thereto is punishable as criminal contempt.
(Nevada Criminal Code 200.377/3771)

Rape and Murder

Murder of the first degree is murder which is committed in the perpetration or attempted perpetration of sexual assault, sexual abuse of a child, or sexual molestation of a child under the age of fourteen years.

Every person convicted of murder of the first degree shall be punished:

(1) by death;

(2) otherwise by imprisonment for life with or without possibility of parole.
(Nevada Criminal Code 200.030)

The complete and unedited text of Nevada's rape laws excerpted above can be found in Nevada Revised Statutes Annotated *and* Statutes of Nevada.

NEW HAMPSHIRE'S RAPE LAWS

Definitions

Actor means a person accused of a crime of sexual assault.

Affinity means a relation which one spouse because of marriage has to blood relatives of the other spouse.

Genital openings means the internal or external genitalia including, but not limited to, the vagina, labia majora, labia minora, vulva, urethra, or perineum.

Pattern of sexual assault means committing more than one act under [the following aggravated felonious sexual assault or felonious sexual assault provisions], or both, upon the same victim over a period of two months or more and within a period of five years.

Retaliation means to undertake action against the interests of the victim, including, but not limited to:

(1) physical or mental torment or abuse;

(2) kidnapping, false imprisonment or extortion; [or]

(3) public humiliation or disgrace.

Serious personal injury means extensive bodily injury or disfigurement, extreme mental anguish or trauma, disease or loss or impairment of a sexual or reproductive organ.

Sexual contact means the intentional touching of the victim's or actor's sexual or intimate parts, including breasts and buttocks, and the intentional touching of the victim's or actor's clothing covering the immediate area of the victim's or actor's sexual or intimate parts. Sexual contact includes only that aforementioned conduct which can be reasonably construed as being for the purpose of sexual arousal or gratification.

Sexual penetration means:

(1) sexual intercourse;

(2) cunnilingus;

(3) fellatio;

(4) anal intercourse;

(5) any intrusion, however slight, of any part of the actors' body or any object manipulated by the actor into genital or anal openings of the victim's body;

(6) any intrusion, however slight, of any part of the victim's body into genital or anal openings of the actor's body; [or]

(7) any act which forces, coerces or intimidates the victim to perform any sexual penetration as defined in [paragraphs (1) through (6) above] on the actor, on another person, or on himself.

Emission is not required as an element of any form of sexual penetration.

(New Hampshire Criminal Code 632-A:1)

Aggravated Felonious Sexual Assault

A person is guilty of the felony of aggravated felonious sexual assault if he engages in sexual penetration with another person under any of the following circumstances:

(1) when the actor overcomes the victim through the actual application of physical force, physical violence, or superior physical strength;

(2) when the victim is physically helpless to resist;

(3) when the actor coerces the victim to submit by threatening to use physical violence or superior physical strength on the victim, and the victim believes that the actor has the present ability to execute these threats;

(4) when the actor coerces the victim to submit by threatening to retaliate against the victim, or any other person, and the victim believes that the actor has the ability to execute these threats in the future;

(5) when the victim submits under circumstances involving false imprisonment, kidnapping, or extortion;

(6) when the actor, without the prior knowledge or consent of the victim, administers or has knowledge of another person administering to the victim any intoxicating substance which mentally incapacitates the victim;

(7) when the actor provides therapy, medical treatment or examination of the victim in a manner or for the purposes which are not professionally recognized as ethical or acceptable;

(8) when, except as between legally married spouses, the victim is mentally defective and the actor knows

or has reason to know that the victim is mentally defective;

(9) when the actor through concealment or by the element of surprise is able to cause sexual penetration with the victim before the victim has an adequate chance to flee or resist;

(10) when, except as between legally married spouses, the victim is thirteen years of age or older and under sixteen years of age and:

    (a) the actor is a member of the same household as the victim; or

    (b) the actor is related by blood or affinity to the victim;

(11) when, except as between legally married spouses, the victim is thirteen years of age or older and under eighteen years of age and the actor is in a position of authority over the victim, and uses this authority to coerce the victim to submit; [or]

(12) when the victim is less than thirteen years of age.

A person is guilty of aggravated felonious sexual assault without penetration when he intentionally touches the genitalia of a person under the age of thirteen under circumstances that can be reasonably construed as being for the purpose of sexual arousal or gratification.

A person is guilty of aggravated felonious sexual assault when such person engages in a pattern of sexual assault against another person, not the actor's legal spouse, who is less than sixteen years of age.

(New Hampshire Criminal Code 632-A:2)

Felonious Sexual Assault

A person is guilty of a Class B felony if he:

    (1) subjects a person to sexual contact and causes serious personal injury to the victim under any of the circumstances named in [the aggravated felonious sexual assault provisions above];

    (2) engages in sexual penetration with a person other than his legal spouse who is thirteen years of age or older and under sixteen years of age; or

(3) engages in sexual contact with a person other than
his legal spouse who is under thirteen years of age.
(New Hampshire Criminal Code 632-A:3)

Sexual Assault

A person is guilty of a misdemeanor if he subjects another person who is thirteen years of age or older to sexual contact under any of the circumstances named in [the Felonious Sexual Assault provisions above]. (New Hampshire Criminal Code 632-A:4)

Spousal Rape

An actor commits a crime under this chapter even though the victim is the actor's legal spouse. Laws attaching a privilege against the disclosure of communications between husband and wife are inapplicable to proceedings under this chapter. (New Hampshire Criminal Code 632-A:5)

The Rape Shield

The testimony of the victim shall not be required to be corroborated in prosecutions under this chapter.

Prior consensual sexual activity between the victim and any person other than the actor shall not be admitted into evidence in any prosecution under this chapter.

Consent is no defense if, at the time of the sexual assault, the victim indicates by speech or conduct that there is not freely given consent to performance of the sexual act. A jury is not required to infer consent from a victim's failure to physically resist a sexual assault.

(New Hampshire Criminal Code 632-A:6)

Rape and Murder

A person is guilty of capital murder if he knowingly causes the death of another before, after, [or] while engaged in the commission of, or while attempting to commit aggravated felonious sexual assault as defined in [the aggravated felonious sexual assault provisions above].

A person is guilty of murder in the first degree if he knowingly causes the death of another before, after, [or] while engaged

in the commission of, or while attempting to commit felonious sexual assault as defined in [the felonious sexual assault provisions above].
(New Hampshire Criminal Code 630:1/1-a)

The complete and unedited text of New Hampshire's rape laws excerpted above can be found in The New Hampshire Revised Statutes Annotated *and* The Laws of the State of New Hampshire.

NEW JERSEY'S RAPE LAWS

Definitions

Actor means a person accused of an offense proscribed [forbidden] under this [law].

Victim means a person alleging to have been subjected to offenses proscribed by this [law].

Sexual penetration means vaginal intercourse, cunnilingus, fellatio, or anal intercourse between persons or insertion of the hand, finger, or object into the anus or vagina either by the actor or upon the actor's instruction. The depth of insertion shall not be relevant as to the question of commission of the crime.

Sexual contact means an intentional touching by the victim or actor, either directly or through clothing, of the victim's or actor's intimate parts for the purpose of degrading or humiliating the victim or sexually arousing or sexually gratifying the actor. Sexual contact of the actor with himself must be in view of the victim whom the actor knows to be present.

Intimate parts means the following body parts: sexual organs, genital area, anal area, inner thigh, groin, buttock, or breast of a person.

Severe personal injury means severe bodily injury, disfigurement, disease, incapacitating mental anguish, or chronic pain.

Physically helpless means that condition in which a person is unconscious or is physically unable to flee or is physically unable to communicate unwillingness to act.

Mentally defective means that condition in which a person suffers from a mental disease or defect which renders that person temporarily or permanently incapable of understanding the nature of his conduct, including, but not limited to, being incapable of providing consent.

Mentally incapacitated means that condition in which a person is rendered temporarily incapable of understanding or controlling his conduct due to the influence of a narcotic, intoxicant, or other substance administered to that person without his prior knowledge or consent, or due to any other act committed upon that person which rendered that person incapable of appraising or controlling his conduct.

(New Jersey Criminal Code 2C:14-1)

Aggravated Sexual Assault

An actor is guilty of aggravated sexual assault if he commits an act of sexual penetration with another person under any one of the following circumstances:

(1) the victim is less than thirteen years old;

(2) the victim is at least thirteen but less than sixteen years old; and

(a) the actor is related to the victim by blood or affinity to the third degree;

(b) the actor has supervisory or disciplinary power over the victim by virtue of the actor's legal, professional, or occupational status; or

(c) the actor is a foster parent, a guardian, or stands *in loco parentis* [in place of the parents] within the household;

(3) the act is committed during the commission, or attempted commission, whether alone or with one or more other persons, of robbery, kidnapping, homicide, aggravated assault on another, burglary, arson, or criminal escape;

(4) the actor is armed with a weapon or any object fashioned in such manner as to lead the victim to reasonably believe it to be a weapon and threatens by word or gesture to use the weapon or object;

(5) the actor is aided or abetted by one or more other persons and either of the following circumstances exists:

(a) the actor uses physical force or coercion; or

(b) the victim is one whom the actor knew or should have known was physically helpless, mentally defective, or mentally incapacitated; [or]

(6) the actor uses physical force or coercion and severe personal injury is sustained by the victim.

Aggravated sexual assault is a crime of the first degree.

(New Jersey Criminal Code 2C:14-2)

Sexual Assault

An actor is guilty of sexual assault if he commits an act of sexual contact with another person under any one of the following circumstances:

(1) the actor uses physical force or coercion, but the victim does not sustain severe personal injury;

(2) the victim is one whom the actor knew or should have known was physically helpless, mentally defective, or mentally incapacitated;

(3) the victim is on probation or parole, or is detained in a hospital, prison, or other institution and the actor has supervisory or disciplinary power over the victim by virtue of the actor's legal, professional, or occupational status;

(4) the victim is at least sixteen but less than eighteen years old and:

(a) the actor is related to the victim by blood or affinity to the third degree;

(b) the actor has supervisory or disciplinary power over the victim; or

(c) the actor is a foster parent, a guardian, or stands *in loco parentis* within the household; or

(5) the victim is at least thirteen but less than sixteen years old and the actor is at least four years older than the victim.

Sexual assault is a crime of the second degree.

(New Jersey Criminal Code 2C:14-2)

Criminal Sexual Contact

An actor is guilty of aggravated criminal sexual contact if he commits an act of sexual contact with the victim under the [aggravated sexual assault provisions above]. Aggravated criminal sexual assault is a crime of the third degree.

An actor is guilty of criminal sexual contact if he commits an act of sexual contact with the victim under the [sexual assault provisions above].

Criminal sexual contact is a crime of the fourth degree.

(New Jersey Criminal Code 2C:14-3)

Community Notification of the Release of Sex Offenders "Megan's Law"

Within forty-five days after receiving notification that an inmate convicted of a sex offense is to be released from incarceration, the chief law enforcement officer of the municipality where the inmate intends to reside shall provide notification of the inmate's release to the community. (New Jersey Criminal Code 2C:7-6)

Rape and Murder

Criminal homicide constitutes murder when it is committed when the actor, acting either alone or with one or more other persons, is engaged in the commission of, or an attempt to commit, or flight after committing or attempting to commit sexual assault and the in course of such crime or of immediate flight therefrom, any person causes the death of a person other than one of the participants. (New Jersey Criminal Code 2C:11-3)

The Rape Shield

In prosecutions for aggravated sexual assault, sexual assault, aggravated criminal sexual conduct or criminal sexual contact, evidence of the victim's previous sexual conduct shall not be admitted nor reference made to it in the presence of the jury except as provided by the court. Evidence of previous sexual conduct shall not be considered relevant unless it is material to negating the element of force or coercion or to proving that the source of semen, pregnancy, or disease is a person other than the defendant. **Sexual conduct** shall mean any conduct or behavior relating to sexual activities of the victim, including but not limited to previous or subsequent experience of sexual penetration or sexual contact, use of contraceptives, living arrangement and life style. (New Jersey Criminal Code 2C:14-7)

Spousal Rape

No actor shall be presumed to be incapable of committing a [sexual] crime because of marriage to the victim. (New Jersey Criminal Code 2C:14-5)

Rape and Murder

Criminal homicide constitutes murder when it is committed when the actor, acting either alone or with one or more other persons, is engaged in the commission of, or an attempt to commit, or flight after committing or attempting to commit sexual assault. (New Jersey Criminal Code 2C:11-3)

The complete and unedited text of New Jersey's rape laws excerpted above can be found in New Jersey Revised Statutes, New Jersey Statutes Annotated, *and* The Laws of New Jersey.

NEW MEXICO'S RAPE LAWS
Definitions

Force or coercion means:

(1) the use of physical force or physical violence;

(2) the use of threats to use physical violence or physical force against the victim or another when the victim believes that there is a present ability to execute the threats;

(3) the use of threats, including threats of physical punishment, kidnapping, extortion or retaliation directed against the victim or another when the victim believes that there is an ability to execute the threats;

(4) the perpetration of criminal sexual penetration or criminal sexual contact when the perpetrator knows or has reason to know that the victim is unconscious, asleep or otherwise physically helpless or suffers from a mental condition that renders the victim incapable of understanding the nature or consequences of the act; or

(5) the perpetration of criminal sexual penetration or criminal sexual contact by a psychotherapist on his patient, with or without the patient's consent, during the course of psychotherapy or within a period of one year following the termination of psychotherapy.

Physical or verbal resistance of the victim is not an element of force or coercion.

Great mental anguish means psychological or emotional damage that requires psychiatric or psychological treatment or care.

Personal injury means bodily injury to a lesser degree than great bodily harm and includes, but is not limited to, disfigurement, mental anguish, chronic or recurrent pain, pregnancy or disease or injury to a sexual or reproductive organ.

Position of authority means that position occupied by a parent, relative, household member, teacher, employer, or other person who, by reason of that position, is able to exercise influence over a child.

(New Mexico Code 30-9-10)

Criminal Sexual Penetration

Criminal sexual penetration is the unlawful and intentional causing of a person to engage in sexual intercourse, cunnilingus, fellatio, or anal intercourse or the causing of penetration, to any extent and with any object, of the genital or anal openings of another, whether or not there is any emission.

Criminal sexual penetration does not include medically indicated procedures.

Criminal sexual penetration in the first degree consists of all sexual penetration perpetrated:

> (1) on a child under thirteen years of age; or
>
> (2) by the use of force or coercion that results in great bodily harm or great mental anguish to the victim.

Whoever commits criminal sexual penetration in the first degree is guilty of a first degree felony.

Criminal sexual penetration in the second degree consists of all criminal sexual penetration perpetrated:

> (1) on a child thirteen to sixteen years of age when the perpetrator is in a position of authority over the child and uses this authority to coerce the child to submit;
>
> (2) by the use of force or coercion that results in personal injury to the victim;
>
> (3) by the use of force or coercion when the perpetrator is aided or abetted by one or more persons;
>
> (4) in the commission of any other felony; or
>
> (5) when the perpetrator is armed with a deadly weapon.

Whoever commits criminal sexual penetration in the second degree is guilty of a second degree felony.

Criminal sexual penetration in the third degree consists of all criminal sexual penetration perpetrated through the use of force or coercion. Whoever commits criminal sexual penetration in the third degree is guilty of a third degree felony.

Criminal sexual penetration in the fourth degree consists of all criminal sexual penetration not defined [above] perpetrated on a child thirteen to sixteen years of age when the perpetrator is at least eighteen years of age and is at least four years older

than and not the spouse of that child. Whoever commits criminal sexual penetration in the fourth degree is guilty of a fourth degree felony.
(New Mexico Criminal Code 30-9-11)

Criminal Sexual Contact

Criminal sexual contact is the unlawful and intentional touching of or application of force, without consent, to the unclothed intimate parts of another who has reached his eighteenth birthday, or intentionally causing another who has reached his eighteenth birthday to touch one's intimate parts.
Criminal sexual contact does not include touching by a psychotherapist on his patient that is:

    (1) inadvertent;

    (2) casual social contact not intended to be sexual in nature; or

    (3) generally recognized by mental health professionals as being a legitimate element of psychotherapy.

Criminal sexual contact in the fourth degree consists of all criminal sexual contact perpetrated:

    (1) by the use of force or coercion that results in personal injury to the victim;

    (2) by the use of force or coercion when the perpetrator is aided or abetted by one or more persons; or

    (3) when the perpetrator is armed with a deadly weapon.

Whoever commits criminal sexual contact in the fourth degree is guilty of a fourth degree felony.
Criminal sexual contact is a misdemeanor when perpetrated with the use of force or coercion.
For the purposes of this section, **intimate parts** means the primary genital area, groin, buttocks, anus, or breast.
(New Mexico Criminal Code 30-9-12)

Criminal Sexual Contact of a Minor

Criminal sexual contact of a minor is the unlawful and intentional touching or applying force to the intimate parts of a minor or the unlawful and intentional causing a minor to touch one's intimate parts. For the purposes of this section, **intimate**

parts means the primary genital area, groin, buttocks, anus, or breast.

Criminal sexual contact of a minor in the third degree consists of all criminal sexual contact perpetrated:

(1) on a child under thirteen years of age; or

(2) on a child thirteen to eighteen years of age when:

(a) the perpetrator is in a position of authority over the child and uses this authority to coerce the child to submit;

(b) the perpetrator uses force or coercion which results in personal injury to the child;

(c) the perpetrator uses force or coercion and is aided or abetted by one or more persons; or

(d) the perpetrator is armed with a deadly weapon.

Whoever commits criminal sexual contact in the third degree is guilty of a third degree felony.

Criminal sexual contact of a minor in the fourth degree consists of all criminal sexual contact [not defined above] of a child thirteen to eighteen years of age perpetrated with force or coercion. Whoever commits criminal sexual contact in the fourth degree is guilty of a fourth degree felony. (New Mexico Criminal Code 30-9-13)

The Rape Shield

[E]vidence of the victim's past sexual conduct, opinion evidence thereof or of reputation for past sexual conduct shall not be admitted unless, and only to the extent that the court finds, that evidence of the victim's past sexual conduct is material and relevant to the case and that its inflammatory or prejudicial nature does not outweigh its probative value. (New Mexico Code 11-413)

Rape and Murder

Murder in the first degree is the killing of one human being by another without lawful justification or excuse, by any of the means with which death may be caused:

(1) by any kind of willful, deliberate and premeditated killing;

(2) in the commission of or attempt to commit a [sexual] felony; or

(3) by any act greatly dangerous to the lives of others, indicating a depraved mind regardless of human life. Whoever commits murder in the first degree is guilty of a capital felony.

(New Mexico Code 30-2-1)

The complete and unedited text of New Mexico's rape laws excerpted above can be found in New Mexico Statutes Annotated *and* The Laws of New Mexico.

NEW YORK'S RAPE LAWS

Definitions

Sexual intercourse has its ordinary meaning and occurs upon any penetration, however slight.

Deviate sexual intercourse means sexual conduct between persons not married to each other consisting of contact between the penis and the anus, the mouth and penis, or the mouth and the vulva.

Sexual contact means any touching of the sexual or other intimate parts of a person not married to the actor for the purpose of gratifying sexual desire of either party. It includes the touching of the actor by the victim, as well as the touching of the victim by the actor, whether directly or through clothing.

Female means any female person who is not married to the actor. **Not married** means:

(1) the lack of an existing relationship of husband and wife between the female and the actor which is recognized by law; or

(2) the existence of the relationship of husband and wife between the actor and the female which is recognized by law at the time the actor commits an offense proscribed [forbidden] by this article by means of forcible compulsion against the female.

Mentally defective means that a person suffers from a mental disease or defect which renders him incapable of appraising the nature of his conduct.

Mentally incapacitated means that a person is rendered temporarily incapable of appraising or controlling his conduct owing to the influence of a narcotic or intoxicating substance administered to him without his consent, or to any other act committed upon him without his consent.

Physically helpless means that a person is unconscious or for any other reason is physically unable to communicate unwillingness to an act.

Forcible compulsion means to compel by either:

(1) use of physical force; or

(2) a threat, express or implied, which places a person in fear of immediate death or physical injury to himself, herself, or another person, or in fear that he, she, or another person will immediately be kidnapped.

Foreign object means any instrument or article which, when inserted in the vagina, urethra, penis, or rectum, is capable of causing physical injury.
(New York Criminal Code 130.00)

Sexual Consent

Whether or not specifically stated, it is an element of every offense defined in this article, except the offense of consensual sodomy, that the sexual act was committed without consent of the victim.

Lack of consent results from:

(1) forcible compulsion;

(2) incapacity to consent; or

(3) where the offense charged is sexual abuse, any circumstances, in addition to forcible compulsion or incapacity to consent, in which the the victim does not expressly or impliedly acquiesce in the actor's conduct.

A person is deemed incapable of consent when he is:

(1) less than seventeen years old;

(2) mentally defective;

(3) mentally incapacitated; or

(4) physically helpless.

(New York Criminal Code 130.05)

Rape

A male is guilty of rape in the first degree when he engages in sexual intercourse with a female:

(1) by forcible compulsion;

(2) who is incapable of consent by reason of being physically helpless; or

(3) who is less than eleven years old.

Rape in the first degree is a Class B felony.

A person is guilty of rape in the second degree when, being eighteen years old or more, he or she engages in sexual intercourse with another person to whom the actor is not married less than fourteen years old. Rape in the second degree is a Class D felony.

A person is guilty of rape in the third degree when:

(1) he or she engages in sexual intercourse with another person to whom the actor is not married who is incapable of consent by reason of some factor other than being less than seventeen years old; or

(2) being twenty-one years old or more, he or she engages in sexual intercourse with another person to whom the actor is not married less than seventeen years old.

Rape in the third degree is a Class E felony.
(New York Criminal Code 130.25/.30/.35)

Sodomy

A person is guilty of sodomy in the first degree when he engages in deviate sexual intercourse with another person:
(1) by forcible compulsion;
(2) who is incapable of consent by reason of being physically helpless; or
(3) who is less than eleven years old.

Sodomy in the first degree is a Class B felony.

A person is guilty of sodomy in the second degree when, being eighteen years old or more, he engages in deviate sexual intercourse with another person less than fourteen years old. Sodomy in the second degree is a Class D felony.

A person is guilty of sodomy in the third degree when:
(1) he engages in deviate sexual intercourse with a person who is incapable of consent by reason of some factor other than being less than seventeen years old; or
(2) being twenty-one years old or more, he engages in deviate sexual intercourse with a person less than seventeen years old.

Sodomy in the third degree is a Class E felony.
(New York Criminal Code 130.50/.45/.40)

Aggravated Sexual Abuse

A person is guilty of aggravated sexual abuse in the first degree when he inserts a foreign object in the vagina, urethra, penis or rectum of another person causing physical injury to such person:

(1) by forcible compulsion;

(2) when the other person is incapable of consent by reason of being physically helpless; or

(3) when the other person is less than eleven years old.

Aggravated sexual abuse in the first degree is a Class B felony.

A person is guilty of aggravated sexual abuse in the second degree when he inserts a finger in the vagina, urethra, penis or rectum of another person causing physical injury to such person:

(1) by forcible compulsion;

(2) when the other person is incapable of consent by reason of being physically helpless; or

(3) when the other person is less than eleven years old.

Aggravated sexual abuse in the second degree is a Class C felony.

(New York Criminal Code 130.70/.67)

Sexual Abuse

A person is guilty of sexual abuse in the first degree when he subjects another person to sexual contact:

(1) by forcible compulsion;

(2) when the other person is incapable of consent by reason of being physically helpless; or

(3) when the other person is less than eleven years old.

Sexual abuse in the first degree is a Class D felony.

A person is guilty of sexual abuse in the second degree when he subjects another person to sexual contact and when such other person is:

(1) incapable of consent by reason of some factor other than being less than seventeen years old; or

(2) less than fourteen years old.

Sexual abuse in the second degree is a Class A misdemeanor.

A person is guilty of sexual abuse in the third degree when he subjects another person to sexual contact without the latter's

consent. Sexual abuse in the third degree is a Class B misdemeanor.
(New York Criminal Code 130.65/.60/.55)

Sexual Misconduct

A person is guilty of sexual misconduct when:
(1) being a male, he engages in sexual intercourse with a female without her consent; or
(2) he engages in deviate sexual intercourse with another person without the latter's consent.
Sexual misconduct is a Class A misdemeanor.
(New York Criminal Code 103.20)

Rape and Murder

A person is guilty of murder in the second degree when, acting either alone or with one or more other persons, he commits or attempts to commit rape in the first degree, sodomy in the first degree, sexual abuse in the first degree, or aggravated sexual abuse.
Murder in the second degree is a Class A-I felony.
(New York Criminal Code 125.25)

The complete and unedited text of New York's rape laws excerpted above can be found in McKinney's Consolidated Laws of New York *and* The Laws of New York.

NORTH CAROLINA'S RAPE LAWS
Definitions

Mentally defective means:

(1) a victim who suffers from mental retardation; or

(2) a victim who suffers from a mental disorder, either of which temporarily or permanently renders the victim substantially incapable of appraising the nature of his or her conduct, or of resisting the act of vaginal intercourse or a sexual act, or of communicating unwillingness to submit to the act of vaginal intercourse or a sexual act.

Mentally incapacitated means a victim who due to any act committed upon the victim is rendered substantially incapable of either appraising the nature of his or her conduct, or resisting the act of vaginal intercourse or a sexual act.

Physically helpless means:

(1) a victim who is unconscious; or

(2) a victim who is physically unable to resist an act of vaginal intercourse or a sexual act or communicate unwillingness to submit to an act of vaginal intercourse or a sexual act.

Sexual act means cunnilingus, fellatio, analingus, or anal intercourse, but does not include vaginal intercourse. Sexual act also means the penetration, however slight, by any object into the genital or anal opening of another person's body; provided, that it shall be an affirmative defense that the penetration was for accepted medical purposes.

(North Carolina Criminal Code 14-27.1)

First Degree Rape

A person is guilty of rape in the first degree if the person engages in vaginal intercourse:

(1) with a victim who is a child under the age of thirteen years and the defendant is at least twelve years old and is at least four years older than the victim; or

(2) with another person by force and against the will of the other person, and:

(a) employs or displays a dangerous or deadly weapon or an article which the other person reasonably believes to be a dangerous or deadly weapon; or

(b) inflicts serious personal injury upon the victim or another person; or

(c) the person commits the offense aided and abetted by one or more other persons.

Any person who commits the offense defined in this section is guilty of a Class B felony.

(North Carolina Criminal Code 14-27.2)

Second Degree Rape

A person is guilty of rape in the second degree if the person engages in vaginal intercourse with another person:

(1) by force and against the will of the other person; or

(2) who is mentally defective, mentally incapacitated, or physically helpless.

Any person who commits the offense defined in this section is guilty of a Class C felony.

(North Carolina Criminal Code 14-27.3)

First Degree Sexual Offense

A person is guilty of a sexual offense in the first degree if the person engages in a sexual act:

(1) with a victim who is a child under the age of thirteen years and the defendant is at least twelve years old and is at least four years older than the victim; or

(2) with another person by force and against the will of the other person, and:

(a) employs or displays a dangerous or deadly weapon or an article which the other person reasonably believes to be a dangerous or deadly weapon;

(b) inflicts serious personal injury upon the victim or another person; or

(c) the person commits the offense aided and abetted by one or more other persons.

Any person who commits an offense defined in this section is guilty of a Class B felony.
(North Carolina Criminal Code 14-27.4)

Second Degree Sexual Offense

A person is guilty of a sexual offense in the second degree if the person engages in a sexual act with another person:

    (1) by force and against the will of the other person; or

    (2) who is mentally defective, mentally incapacitated, or physically helpless.

Any person who commits the offense defined in this section is guilty of a Class C felony.
(North Carolina Criminal Code 14-27.5)

Taking Indecent Liberties with Children

A person is guilty of taking indecent liberties with children if, being sixteen years of age or more and at least five years older than the child in question, he either:

    (1) willfully takes or attempts to take any immoral, improper, or indecent liberties with any child of either sex under the age of sixteen years for the purpose of arousing or gratifying sexual desire; or

    (2) willfully commits or attempts to commit any lewd or lascivious act upon or with the body or any part or member of the body of any child of either sex under the age of sixteen years.

Taking indecent liberties with children is punishable as a Class F felony.
(North Carolina Criminal Code 14-202.1)

Evidence of Rape

It shall not be necessary upon the trial of any indictment for [first degree rape, second degree rape, first degree sexual offense, or second degree sexual offense] where the sex act alleged is vaginal intercourse or anal intercourse to prove the actual emission of semen in order to constitute the offense; but the offense shall be completed upon proof of penetration only.

Penetration, however slight, is vaginal intercourse or anal intercourse. (North Carolina Criminal Code 14-27.10)

Inability to Rape

In prosecution [for first degree rape, second degree rape, first degree sexual offense, or second degree sexual offense], there shall be no presumption that any person under the age of fourteen years is physically incapable of committing a sex offense of any degree or physically incapable of committing rape, or that a male child under the age of fourteen years is incapable of engaging in sexual intercourse. (North Carolina Criminal Code 14-27.9)

Punishment

An attempt to commit first degree rape [as defined above] or an attempt to commit a first degree sexual offense [as defined above] is a Class F felony. An attempt to commit second degree rape [as defined above] or an attempt to commit a second degree sexual offense [as defined above] is a Class H felony. (North Carolina Criminal Code 14-27.6)

Spousal Rape

A person may be prosecuted under [the above provisions] whether or not the victim is the person's legal spouse at the time of the commission of the alleged rape or sexual offense. (North Carolina Criminal Code 14-27.8)

Custody Rape

If a defendant who has assumed the position of a parent in the home of a minor victim engages in vaginal intercourse or a sexual act with a victim who is a minor residing in the home, or if a person having custody of a victim of any age or a person who is an agent or employee of any person, or institution, whether such institution is private, charitable, or governmental, having custody of a victim of any age engages in vaginal intercourse or a sexual act with such victim, the defendant is guilty of a Class E felony. (North Carolina Criminal Code 14-27.7)

Rape and Murder

A murder which shall be committed in the perpetration or attempted perpetration of any rape or sex offense shall be deemed murder in the first degree.

Any person who commits such murder shall be punished with death or imprisonment for life.

(North Carolina Criminal Code 14-17)

The complete and unedited text of North Carolina's rape laws excerpted above can be found in The General Statutes of North Carolina *and* The Laws of North Carolina.

NORTH DAKOTA'S RAPE LAWS

Definitions

Sexual act means sexual contact between human beings consisting of contact between the penis and the vulva, the penis and the anus, the mouth and the penis, or the mouth and the vulva; or the use of an object which comes in contact with the victim's anus, vulva, or penis. For the purposes of this [provision], sexual contact between the penis and the vulva, or between the penis and the anus or an object and the anus, vulva, or penis of the victim, occurs upon penetration, however slight. Emission [of semen] is not required.

Sexual contact means any touching of the sexual or other intimate parts of the person for the purpose of arousing or satisfying sexual or aggressive desires.

Object means anything used in the commission of a sexual act other than the person of the actor.

Deviate sexual act means any form of sexual contact with an animal, bird, or dead person.

(North Dakota Criminal Code 12.1-20-2)

Gross Sexual Imposition

A person who engages in a sexual act with another, or who causes another to engage in a sexual act, is guilty of an offense if:

(1) he compels the victim to submit by force or by threat of imminent death, serious bodily injury, or kidnapping, to be inflicted on any human being;

(2) he or someone with his knowledge has substantially impaired the victim's power to appraise or control his or her conduct by administering or employing without his or her knowledge intoxicants or other means with intent to prevent resistance;

(3) he knows that the victim is unaware that a sexual act is being committed upon him or her;

(4) the victim is less than fifteen years old; or

(5) he knows or has reasonable cause to believe that the other person suffers from a mental disease or defect which renders him or her incapable of understanding the nature of his or her conduct.

A person who engages in sexual contact with another, or who causes another to engage in sexual contact, is guilty of an offense if:

> (1) the victim is less than fifteen years old; or
>
> (2) he compels the victim to submit by force or by threat of imminent death, serious bodily injury, or kidnapping, to be inflicted on any human being.

The offense of [gross sexual imposition] is a Class A felony if in the course of the offense the actor inflicts serious bodily injury upon the victim. Otherwise the offense of [gross sexual imposition] is a class B felony.

(North Dakota Criminal Code 12.1-20-3)

Sexual Imposition

A person who engages in a sexual act or sexual contact with another, or who causes another to engage in a sexual act or sexual contact, is guilty of an offense if the actor compels the other person to submit by any threat that would render a person of reasonable firmness incapable of resisting.

The offense of [sexual imposition] is a Class C felony unless the victim is a minor, fifteen years of age or older, in which case the offense of [sexual imposition] is a Class B felony.

(North Dakota Criminal Code 12.1-20-4)

Sexual Assault

A person who knowingly has sexual contact with another, or who causes such other person to have sexual contact with him, is guilty of an offense if:

> (1) he knows or has reasonable cause to believe that the contact is offensive to the other person;
>
> (2) he knows or has reasonable cause to believe that the other person suffers from a mental disease or defect which renders him or her incapable of understanding the nature of his or her conduct;
>
> (3) he or someone with his knowledge has substantially impaired the [victim's] power to appraise or control his or her conduct, by administering or employing without [his or her] knowledge intoxicants or other means for the purpose of preventing resistance;

(4) the other person is in official custody or detained in a hospital, prison, or other institution and the actor has supervisory or disciplinary authority over him or her;

(5) the other person is a minor, fifteen years of age or older, and the actor is his or her parent, guardian, or is otherwise responsible for general supervision of the other person's welfare; or

(6) the other person is a minor, fifteen years of age or older, and the actor is an adult.

The offense of [sexual assault] is a Class A misdemeanor if the actor's conduct violates [the above provisions pertaining to a minor], otherwise the offense of [sexual assault] is a Class B misdemeanor.
(North Dakota Criminal Code 12.1-20-7)

AIDS/HIV Rape

A person who, knowing that that person is or has been afflicted with acquired immune deficiency syndrome, afflicted with acquired immune deficiency syndrome related complexes, or infected with the human immunodeficiency virus, willfully transfers any of that person's body fluid to another person is guilty of a Class A felony. (North Dakota Criminal Code 12.1-20-17)

Deviate Sexual Act

A person who performs a deviate sexual act with the intent to arouse or gratify his sexual desire is guilty of a Class A misdemeanor. (North Dakota Criminal Code 12.1-20-12)

Rape and Murder

A person is guilty of murder, a Class AA felony, if the person causes the death of another human being [when] acting either alone or with one or more other persons, [he or she] commits or attempts to commit gross sexual imposition. (North Dakota Criminal Code 12.1-16-01)

The complete and unedited text of North Dakota's rape laws excerpted above can be found in *The North Dakota Century Code* and *The Laws of North Dakota.*

OHIO'S RAPE LAWS

Definitions

Sexual conduct means vaginal intercourse between a male and female, and anal intercourse, fellatio, and cunnilingus between persons regardless of sex. Penetration, however slight, is sufficient to complete vaginal or anal intercourse.

Sexual contact means any touching of an erogenous zone of another, including without limitation the thigh, genitals, buttock, pubic region, or, if the person is a female, a breast, for the purpose of sexually arousing or gratifying either person.

Spouse means a person married to an offender at the time of an alleged offense.

(Ohio Criminal Code 2907.01)

Rape

No person shall engage in sexual conduct with another who is not the spouse of the offender or who is the spouse of the offender but is living separate and apart from the offender, when any of the following applies:

> (1) for the purpose of preventing resistance, the offender substantially impairs the other person's judgment or control by administering any drug or intoxicant to the other person, surreptitiously or by force, threat of force, or deception;
>
> (2) the other person is less than thirteen years of age, whether or not the offender knows the age of the other person; [or]
>
> (3) the other person's ability to resist or consent is substantially impaired because of a mental or physical condition or because of advanced age, and the offender knows or has reasonable cause to believe that the other person's ability to resist or consent is substantially impaired because of a mental or physical condition or because of advanced age.

No person shall engage in sexual conduct with another when the offender purposely compels the other person to submit by force or threat of force.

Whoever violates this section is guilty of rape, an aggravated felony of the first degree.

(Ohio Criminal Code 2907.02)

Spousal Rape

No person shall engage in sexual conduct with another when the offender purposely compels the other person to submit by force or threat of force.

It is not a defense to a charge under this section that the offender and the victim were married or were cohabiting at the time of the commission of the offense.

Whoever violates this section is guilty of rape, an aggravated felony of the first degree.

(Ohio Criminal Code 2907.02)

Sexual Battery

No person shall engage in sexual conduct with another, not the spouse of the offender, when any of the following apply:

(1) the offender knowingly coerces the other person to submit by any means that would prevent resistance by a person of ordinary resolution;

(2) the offender knows that the other person's ability to appraise the nature of or control his or her own conduct is substantially impaired;

(3) the offender knows that the other person submits because he or she is unaware that the act is being committed;

(4) the offender knows that the other person submits because such person mistakenly identifies the offender as his or her spouse;

(5) the offender is the other person's natural or adoptive parent, or a stepparent, or guardian, custodian, or person in loco parentis [in place of the parents];

(6) the other person is in custody of law or a patient in a hospital or other institution, and the offender has supervisory or disciplinary authority over such other person; [or]

(7) the offender is a teacher, administrator, coach, or other person in authority employed by or serving in a school for which the other person is enrolled or that the other person attends.

Whoever violates this section is guilty of sexual battery, a felony of the third degree.
(Ohio Criminal Code 2907.03)

Gross Sexual Imposition

No person shall have sexual contact with another, not the spouse of the offender; cause another, not the spouse of the offender, to have sexual contact with the offender; or cause two or more other persons to have sexual contact when any of the following applies:

(1) the offender purposely compels the other person, or one of the other persons, to submit by force or threat of force;

(2) for the purpose of preventing resistance, the offender substantially impairs the other person's judgment or control by administering any drug or intoxicant to the other person, surreptitiously or by force, threat of force, or deception;

(3) the offender knows that the judgement or control of the other person or one of the other persons is substantially impaired as a result of the influence of any drug or intoxicant administered to the other person with his consent for the purpose of any kind of medical or dental examination, treatment, or surgery;

(4) the ability of the other person to resist or consent or the ability of one of the other persons to resist or consent is substantially impaired because of a mental or physical condition or because of advanced age, and the offender knows or has reasonable cause to believe that the other person's ability to resist or consent of the other person or one or of the other persons is substantially impaired because of a mental or physical condition or because of advanced age; or

(5) the other person, or one of the other persons, is less than thirteen years of age, whether or not the offender knows the age of that person.

Whoever violates this [provision] is guilty of gross sexual imposition, a felony of the third or fourth degree.
(Ohio Criminal Code 2907.05)

Sexual Imposition

No person shall have sexual contact with another, not the spouse of the offender; cause another, not the spouse of the offender, to have sexual contact with the offender; or cause two or more other persons to have sexual contact when any of the following applies:

> (1) the offender knows that the sexual contact is offensive to the other person, or one of the other persons, or is reckless in that regard;
>
> (2) the offender knows that the other person's, or one of the other person's, ability to appraise the nature of or control the offender's or touching person's conduct is substantially impaired;
>
> (3) the offender knows that the other person, or one of the other persons, submits because of being unaware of the sexual contact; or
>
> (4) the other person, or one of the other persons, is thirteen years of age or older but less than sixteen years of age, whether or not the offender knows the age of such person, and the offender is at least eighteen years of age and four or more years older than such other person.

Whoever violates this section is guilty of sexual imposition, a misdemeanor of the third degree.
(Ohio Criminal Code 2907.06)

Object Rape

No person, without privilege to do so, shall insert any part of the body or any instrument, apparatus, or other object into the vaginal or anal cavity of another.

It is not a defense that the offender and the victim were married or were cohabiting at the time of the commission of the offense.

Whoever violates this section is guilty of felonious sexual penetration, an aggravated felony of the first degree.
(Ohio Criminal Code 2907.12)

The Rape Shield

Evidence of specific instances of the victim's sexual activity, opinion evidence of the victim's sexual activity, and reputation evidence of the victim's sexual activity shall not be admitted [into evidence] unless it involves evidence of the origin of semen, pregnancy, or disease, or the victim's past sexual activity with the offender, and only to the extent that the [judge] finds that the evidence is material to a fact at issue in the case and that its inflammatory or prejudicial nature does not outweigh its probative value. (Ohio Criminal Code 2907.02)

Rape and Murder

No person shall purposely cause the death of another while committing or attempting to commit, or while fleeing immediately after committing or attempting to commit rape.
Whoever violates this provision is guilty of aggravated murder.
Whoever is convicted of, pleads guilty to, or pleads no contest and is found guilty of aggravated murder shall suffer death or be imprisoned for life.
(Ohio Criminal Code 2903.01/2929.02)

The complete and unedited text of Ohio's rape laws excerpted above can be found in The Ohio Revised Code Annotated *and* Ohio Laws.

OKLAHOMA'S RAPE LAWS
Definitions

Rape is an act of sexual intercourse involving vaginal or anal penetration accomplished with a male or female who is not the spouse of the perpetrator and who may be of the same or the opposite sex as the perpetrator under any of the following circumstances:

(1) where the victim is under sixteen years of age;

(2) where the victim is incapable through mental illness or any other unsoundness of mind, whether temporary or permanent, of giving legal consent;

(3) where force or violence is used or threatened, accompanied by apparent power of execution to the victim or to another person;

(4) where the victim is intoxicated by a narcotic or anesthetic agent, administered by or with the privity of the accused as a means of forcing the victim to submit;

(5) where the victim is at the time unconscious of the nature of the act and this is known to the accused;

(6) where the victim submits to sexual intercourse under the belief that the person committing the act is a spouse, and this belief is induced by artifice, pretense, or concealment practiced by the accused or by the accused in collusion with such spouse with intent to induce such belief. In all cases of collusion between the accused and the spouse to accomplish such act, both the spouse and the accused, upon conviction, shall be deemed guilty or rape; or

(7) where the victim is under the legal custody of a state agency and submits to sexual intercourse with a state employee in the belief that such intercourse or activity will influence the professional responsibility of the employee or if not submitted to will result in detrimental condition for the victim.

Rape is an act of sexual intercourse accomplished with a male or female who is the spouse of the perpetrator if force or violence is used or threatened, accompanied by apparent power of execution to the victim or to another person.

(Oklahoma Criminal Code 21-1111)

Rape

Rape in the first degree shall include:

    (1) rape committed by a person over eighteen years of age upon a person under fourteen years of age;

    (2) rape committed upon a person incapable through mental illness or any unsoundness of mind of giving legal consent regardless of the age of the person committing the crime;

    (3) rape accomplished with any person by means of force, violence, or threats of force or violence accompanied by apparent power of execution regardless of the age of the person committing the crime;

    (4) rape by instrumentation resulting in bodily harm regardless of the age of the person committing the crime; or

    (5) rape by instrumentation committed upon a person under fourteen years of age.

In all other cases, rape or rape by instrumentation is rape in the second degree.

(Oklahoma Criminal Code 21-1114)

Punishment for Rape

Rape in the first degree is punishable by death or imprisonment not less than five years, in the discretion of the jury, or in case the jury fail or refuse to fix the punishment then the same shall be pronounced by the court.

Rape in the second degree is punishable by imprisonment not less than one year nor more than fifteen years.

(Oklahoma Criminal Code 21-1115/1116)

Object Rape

Rape by instrumentation is an act within or without the bonds of matrimony in which any inanimate object or any part of the human body, not amounting to sexual intercourse is used in the carnal knowledge of another person, without his or her consent and penetration of the anus or vagina occurs to that person.

(Oklahoma Criminal Code 21-1111.1)

Penetration

The essential guilt of rape or rape by instrumentation, except with the consent of a male or female over fourteen years of age, consists in the outrage to the person and feelings of the victim. Any sexual penetration, however slight, is sufficient to complete the crime. (Oklahoma Criminal Code 21-1113)

The Rape Shield

In a criminal case in which a person is accused of a sexual offense against another person, the following is not admissible:

(1) evidence of reputation or opinion regarding other sexual behavior of a victim or the sexual offense alleged;

(2) evidence of specific instances of sexual behavior of an alleged victim with persons other than the accused offered on the issue of whether the alleged victim consented to the sexual behavior with respect to the sexual offense alleged.

The above provisions do not require the exclusion of evidence of:

(1) specific instances of sexual behavior if offered for a purpose other than the issue of consent, including proof of the source of semen, pregnancy, disease or injury;

(2) false allegations of sexual offenses; or

(3) similar sexual acts in the presence of the accused with persons other than the accused which occurs at the time of the event giving rise to the sexual offense alleged.

(Oklahoma Criminal Code 12-2412)

Rape and Murder

A person commits the crime of murder in the first degree when he takes the life of a human being, regardless of malice, in the commission of forcible rape.

A person who is convicted of or pleads guilty or nolo contendere [no contest] to murder in the first degree shall be pun-

ished by death, by imprisonment for life without parole or by imprisonment for life.
(Oklahoma Criminal Code 21-701.7/.9)

The complete and unedited text of Oklahoma's rape laws excerpted above can be found in Oklahoma Statutes *and* Oklahoma Statutes Annotated.

OREGON'S RAPE LAWS

Definitions

Deviate sexual intercourse means sexual conduct between persons consisting of contact between the sex organs of one person and the mouth or anus of another.

Forcible compulsion means physical force that overcomes earnest resistance; or a threat, express or implied, that places a person in fear of immediate or future death or physical injury to self or another person, or in fear that the person or another person will immediately or in the future be kidnapped.

Mentally defective means that a person suffers from a mental disease or defect that renders the person incapable of appraising the nature of the conduct of the person.

Mentally incapacitated means that a person is rendered incapable of appraising or controlling the conduct of the person at the time of the alleged offense because of the influence of a controlled or other intoxicating substance administered to the person without the consent of the person or because of any other act committed upon the person without the consent of the person.

Physically helpless means that a person is unconscious or for any other reason is physically unable to communicate unwillingness to an act.

Sexual contact means any touching of the sexual or other intimate parts of a person or causing such person to touch the sexual or other intimate parts of the actor for the purpose of arousing or gratifying the sexual desire of either party.

Sexual intercourse has its ordinary meaning and occurs upon any penetration, however slight; emission [of semen] is not required.

(Oregon Criminal Code 163.305)

Sexual Consent

A person is considered incapable of consenting to a sexual act if the person is:

    (1) under eighteen years of age;

    (2) mentally defective;

    (3) mentally incapacitated; or

(4) physically helpless.
(Oregon Criminal Code 163.315)

First Degree Rape

A person who has sexual intercourse with another person commits the crime of rape in the first degree if:

(1) the victim is subjected to forcible compulsion by the person;

(2) the victim is under twelve years of age;

(3) the victim is under sixteen years of age and is the person's sibling, of the whole or half blood, the person's child or the person's spouse's child; or

(4) the victim is incapable of consent by reason of mental defect, mental incapacitation or physical helplessness.

Rape in the first degree is a Class A felony.
(Oregon Criminal Code 163.375)

Second Degree Rape

A person who has sexual intercourse with another person commits the crime of rape in the second degree if the other person is under fourteen years of age.

Rape in the second degree is a Class B felony.
(Oregon Criminal Code 163.365)

Third Degree Rape

A person commits the crime of rape in the third degree if the person has sexual intercourse with another person under sixteen years of age.

Rape in the third degree is a Class C felony.
(Oregon Criminal Code 163.355)

First Degree Sodomy

A person who engages in deviate sexual intercourse with another person or causes another to engage in deviate sexual intercourse commits the crime of sodomy in the first degree if:

(1) the victim is subjected to forcible compulsion by the actor;

(2) the victim is under twelve years of age;

(3) the victim is under sixteen years of age and is the actor's brother or sister, of the whole or half blood, the son or daughter of the actor or the son or daughter of the actor's spouse; or

(4) the victim is incapable of consent by reason of mental defect, mental incapacitation, or physical helplessness.

Sodomy in the first degree is a Class A felony.
(Oregon Criminal Code 163.405)

Second Degree Sodomy

A person who engages in deviate sexual intercourse with another person or causes another to engage in deviate sexual intercourse commits the crime of sodomy in the second degree if the victim is under fourteen years of age.

Sodomy in the second degree is a Class B felony.
(Oregon Criminal Code 163.395)

Third Degree Sodomy

A person commits the crime of sodomy in the third degree if the person engages in deviate sexual intercourse with another person under sixteen years of age or causes that person to engage in deviate sexual intercourse.

Sodomy in the third degree is a Class C felony.
(Oregon Criminal Code 163.385)

First Degree Sexual Abuse

A person commits the crime of sexual abuse in the first degree when that person subjects another person to sexual contact and:

(1) the victim is less than fourteen years of age; or

(2) the victim is subjected to forcible compulsion by the actor.

Sexual abuse in the first degree is a Class B felony.
(Oregon Criminal Code 163.427)

Second Degree Sexual Abuse

A person commits the crime of sexual abuse in the second degree when that person subjects another person to sexual intercourse, deviate sexual intercourse or penetration of the vagina, anus or penis with any object other than the penis or mouth of the actor and the victim does not consent thereto.

Sexual abuse in the second degree is a Class C felony.

(Oregon Criminal Code 163.425)

Third Degree Sexual Abuse

A person commits the crime of sexual abuse in the third degree if the person subjects another person to sexual contact; and

> (1) the victim does not consent to the sexual contact; or
>
> (2) the victim is incapable of consent by reason of being under eighteen years of age, mentally defective, mentally incapacitated or physically helpless.

Sexual abuse in the third degree is a Class A misdemeanor.

(Oregon Criminal Code 163.415)

Unlawful Sexual Penetration

A person commits the crime of unlawful sexual penetration in the first degree if the person penetrates the vagina, anus or penis of another with any object other than the penis or mouth of the actor and:

> (1) the victim is subjected to forcible compulsion;
>
> (2) the victim is under twelve years of age; or
>
> (3) the victim is incapable of consent by reason of mental defect, mental incapacitation or physical helplessness.

A person commits the crime of unlawful sexual penetration in the second degree if the person penetrates the vagina, anus or penis of another with any object other than the penis or mouth of the actor and the victim is under fourteen years of age.

Unlawful sexual penetration in the first degree is a Class A felony. Unlawful sexual penetration in the second degree is a Class B felony.

Nothing in the first and second degree unlawful sexual penetration provisions above prohibits a penetration when the penetration is a part of:

(1) a medically recognized treatment or diagnostic procedure; or

(2) a penetration accomplished by a peace or corrections officer acting in an official capacity in order to search for weapons, contraband or evidence of a crime.

(Oregon Criminal Code 163.408/.411/.412)

Rape and Murder

Criminal homicide constitutes murder when it is committed by a person, acting either alone or with one or more persons, who commits or attempts to commit [any felony sexual offense in the first degree as defined above] and in the course of and in furtherance of the crime the person is committing or attempting to commit, or during flight therefrom, the person, or another participant if there be any, causes the death of a person other than one of the participants. (Oregon Criminal Code 163.115)

The complete and unedited text of Oregon's rape laws excerpted above can be found in Oregon Revised Statutes *and* Oregon Laws.

PENNSYLVANIA'S RAPE LAWS

Definitions

Deviate sexual intercourse means sexual intercourse per os [mouth] or per anus between human beings who are not husband and wife, except as provided in "spousal sexual assault," The term also includes penetration, however slight, of the genitals or anus of another person with a foreign object for any purpose other than good faith medical, hygienic, or law enforcement procedures.

Foreign object includes any physical object not a part of the actor's body.

Indecent contact means any touching of the sexual or other intimate parts of the person for the purpose of arousing or gratifying sexual desire, in either person.

Sexual intercourse, in addition to its ordinary meaning, includes intercourse per os or per anus, with some penetration however slight; emission [of semen] is not required. (Pennsylvania Criminal Code 3101)

Rape

A person commits a felony of the first degree when he engages in sexual intercourse with another person not his spouse:

    (1) by forcible compulsion;

    (2) by threat of forcible compulsion that would prevent resistance by a person of reasonable resolution;

    (3) who is unconscious; or

    (4) who is so mentally deranged or deficient that such person is incapable of consent.

Whenever the term **rape** is used it is deemed to include spousal sexual assault as further defined in **spousal sexual assault** [below]. (Pennsylvania Criminal Code 3121)

Statutory Rape

A person who is eighteen years of age or older commits statutory rape, a felony of the second degree, when he engages in sexual intercourse with another person not his spouse who is less than fourteen years of age. (Pennsylvania Criminal Code 3122)

Deviate Sexual Intercourse

Involuntary deviate sexual intercourse. A person commits a felony of the first degree when he engages in deviate sexual intercourse with another person:

(1) by forcible compulsion;

(2) by threat of forcible compulsion that would prevent resistance by a person of reasonable resolution;

(3) who is unconscious;

(4) who is so mentally deranged or deficient that such person is incapable of consent; or

(5) who is less than sixteen years of age.

Voluntary deviate sexual intercourse. A person who engages in deviate sexual intercourse under circumstances not covered [in the "involuntary deviate sexual intercourse" provisions above] is guilty of a misdemeanor of the second degree. (Pennsylvania Criminal Code 3123/3124)

Aggravated Indecent Assault

Except as provided in the "rape," "statutory rape," and "involuntary deviate sexual intercourse" provisions above, a person commits a felony of the second degree [when] he engages in penetration, however slight, of the genitals or anus of another with a part of the actor's body for any purpose other than good faith medical, hygienic, or law enforcement procedure if:

(1) he does so without the consent of the other person;

(2) he knows that the other person suffers from a mental disease or defect which renders him or her incapable of appraising the nature of his or her conduct;

(3) he knows that the other person is unaware that the indecent contact is being committed;

(4) he has substantially impaired the other person's power to appraise or control his or her conduct by administering or employing, without the knowledge of the other, drugs, intoxicants, or other means for the purpose of preventing resistance;

(5) the other person is in custody of law or detained in a hospital or other institution and the actor has supervisory or disciplinary authority over him; or

(6) he is over eighteen years of age and the other person is under fourteen years of age.

(Pennsylvania Criminal Code 3125)

Indecent Assault

A person who has indecent contact with another not his spouse, or causes another to have indecent contact with him, is guilty of indecent assault if:

(1) he does so without the consent of the other person;

(2) he knows that the other person suffers from a mental disease or defect which renders him or her incapable of appraising the nature of his or her conduct;

(3) he knows that the other person is unaware that the indecent contact is being committed;

(4) he has substantially impaired the other person's power to appraise or control his or her conduct by administering or employing, without the knowledge of the other, drugs, intoxicants, or other means for the purpose of preventing resistance;

(5) the other person is in custody of law or detained in a hospital or other institution and the actor has supervisory or disciplinary authority over him; or

(6) he is over eighteen years of age and the other person is under fourteen years of age.

Indecent assault under section (6) above is a misdemeanor of the first degree. Indecent assault under sections (1)-(5) is a misdemeanor of the second degree.

(Pennsylvania Criminal Code 3126)

Spousal Sexual Assault

Sexual assault. A person commits a felony of the second degree when that person engages in sexual intercourse with that person's spouse:

(1) by forcible compulsion;

(2) by threat of forcible compulsion that would prevent resistance by a person of reasonable resolution; or

(3) who is unconscious.

Involuntary spousal deviate sexual intercourse. A person commits a felony of the second degree when that person engages in deviate sexual intercourse with that person's spouse:

(1) by forcible compulsion;

(2) by threat of forcible compulsion that would prevent resistance by a person of reasonable resolution; or

(3) who is unconscious.

Reporting. The crime of spousal sexual assault shall be personally reported by the victim or her agent to a law enforcement agency having the requisite jurisdiction within ninety days of the commission of the offense.

(Pennsylvania Criminal Code 3128)

The Rape Shield

Evidence of specific instances of the alleged victim's past sexual conduct, opinion evidence of the alleged victim's past sexual conduct, and reputation evidence of the alleged victim's past sexual conduct shall not be admissible in prosecutions under this chapter except evidence of the alleged victim's past sexual conduct with the defendant where consent of the alleged victim is at issue. (Pennsylvania Criminal Code 3104)

Rape and Murder

A person is guilty of criminal homicide if he intentionally, knowingly, recklessly, or negligently causes the death of another human being.

A criminal homicide constitutes murder of the second degree when it is committed while a defendant was engaged as a principal or accomplice in the perpetration of felony rape or felony deviate sexual intercourse by force or threat of force.

(Pennsylvania Criminal Code 2501/2)

The complete and unedited text of Pennsylvania's rape laws ex-cerpted above can be found in Pennsylvania Consolidated Statutes *and* The Laws of Pennsylvania.

RHODE ISLAND'S RAPE LAWS
Definitions

Accused is a person accused of sexual assault.

Force or **coercion** shall mean when the accused does any of the following:

> (1) uses or threatens to use a weapon, or any article used or fashioned in a manner to lead the victim to reasonably believe it to be a weapon;
>
> (2) overcomes the victim through the application of physical force or physical violence;
>
> (3) coerces the victim to submit by threatening to use force or violence on the victim and the victim reasonably believes that the accused has the present ability to execute these threats; or
>
> (4) coerces the victim to submit by threatening to at some time in the future murder, inflict serious bodily injury upon, or kidnap the victim or any other person and the victim reasonably believes that the accused has the ability to execute this threat.

Intimate parts means the genital or anal areas, groin, inner thigh, or buttock of any person or the breast of a female.

Mentally disabled means a person who suffers from a mental impairment which renders that person incapable of appraising the nature of the act.

Mentally incapacitated means a person who is rendered temporarily incapable of appraising or controlling his or her conduct due to the influence of a narcotic, anesthetic, or other substance administered to that person without his or her consent, or who is mentally unable to communicate unwillingness to engage in the act.

Physically helpless means a person who is unconscious, asleep, or for any other reason is physically unable to communicate unwillingness to an act.

Sexual contact is the intentional touching of the victim's or accused intimate parts, clothed or unclothed, if that intentional touching can be reasonably construed as intended by the accused to be for the purpose of sexual arousal, gratification, or assault.

Sexual penetration is sexual intercourse, cunnilingus, fellatio, and anal intercourse, or any other intrusion, however slight, by

any part of a person's body or by any object into the genital or
anal openings of another person's body, but emission of semen
is not required.

Spouse is a person married to the accused at the time of the alleged sexual assault, except that such person shall not be considered the spouse if the couple are living apart and a decision
for divorce has been granted, whether or not a final decree has
been entered.

Victim is the person alleging to have been subjected to sexual
assault.

(Rhode Island Criminal Code 11-37-1)

First Degree Sexual Assault

A person is guilty of first degree sexual assault if he or she engages in sexual penetration with another person, and if any of
the following circumstances exist:

(1) the accused, not being the spouse, knows or has
reason to know that the victim is mentally incapacitated, mentally disabled, or physically helpless;

(2) the accused uses force or coercion;

(3) the accused, through concealment or by the element of surprise, is able to overcome the victim; or

(4) the accused engages in the medical treatment or
examination of the victim for the purpose of sexual
arousal, gratification, or stimulation.

Every person who shall commit sexual assault in the first degree shall be imprisoned for a period not less than ten years
and may be imprisoned for life.

(Rhode Island Criminal Code 11-37-2/3)

Reporting First Degree Sexual Assault

Any person, other than the victim, who knows or has reason to
know that a first degree sexual assault or attempted first degree
sexual assault is taking place in his or her presence shall immediately notify the police where the attempted assault is taking
place.

No person shall be charged under [this section] unless and until
the police department investigating the incident obtains from

the victim a signed complaint against the person alleging a violation of [this section].

Any person who knowingly fails to report a sexual assault or attempted sexual assault as required under [this section] shall be guilty of a misdemeanor and, upon conviction, shall be punished by imprisonment for not more than one year or fined not more than five hundred dollars, or both.
(Rhode Island Criminal Code 11-37-3.1/.2/.3)

Second Degree Sexual Assault

A person is guilty of second degree sexual assault if he or she engages in sexual contact with another person, and if any of the following circumstances exist:

(1) the accused knows or has reason to know that the victim is mentally incapacitated, mentally disabled, or physically helpless;

(2) the accused uses force or coercion; or

(3) the accused engages in the medical treatment or examination of the victim for the purpose of sexual arousal, gratification, or stimulation.

Every person who shall commit sexual assault in the second degree shall be imprisoned for not less than three years and not more than fifteen years.
(Rhode Island Criminal Code 11-37-4/5)

Third Degree Sexual Assault

A person is guilty of third degree sexual assault if he or she is over the age of eighteen years and engaged in sexual penetration with another person over the age of fourteen years and under the age of consent, sixteen years of age.

Every person who shall commit sexual assault in the third degree shall be imprisoned for not more than five years.
(Rhode Island Criminal Code 11-37-6/7)

Child Molestation Sexual Assault

A person is guilty of first degree child molestation sexual assault if he or she engages in sexual penetration with a person fourteen years of age or under.

Every person who shall commit first degree child molestation sexual assault shall be imprisoned for a period of not less than twenty years and may be imprisoned for life.

A person is guilty of second degree child molestation sexual assault if he or she engages in sexual contact with a person fourteen years of age or under.

Every person who shall commit second degree child molestation sexual assault shall be imprisoned for not less than six years nor more than thirty years.

All court records which concern the identity of a victim of child molestation sexual assault shall be confidential and shall not be made public.

(Rhode Island Criminal Code 11-37-8.1/.2/.3/.4/.5)

Subsequent Sexual Offenses

If a person is convicted of a second or subsequent offense under the provisions of [first or second degree sexual assault or first or second degree child molestation sexual assault] the sentence imposed under these sections for the second or subsequent offenses shall not be less than twice the minimum number of years of sentence for the most recent offense. (Rhode Island Criminal Code 11-37-10)

Domestic Rape

Domestic violence includes, but is not limited to, sexual assault in the first and second degree [as defined above] committed by one family or household member against another.

Family or household members include spouses, former spouses, adult persons related by blood or marriage, adult persons who are presently residing together or who have resided together in the past three years, and persons who have a child in common regardless of whether they have been married or have lived together, or persons who are or have been in a substantive dating or engagement relationship.

(Rhode Island Criminal Code 12-29-2)

Rape and Murder

The unlawful killing of a human being with malice aforethought is murder. Every murder committed in the perpetration of, or attempt to perpetrate, rape, any degree of sexual assault or child molestation is murder in the first degree. (Rhode Island Criminal Code 11-23-1)

The complete and unedited text of Rhode Island's rape laws excerpted above can be found in The General Laws of Rhode Island *and* The Public Laws of Rhode Island.

SOUTH CAROLINA'S RAPE LAWS
Definitions

Actor means a person accused of criminal sexual conduct.

Aggravated coercion means that the actor threatens to use force or violence of a high and aggravated nature to overcome the victim or another person, if the victim reasonably believes that the actor has the present ability to carry out the threat, or threatens to retaliate in the future by the infliction of physical harm, kidnapping, or extortion, under circumstances of aggravation, against the victim or any other person.

Aggravated force means that the actor uses physical force or physical violence of a high and aggravated nature to overcome the victim or includes the threat of the use of a deadly weapon.

Intimate parts includes the primary genital area, anus, groin, inner thighs, or buttocks of a male or female and the breasts of a female.

Mentally incapacitated means that a person is rendered temporarily incapable of appraising or controlling his or her conduct whether this condition is produced by illness, defect, the influence of a substance, or from some other cause.

Physically helpless means that a person is unconscious, asleep, or for any other reason physically unable to communicate unwillingness to act.

Sexual battery means sexual intercourse, cunnilingus, fellatio, anal intercourse, or any intrusion, however slight, of any part of a person's body or of any object into the genital or anal openings of another person's body, except when such intrusion is accomplished for medically recognized treatment or diagnostic purposes.

Victim means the person alleging to have been subjected to criminal sexual conduct.

(South Carolina Criminal Code 16-3-651)

First Degree Criminal Sexual Conduct

A person is guilty of criminal sexual conduct in the first degree if the actor engages in sexual battery with the victim and if any one or more of the following circumstances are proven:

> (1) the actor uses aggravated force to accomplish sexual battery; or

(2) the victim submits to sexual battery by the actor under circumstances where the victim is also the victim of forcible confinement, kidnapping, robbery, extortion, burglary, housebreaking, or any other similar offense or act.

Criminal sexual conduct in the first degree is a felony punishable by imprisonment for not more than thirty years, according to the discretion of the court.

(South Carolina Criminal Code 16-3-652)

Second Degree Criminal Sexual Conduct

A person is guilty of criminal sexual conduct in the second degree if the actor uses aggravated coercion to accomplish sexual battery.

Criminal sexual conduct in the second degree is a felony punishable by imprisonment for not more than twenty years according to the discretion of the court.

(South Carolina Criminal Code 16-3-653)

Third Degree Criminal Sexual Conduct

A person is guilty of criminal sexual conduct in the third degree if the actor engages in sexual battery with the victim and if any one or more of the following circumstances are proven:

(1) the actor uses force or coercion to accomplish the sexual battery in the absence of aggravating circumstances; or

(2) the actor knows or has reason to know that the victim is mentally defective, mentally incapacitated, or physically helpless and aggravated force or aggravated coercion was not used to accomplish sexual battery.

Criminal sexual conduct in the third degree is a felony punishable by imprisonment for not more than ten years, according to the discretion of the court.

(South Carolina Criminal Code 16-3-654)

Criminal Sexual Conduct with a Minor

A person is guilty of criminal sexual conduct in the first degree if the actor engages in sexual battery with a victim who is less than eleven years of age.

A person is guilty of criminal sexual conduct in the second degree if the actor engages in sexual battery with a victim who is fourteen years of age or less but who is at least eleven years of age.

A person is guilty of criminal sexual conduct in the second degree if the actor engages in sexual battery with a victim who is at least fourteen years of age but who is less than sixteen years of age and the actor is in a position of familial, custodial, or official authority to coerce the victim to submit or is older than the victim.

(South Carolina Criminal Code 16-3-655)

Spousal Sexual Battery

Sexual battery, when accomplished through use of aggravated force, defined as the use of physical force or physical violence of a high and aggravated nature which results in some physical manifestation of that force or violence to overcome the victim, by one spouse against the other spouse if they are living together, constitutes the felony of spousal sexual battery and, upon conviction, a person must be imprisoned not more than ten years.

The offending spouse's conduct must be reported to appropriate law enforcement authorities within thirty days in order for that spouse to be prosecuted for this offense.

(South Carolina Criminal Code 16-3-615)

Spousal Criminal Sexual Conduct

A person cannot be guilty of criminal sexual conduct [as defined above] if the victim is the legal spouse unless the couple is living apart and the offending spouse's conduct constitutes criminal sexual conduct in the first or second degree as defined in first degree criminal sexual conduct and second degree criminal sexual conduct.

The offending spouse's conduct must be reported to appropriate law enforcement authorities within thirty days in order for a person to be prosecuted for these offenses. (South Carolina Criminal Code 16-3-658)

The Rape Shield

Evidence of specific instances of the victim's sexual conduct, opinion evidence of the victim's sexual conduct and reputation evidence of the victim's sexual conduct shall not be admitted in prosecutions for criminal sexual conduct. (South Carolina Criminal Code 16-3-659.1)

Publishing the Name of the Victim

Whoever publishes or causes to be published the name of any person upon whom the crime of criminal sexual conduct has been committed or alleged to have been committed in this State in any newspaper, magazine, or other publication shall be deemed guilty of a misdemeanor and, upon conviction thereof, shall be punished by a fine of not more than one thousand dollars or imprisonment of not more than three years. (South Carolina Criminal Code 16-3-730)

Rape and Murder

Murder is the killing of any person with malice aforethought, either express or implied.
Murder committed while in the commission of criminal sexual conduct in any degree is an aggravating circumstance.
(South Carolina Criminal Code 16-3-10/20)

The complete and unedited text of South Carolina's rape laws excerpted above can be found in The Code of Laws of South Carolina *and* The Acts of South Carolina.

SOUTH DAKOTA'S RAPE LAWS

Rape

Rape is an act of sexual penetration accomplished with any person under any of the following circumstances:

(1) if the victim is less than ten years of age;

(2) through the use of force, coercion, or threats of immediate and great bodily harm against the victim or other persons within the victim's presence, accompanied by apparent power of execution;

(3) if the victim is incapable, because of physical or mental incapacity, of giving consent to such act;

(4) if the victim is incapable of giving consent because of any intoxicating, narcotic, or anesthetic agent or hypnosis;

(5) if the victim is ten years of age, but less than sixteen years of age, and the perpetrator is at least three years older than the victim; or

(6) if persons who are not legally married and who are within degrees of consanguinity within which marriages are by the laws of this state declared void pursuant to [the provisions] defining incest.

A violation of section (1) is rape in the first degree, a Class 1 felony. If any adult is convicted of section (1) the court shall impose the following minimum sentences: ten years for a first offense and twenty years for a subsequent offense. A violation of sections (2), (3) or (4) is rape in the second degree, a Class 2 felony. A violation of sections (5) or (6) is rape in the third degree, a Class 3 felony.

A charge brought [under] this section may be commenced at any time prior to the time the victim becomes age twenty-five or within seven years of the commission of the crime, whichever is longer.

(South Dakota Criminal Code 22-22-1/1.2)

Spousal Rape

Spousal rape is an act of sexual penetration accomplished with a person's spouse, provided, that at the time of the act the actor and his spouse are no longer cohabiting or are legally separated, through the use of force, coercion, or threat of immediate and great bodily harm against the spouse or other persons within the spouse's presence, accompanied by the apparent power of execution if the evidence is sufficient to support a finding of rape had the accused and the spouse been strangers. Complaint for spousal rape must be made to a law enforcement officer within ninety days of the occurrence. A violation of this section is a Class 2 felony. (South Dakota Criminal Code 22-22-1.1)

Sexual Penetration

Sexual penetration means an act, however slight, of sexual intercourse, cunnilingus, fellatio, anal intercourse, or any intrusion, however slight, of any part of the body or of any object into the genital and anal openings of another person's body. All of the the foregoing acts of sexual penetration, except sexual intercourse, are also defined as sodomy. Practitioners of the healing arts lawfully practicing within the scope of their practice are not included within the provisions of this section. (South Dakota Criminal Code 22-22-2)

Sexual Contact

Sexual contact means any touching, not amounting to rape, of the breasts of a female or the genitalia or anus of any person with the intent to arouse or gratify the sexual desire of either party. Practitioners of the healing arts lawfully practicing within the scope of their practice are not included within the provisions of this section. (South Dakota Criminal Code 22-22-7.1)

Sexual Contact with a Person Incapable of Consent

Any person, fifteen years of age or older, who knowingly engages in sexual contact with another person, other than his spouse if the other person is sixteen years of age or older, and the other person is incapable, because of physical or mental incapacity, of consenting to sexual contact, is guilty of a Class 4 felony. (South Dakota Criminal Code 22-22-7.2)

Sexual Contact with a Minor Under the Age of Sixteen Years

Any person, sixteen years of age or older, who knowingly engages in sexual contact with another person, other than that person's spouse if the other person is under the age of sixteen years is guilty of a Class 3 felony. If the actor is less than three years older than the other person, the actor is guilty of a Class 1 misdemeanor. A charge brought [under] this section may be commenced at any time before the victim becomes age twenty-five or within seven years of the commission of the crime, whichever is longer.

If any adult is convicted of the [above] provision the court shall impose the following minimum sentence: if the victim is less than ten years of age, five years for a first offense and ten years for a subsequent offense.
(South Dakota Criminal Code 22-22-7/1.2)

Psychotherapy Rape

Psychotherapist means a physician, psychologist, nurse, chemical dependency counselor, social worker, member of the clergy, marriage and family therapist, mental health service provider, or other person, state licensed or not, who performs or purports to perform psychotherapy.

Psychotherapy means the professional treatment, assessment or counseling of a mental or emotional illness, symptom, or condition.

Patient means a person who seeks or obtains psychotherapeutic services from a psychotherapist on a regular and ongoing basis.

Emotionally dependent means a condition of the patient brought about by the nature of the patient's own emotional condition or the nature of the treatment provided by the psychotherapist which is characterized by significant impairment of the patient's ability to withhold consent to sexual acts or contact with the psychotherapist and which the psychotherapist knows or has reason to know exists.

A psychotherapist who knowingly engages in sexual contact [as defined in "sexual contact" above] with a person who is not his spouse and who is his emotionally dependent patient at the time, commits a Class 4 felony. Consent by the patient is not a defense.

A psychotherapist who knowingly engages in an act of sexual penetration [as defined in "sexual penetration" above] with a person who is not his spouse and who is his emotionally dependent patient at the time, commits a Class 4 felony. Consent by the patient is not a defense.

(South Dakota Criminal Code 22-22-27/28/29)

Rape and Murder

Homicide is the killing of one human being by another.

Homicide is murder in the first degree when committed by a person engaged in the perpetration of, or attempt to perpetrate, any rape.

Murder in the first degree is a Class A felony.

(South Dakota Criminal Code 22-16-1/4/12)

The complete and unedited text of South Dakota's rape laws excerpted above can be found in South Dakota Codified Laws Annotated *and* The Laws of South Dakota.

TENNESSEE'S RAPE LAWS

Definitions

Coercion means threat of kidnapping, extortion, force or violence to be performed immediately or in the future or the use of parental, custodial, or official authority over a child less than fifteen years of age.

Intimate parts includes the primary genital area, groin, inner thigh, buttock or breast of a human being.

Mentally defective means that a person suffers from a mental disease or defect which renders that person temporarily or permanently incapable of appraising the nature of his conduct.

Mentally incapacitated means that a person is rendered temporarily incapable of appraising or controlling his conduct due to the influence of a narcotic, anesthetic or other substance administered to that person without his consent, or due to any other act committed upon that person without his consent.

Physically helpless means that a person is unconscious, asleep or for any other reason physically or verbally unable to communicate unwillingness to do an act.

Sexual contact includes the intentional touching of the victim's, the defendant's, or any other person's intimate parts, or the intentional touching of the clothing covering the immediate area of the victim's, the defendant's, or any other person's intimate parts, if that intentional touching can be reasonably construed as being for the purpose of sexual arousal or gratification.

Sexual penetration means sexual intercourse, cunnilingus, fellatio, anal intercourse, or any other intrusion, however slight, of any part of a person's body or of any object into the genital or anal openings of the victim's, the defendant's, or any other person's body, but the emission of semen is not required.

Victim means the person alleged to have been subjected to criminal sexual conduct.

(Tennessee Criminal Code 39-13-501)

Aggravated Rape

Aggravated rape is unlawful sexual penetration of a victim by the defendant or of the defendant by a victim accompanied by any of the following circumstances:

(1) force or coercion is used to accomplish the act and the defendant is armed with a weapon or any article used or fashioned in a manner to lead the victim to believe it to be a weapon;

(2) the defendant causes bodily injury to the victim; or

(3) the defendant is aided or abetted by one or more other persons; and

(a) force or coercion is used to accomplish the act; or

(b) the defendant knows or has reason to know that the victim is mentally defective, mentally incapacitated or physically helpless.

Aggravated rape is a Class A felony.
(Tennessee Criminal Code 39-13-502)

Rape

Rape is unlawful sexual penetration of a victim by the defendant or of the defendant by a victim accompanied by any of the following circumstances:

(1) force or coercion is used to accomplish the act;

(2) the defendant knows or has reason to know that the victim is mentally defective, mentally incapacitated or physically helpless; or

(3) the sexual penetration is accomplished by fraud.

Rape is a Class B felony.
(Tennessee Criminal Code 39-13-503)

Aggravated Sexual Battery

Aggravated sexual battery is unlawful sexual contact with a victim by the defendant or of the defendant by a victim accompanied by any of the following circumstances:

(1) force or coercion is used to accomplish the act and the defendant is armed with a weapon or any article used or fashioned in a manner to lead the victim to reasonably believe it to be a weapon;

(2) the defendant causes bodily injury to the victim;

(3) the defendant is aided or abetted by one or more other persons; and

(a) force or coercion is used to accomplish the act; or

(b) the defendant knows or has reason to know that the victim is mentally defective, mentally incapacitated or physically helpless; or

(4) the victim is less than thirteen years of age.

Aggravated sexual battery is a Class B felony.

(Tennessee Criminal Code 39-13-504)

Sexual Battery

Sexual battery is unlawful sexual contact with a victim by the defendant or of the defendant by a victim accompanied by any of the following circumstances:

(1) force or coercion is used to accomplish the act;

(2) the defendant knows or has reason to know that the victim is mentally defective, mentally incapacitated or physically helpless; or

(3) the sexual penetration is accomplished by fraud.

Sexual battery is a Class E felony.

(Tennessee Criminal Code 39-13-505)

Statutory Rape

Statutory rape is sexual penetration of a victim by the defendant or of the defendant by a victim when the victim is at least thirteen but less than eighteen years of age and the defendant is at least four years older than the victim.

Statutory rape is a Class E felony.

(Tennessee Criminal Code 39-13-506)

Child Rape

Rape of a child is the unlawful sexual penetration of a victim by the defendant or of the defendant by a victim, if such victim is less than thirteen years of age.

Rape of a child is a Class A felony.

(Tennessee Criminal Code 39-13-522)

Spousal Rape

A person does not commit spousal rape if the victim is the legal spouse of the perpetrator except as provided:

(1) **spousal rape** means the unlawful sexual penetration of one spouse by the other where:

(a) the defendant is armed with a weapon or any article used or fashioned in a manner to lead the victim to reasonably believe it to be a weapon;

(b) the defendant causes serious bodily injury to the victim; or

(c) the spouses are living apart and one of them has filed for separate maintenance or divorce.

Spousal rape can be a Class A, B, or C felony.

(Tennessee Criminal Code 39-13-507)

Spousal Sexual Battery

A person does not commit spousal sexual battery if the victim is the legal spouse of the perpetrator except as provided here:

(1) **spousal sexual battery** means the unlawful sexual contact by one spouse of another where:

(a) the defendant is armed with a weapon or any article used or fashioned in a manner to lead the victim to reasonably believe it to be a weapon;

(b) the defendant causes serious bodily injury to the victim; or

(c) the spouses are living apart and one of them has filed for separate maintenance or divorce.

Spousal sexual battery can be a Class B, E, or D felony.

(Tennessee Criminal Code 39-13-507)

Rape and Murder

First degree murder is a reckless killing of another committed in the penetration of, or attempt to perpetrate, any first degree rape.

A person convicted of first degree murder shall be punished by:

(1) death;

(2) imprisonment for life without possibility of parole; or

(3) imprisonment for life.

(Tennessee Criminal Code 39-13-202)

The complete and unedited text of Tennessee's rape laws excerpted above can be found in The Tennessee Code Annotated, *and* The Public Acts of Tennessee.

TEXAS' RAPE LAWS

Definitions

Sexual contact means any touching of the anus, breast, or any part of the genitals of another person with intent to arouse or gratify the sexual desire of any person.

Sexual intercourse means any penetration of the female organ by the male sex organ.

Deviate sexual intercourse means:

(1) any contact between any part of the genitals of one person and the mouth or anus of another person; or

(2) the penetration of the genitals or the anus of another person with an object.

(Texas Criminal Code 21.01)

Sexual Assault

A person commits an offense of sexual assault if the person:

(1) intentionally or knowingly:

(a) causes the penetration of the anus or female sexual organ of another person by any means, without that person's consent;

(b) causes the penetration of the mouth of another person by the sexual organ of the actor, without that person's consent; or

(c) causes the sexual organ of another person, without that person's consent, to contact or penetrate the mouth, anus, or sexual organ of another person, including the actor; or

(2) intentionally or knowingly:

(a) causes the penetration of the anus or female sexual organ of a child by any means;

(b) causes the penetration of the mouth of a child by the sexual organ of the actor;

(c) causes the sexual organ of a child to contact or penetrate the mouth, anus, or sexual organ of another person, including the actor; or

(d) causes the anus of a child to contact the mouth, anus, or sexual organ of another person, including the actor.

It is a defense to prosecution under [this section] that the conduct consisted of medical care for the child and did not include any contact between the anus or sexual organ of the child and the mouth, anus, or sexual organ of the actor or a third party.

It is an affirmative defense to prosecutions under [this section] that the actor was not more than three years older than the victim, and the victim was a child of fourteen years of age or older.

A sexual assault under [the above provisions] is without the consent of the other person if:

(1) the actor compels the other person to submit or participate by the use of physical force or violence;

(2) the actor compels the other person to submit or participate by threatening to use force or violence against the other person, and the other person believes that the actor has the present ability to execute the threat;

(3) the other person has not consented and the actor knows the other person is unconscious or physically unable to resist;

(4) the actor knows that as a result of mental disease or defect the other person is at the time of the sexual assault incapable either of appraising the nature of the act or of resisting it;

(5) the other person has not consented and the actor knows the other person is unaware that the sexual assault is occurring;

(6) the actor has intentionally impaired the other person's power to appraise or control the other person's conduct by administering any substance without the other person's knowledge;

(7) the actor compels the other person to submit or participate by threatening to use force or violence against any person, and the other person believes that the actor has the ability to execute the threat; or

(8) the actor is a public servant who coerces the other person to submit or participate.

In this section:

(1) **child** means a person younger than seventeen years of age who is not the spouse of the actor; [and]

(2) **spouse** means a person who is legally married to another, except that persons married to each other are not treated as spouses if they do not reside together or if there is an action pending between them for dissolution of the marriage or for separate maintenance.

An offense under this section is a felony of the second degree. (Texas Criminal Code 22.011)

Aggravated Sexual Assault

A person commits an offense of aggravated sexual assault if the person:

(1) intentionally or knowingly:

(a) causes the penetration of the anus or female sexual organ of another person by any means, without that person's consent;

(b) causes the penetration of the mouth of another person by the sexual organ of the actor, without that person's consent; or

(c) causes the sexual organ of another person, without that person's consent, to contact or penetrate the mouth, anus, or sexual organ of another person, including the actor; or

(2) intentionally or knowingly:

(a) causes the penetration of the anus or female sexual organ of a child by any means;

(b) causes the penetration of the mouth of a child by the sexual organ of the actor;

(c) causes the sexual organ of a child to contact or penetrate the mouth, anus, or sexual organ of another person, including the actor; or

(d) causes the anus of a child to contact the mouth, anus, or sexual organ of another person, including the actor; and

(2) if:

(a) the person:

(i) causes serious bodily injury or attempts to cause the death of the victim or another person in the course of the same criminal episode;

(ii) by acts or words places the victim in fear that death, serious bodily injury, or kidnapping will be imminently inflicted on any person;

(iii) by acts or words occurring in the presence of the victim threatens to cause the death, serious bodily injury, or kidnapping of any person;

(iv) uses or exhibits a deadly weapon in the course of the same criminal episode; or

(v) acts in concert with another who engages in conduct described [in the first section above] directed toward the same victim and occurring during the course of the same criminal episode; or

(b) the victim is younger than fourteen years of age.

An aggravated sexual assault under this section is without the consent of the other person if the aggravated sexual assault occurs under the same circumstances listed in the [sexual assault provisions above].

An offense of aggravated sexual assault is a felony of the first degree.

(Texas Criminal Code 22.021)

Rape and Murder

A person commits an offense of capital murder if he intentionally or knowingly causes the death of an individual in the course of committing or attempting to commit aggravated sexual assault.

An offense of murder is a capital felony.

(Texas Criminal Code 19.02/.03)

The complete and unedited text of Texas' rape laws excerpted above can be found in Texas Revised Statutes Annotated, Texas Statutes Annotated, *and* The Laws of the State of Texas.

UTAH'S RAPE LAWS

Rape

A person commits rape when the actor has sexual intercourse with another person without the victim's consent.

This section applies whether or not the actor is married to the victim.

Rape is a felony of the first degree.

(Utah Criminal Code 76-5-402)

Child Rape

A person commits rape of a child when the person has sexual intercourse with a child who is under the age of fourteen.

Rape of a child is punishable, as a felony of the first degree, by imprisonment for a term which is a minimum mandatory term of five, ten, or fifteen years and which may be for life.

(Utah Criminal Code 76-5-402.1)

Object Rape

A person who, without the victim's consent, causes the penetration, however slight, of the genital or anal opening of another person who is fourteen years of age or older, by any foreign object, substance, instrument, or device, not including a part of the human body, with intent to cause substantial emotional or bodily pain to the victim or with the intent to arouse or gratify the sexual desire of any person, commits an offense which is punishable as a felony of the first degree. (Utah Criminal Code 76-5-402.2)

Object Rape of a Child

A person who causes the penetration, however slight, of the genital or anal opening of a child who is under the age of fourteen by any foreign object, substance, instrument, or device, not including a part of the human body, with intent to cause substantial emotional or bodily pain to the child or with the intent to arouse or gratify the sexual desire of any person, commits an offense which is punishable as a felony of the first degree, by imprisonment for a term which is a minimum mandatory term of five, ten, or fifteen years and which may be for life. (Utah Criminal Code 76-5-402.3)

Sodomy

A person commits sodomy when the actor engages in any sexual act with a person who is fourteen years of age or older involving the genitals of one person and mouth or anus of another person, regardless of the sex of either participant. Sodomy is a Class B misdemeanor.

A person commits forcible sodomy when the actor commits sodomy upon another without the other's consent. Forcible sodomy is a felony in the first degree.

(Utah Criminal Code 76-5-403)

Sodomy on a Child

A person commits sodomy upon a child if the actor engages in any sexual act upon or with a child who is under the age of fourteen, involving the genitals of one person and mouth or anus of another person, regardless of the sex of either participant.

Sodomy upon a child is punishable as a felony of the first degree, by imprisonment for a term which is a minimum mandatory term of five, ten, or fifteen years and which may be for life.

(Utah Criminal Code 76-5-403.1)

Forcible Sexual Abuse

A person commits forcible sexual abuse if the victim is fourteen years of age or older and, under circumstances not amounting to rape, object rape, sodomy, or attempted rape or sodomy, the actor touches the anus, buttocks, or any part of the genitals of another, or touches the breast of a female, or otherwise takes indecent liberties with another, or causes another to take indecent liberties with the actor or another, with intent to cause substantial emotional or bodily pain to any person or with the intent to arouse or gratify the sexual desire of any person, without the consent of the other, regardless of the sex of any participant.

Forcible sexual abuse is a felony of the second degree.

(Utah Criminal Code 76-5-404)

Aggravated Sexual Assault

A person commits aggravated sexual assault if in the course of a rape or attempted rape, object rape or attempted object rape, forcible sodomy or attempted forcible sodomy, or forcible sexual abuse or attempted forcible sexual abuse the actor:

(1) causes bodily injury to the victim;

(2) uses or threatens the victim by use of a dangerous weapon;

(3) compels, or attempts to compel, the victim to submit to rape, object rape, forcible sodomy, or forcible sexual abuse, by threat of kidnapping, death, or serious bodily injury to be inflicted imminently on any person; or

(4) is aided or abetted by one or more persons.

Aggravated sexual assault is a first degree felony punishable by imprisonment for a term which is a minimum mandatory term of five, ten, or fifteen years and which may be for life. (Utah Criminal Code 76-5-405)

Sexual Intercourse, Rape, Sodomy or Sexual Abuse Without Consent

An act of sexual intercourse, rape, attempted rape, rape of a child, attempted rape of a child, object rape, attempted object rape, object rape of a child, attempted object rape of a child, sodomy, attempted sodomy, sodomy upon a child, attempted sodomy upon a child, forcible sexual abuse, attempted forcible sexual abuse, sexual abuse of a child, attempted sexual abuse of a child, or simple sexual abuse is without consent of the victim under any of the following circumstances:

(1) the victim expresses lack of consent through words or conduct;

(2) the actor overcomes the victim through the actual application of physical force or violence;

(3) the actor is able to overcome the victim through concealment or by the element of surprise;

(4) the actor coerces the victim to submit by threatening to retaliate [by threats of physical force, kidnapping, or extortion] in the immediate future against the

victim or any other person, and the victim perceives at the time that the actor has the ability to execute this threat;

(5) the victim has not consented and the actor knows the victim is unconscious, unaware that the act is occurring, or physically unable to resist;

(6) the actor knows that as a result of mental disease or defect, the victim is at the time of the act incapable either of appraising the nature of the act or of resisting it;

(7) the actor knows that the victim submits or participates because the victim erroneously believes that the actor is the victim's spouse;

(8) the actor intentionally impaired the power of the victim to appraise or control his or her conduct by administering any substance without the victim's knowledge;

(9) the victim is younger than fourteen years of age;

(10) the victim is younger than eighteen years of age and at the time of the offense the actor was the victim's parent, stepparent, adoptive parent, or legal guardian or occupied a position of special trust in relation to the victim; or

(11) the victim is fourteen years of age or older, but not older than seventeen, and the actor is more than three years older than the victim and entices or coerces the victim to submit or participate.

(Utah Criminal Code 76-5-406)

Rape and Murder

Criminal homicide constitutes aggravated murder if the actor intentionally or knowingly causes the death of another and the homicide was committed while the actor was engaged in the commission of, or an attempt to commit, or flight after committing or attempting to commit rape, rape of a child, object rape, object rape of a child, forcible sodomy, sodomy upon a child, sexual abuse of a child, or aggravated sexual assault.

Aggravated murder is a capital offense.
(Utah Criminal Code 76-5-202)

The complete and unedited text of Utah's rape laws excerpted above can be found in The Utah Code Annotated, *and* The Laws of Utah.

VERMONT'S RAPE LAWS

Definitions

A **sexual act** means conduct between persons consisting of contact between the penis and the vulva, the penis and the anus, the mouth and the penis, the mouth and the vulva, or any intrusion, however slight, by any part of a person's body or any object into the genital or anal opening of another.

Sexual conduct means any conduct or behavior relating to sexual activities of the complaining witness, including but not limited to prior experience of sexual acts, use of contraceptives, living arrangement and mode of living.

Consent means words or actions by a person indicating a voluntary agreement to engage in a sexual act.

Serious bodily injury means bodily injury which creates a substantial risk of death or which causes substantial loss or impairment of the function of any bodily member or organ, or substantial impairment of health, or substantial disfigurement.

Bodily injury means physical pain, illness or any impairment of physical condition.

Actor means a person charged with sexual assault or aggravated sexual assault.

Deadly force means physical force which a person uses with the intent of causing, or which the person knows or should have known would create a substantial risk of causing, death or serious bodily injury.

Deadly weapon means:

(1) any firearm; or

(2) any weapon, device, instrument, material or substance, whether animate or inanimate, which in the manner it is used or is intended to be used, is known to be capable of producing death or serious bodily injury.

(Vermont Criminal Code 3251)

Sexual Assault

A person who engages in a sexual act with another person and:

(1) compels the other person to participate in a sexual act:

(a) without the consent of the other person;

(b) by threatening or coercing the other person; or

(c) by placing the other person in fear that any person will suffer imminent bodily injury;

(2) has impaired substantially the ability of the other person to appraise or control conduct by administering or employing drugs or intoxicants without the knowledge or against the will of the other person;

(3) the other person is under the age of sixteen, except where the persons are married to each other and the sexual act is consensual; or

(4) the other person is under the age of eighteen and is entrusted to the actor's care by authority of law or is the actor's child, grandchild, foster child, adopted child or step-child;

shall be imprisoned for not more than twenty years, or fined not more than $10,000, or both.

A person who engages in a sexual act with another person under the age of sixteen and:

(1) the victim is entrusted to the actor's care by authority of law or is the actor's child, grandchild, foster child, adopted child, or step-child; or

(2) the actor is at least eighteen years of age, resides in the victim's household and serves in a parental role with respect to the victim; shall be imprisoned for not more than thirty-five years, or fined not more than $25,000, or both.

(Vermont Criminal Code 3252)

Aggravated Sexual Assault

A person commits the crime of aggravated sexual assault if the person commits sexual assault under any of the following circumstances:

(1) at the time of the sexual assault, the actor causes serious bodily injury to the victim or to another;

(2) the actor is joined or assisted by one or more persons in physically restraining, assaulting, or sexually assaulting the victim;

(3) the actor commits the sexual act under circumstances which constitute the crime of kidnapping;

(4) the actor has previously been convicted in this state of sexual assault or aggravated sexual assault or has been convicted in any jurisdiction in the United States or territories of an offense which would constitute sexual assault or aggravated sexual assault if committed in this state;

(5) at the time of the sexual assault, the actor is armed with a deadly weapon and uses or threatens to use the deadly weapon on the victim or on another;

(6) at the time of the sexual assault, the actor threatens to cause imminent serious bodily injury to the victim or to another and the victim reasonably believes that the actor has the present ability to carry out the threat;

(7) at the time of the sexual assault, the actor applies deadly force to the victim;

(8) the victim is under the age of ten and the actor is at least eighteen years of age; or

(9) the victim is subjected by the actor to repeated nonconsensual sexual acts as part of the same occurrence or the victim is subjected to repeated nonconsensual sexual acts as part of the actor's common scheme and plan.

A person who commits the crime of aggravated sexual assault shall be punishable by a maximum sentence of life imprisonment or a fine of not more than $50,000, or both.
(Vermont Criminal Code 3253)

Sexual Consent

In prosecutions for the crimes of sexual assault or aggravated sexual assault:

(1) lack of consent may be shown without proof of resistance;

(2) a person shall be deemed to have acted without the consent of the other person where the actor:

(a) knows that the other person is mentally incapable of understanding the nature of the sexual act;

(b) knows that the other person is not physically capable of resisting, or declining consent to, the sexual act;

(c) knows that the other person is unaware that a sexual act is being committed; or

(d) knows that the other person is mentally incapable of resisting, or declining consent to, the sexual act due to mental illness or mental retardation.

(Vermont Criminal Code 3254)

The Rape Shield

In prosecutions for the crimes of sexual assault or aggravated sexual assault:

(1) neither opinion evidence of, nor evidence of the reputation of the complaining witness' sexual conduct shall be admitted;

(2) evidence of prior sexual conduct of the complaining witness shall not be admitted [except] where it bears on the credibility of the complaining witness.

(Vermont Criminal Code 3255)

Rape and Murder

Murder committed in perpetrating or attempting to perpetrate sexual assault [or] aggravated sexual assault shall be murder in the first degree.

The punishment for murder in the first degree shall be imprisonment for life and for a minimum term of thirty-five years.

(Vermont Criminal Code 2301/2303)

The complete and unedited text of Vermont's rape laws excerpted above can be found in Vermont Statutes Annotated *and* The Laws of Vermont.

VIRGINIA'S RAPE LAWS
Definitions

Complaining witness means the person alleged to have been subjected to rape, forcible sodomy, inanimate or animate sexual penetration, marital sexual assault, aggravated sexual battery, or sexual battery.

Mental incapacity means that condition of the complaining witness existing at the time of an offense which prevents the complaining witness from understanding the nature or consequences of the sexual act involved in such offense and about which the accused knew or should have known.

Physical helplessness means unconsciousness or any other condition existing at the time of an offense which otherwise rendered the complaining witness physically unable to communicate an unwillingness to act and about which the accused knew or should have known.

Sexual abuse means an act committed with the intent to sexually molest, arouse or gratify any person where:

(1) the accused intentionally touches the complaining witness' intimate parts or material directly covering such intimate parts;

(2) the accused forces the complaining witness to touch the accused's, the witness' own, or another person's intimate parts or material directly covering such intimate parts; or

(3) the accused forces another person to touch the complaining witness' intimate parts or material directly covering such intimate parts.

(Virginia Criminal Code 18-2-67.10)

Rape

If any person has sexual intercourse with a complaining witness who is not his or her spouse or causes a complaining witness, whether or not his or her spouse, to engage in sexual intercourse with any other person and such act is accomplished:

(1) against the complaining witness' will, by force, threat or intimidation of or against the complaining witness or another person;

(2) through the use of the complaining witness' mental incapacity or physical helplessness; or

(3) with a child under age thirteen as the victim, he or
she shall be guilty of rape.

If any person has sexual intercourse with his or her spouse and
such act is accomplished against the spouse's will by force,
threat or intimidation of or against the spouse or another, he or
she shall be guilty of rape.

A violation of this section shall be punishable by confinement
for life or any term not less than five years.

(Virginia Criminal Code 18-2-61)

Forcible Sodomy

An accused shall be guilty of forcible sodomy if he or she engages in cunnilingus, fellatio, analingus or anal intercourse with
a complaining witness who is not his or her spouse, or causes a
complaining witness, whether or not his or her spouse, to engage in such acts with any other person, and:

(1) the complaining witness is less than thirteen years
of age; or

(2) the act is accomplished against the will of the
complaining witness, by force, threat or intimidation
of or against the complaining witness or another person, or through the use of the complaining witness'
mental incapacity or physical helplessness.

An accused shall be guilty of forcible sodomy if:

(1) he or she engages in cunnilingus, fellatio, analingus or anal intercourse with his or her spouse; and

(2) such act is accomplished against the will of the
spouse by force, threat or intimidation of or against
the spouse or another person.

Forcible sodomy is a felony punishable by confinement for life
or any term not less than five years.

(Virginia Criminal Code 18-2-67.1)

Object Sexual Penetration

An accused shall be guilty of inanimate or animate object sexual penetration if he or she penetrates the labia majora or anus
of a complaining witness who is not his or her spouse with any
object, other than for a bona fide medical purpose, or causes
such complaining witness to so penetrate his or her own body

with an object or causes a complaining witness, whether or not his or her spouse, to engage in such acts with any other person; and

> (1) the complaining witness is less than thirteen years of age; or
>
> (2) the act is accomplished against the will of the complaining witness, by force, threat or intimidation of or against the complaining witness or another person, or through the use of the complaining witness' mental incapacity or physical helplessness.

An accused shall be guilty of inanimate or animate object sexual penetration if:

> (1) he or she penetrates the labia majora or anus of his or her spouse with any object, other than for a bona fide medical purpose, or causes such spouse to so penetrate his or her own body with an object; and
>
> (2) such act is accomplished against the spouse's will by force, threat or intimidation of or against the spouse or another person.

Inanimate or animate object sexual penetration is a felony punishable by confinement for life or any term not less than five years.

(Virginia Criminal Code 18-2-67.2)

Marital Sexual Assault

An accused shall be guilty of marital sexual assault if:

> (1) he or she engages in sexual intercourse, cunnilingus, fellatio, analingus or anal intercourse with his or her spouse, or penetrates the labia majora or anus of his or her spouse with any object other than for a bona fide medical purpose, or causes such spouse to so penetrate his or her own body with an object; and
>
> (2) such the act is accomplished against the spouse's will, by force or a present threat of force against the spouse or another person.

A violation of this section shall be punishable by confinement for a term of not less than one year nor more than twenty years.

(Virginia Criminal Code 18-2-67.2:1)

Aggravated Sexual Battery

An accused shall be guilty of aggravated sexual battery if he or she sexually abuses the complaining witness; and

(1) the complaining witness is less than thirteen years of age; or

(2) the act is accomplished against the will of the complaining witness, by force, threat or intimidation or through the use of the complaining witness' mental incapacity or physical helplessness; and

(a) the complaining witness is at least thirteen but less than fifteen years of age;

(b) the accused causes serious bodily or mental injury to the complaining witness; or

(c) the accused uses or threatens to use a dangerous weapon.

Aggravated sexual battery is a felony punishable by confinement for a term of not less than one nor more than twenty years.

(Virginia Criminal Code 18-2-67.3)

Sexual Battery

An accused shall be guilty of sexual battery if he or she sexually abuses the complaining witness against the will of the complaining witness, by force, threat or intimidation or through the use of the complaining witness' mental incapacity or physical helplessness.

Sexual battery is a Class 1 misdemeanor.

(Virginia Criminal Code 18-2-67.4)

Rape and Murder

The willful, deliberate and premeditated killing of a person in the commission of, or subsequent to, rape shall constitute capital murder. Capital murder is punishable as a Class 1 felony.

Murder, other than capital murder, committed in the commission of, or attempt to commit rape, forcible sodomy, or inanimate object sexual penetration is murder in the first degree. Murder in the first degree is punishable as a Class 2 felony.

(Virginia Criminal Code 18-2-31/32)

The complete and unedited text of Virginia's rape laws excerpted above can be found in The Code of Virginia Annotated *and* Acts of the Commonwealth of Virginia.

WASHINGTON'S RAPE LAWS
Definitions

Sexual intercourse:

(1) has its ordinary meaning and occurs upon any penetration, however slight;

(2) also means any penetration of the vagina or anus however slight, by an object, when committed on one person by another, whether such persons are of the same or opposite sex, except when such penetration is accomplished for medically recognized treatment or diagnostic purposes; and

(3) also means any act of sexual contact between persons involving the sex organs of one person and the mouth or anus of another whether such persons are of the same or opposite sex.

Married means one who is legally married to another, but does not include a person who is living separate from his or her spouse and who has filed for legal separation or for dissolution of his or her marriage.

Mental incapacity is that condition existing at the time of the offense which prevents a person from understanding the nature or consequences of the act of sexual intercourse, whether that condition is produced by illness, defect, the influence of a substance or from some other cause.

Physically helpless means a person who is unconscious, or for any other reason is physically unable to communicate unwillingness to an act.

Forcible compulsion means physical force which overcomes resistance, or a threat, express or implied, that places a person in fear of death or physical injury to herself or himself or another person, or in fear that she or he or another person will be kidnapped.

Consent means that at the time of the act of sexual intercourse or sexual contact there are actual words or conduct indicating freely given agreement to have sexual intercourse or sexual contact.

(Washington Criminal Code 9A.44.010)

First Degree Rape

A person is guilty of rape in the first degree when such person engages in sexual intercourse with another person by forcible compulsion where the perpetrator or an accessory:

> (1) uses or threatens to use a deadly weapon or what appears to be a deadly weapon;
> (2) kidnaps the victim;
> (3) inflicts serious physical injury; or
> (4) feloniously enters into the building or vehicle where the victim is situated.

Rape in the first degree is a Class A felony.
(Washington Criminal Code 9A.44.040)

Second Degree Rape

A person is guilty of rape in the second degree when, under circumstances not constituting rape in the first degree, the person engages in sexual intercourse with another person:

> (1) by forcible compulsion;
> (2) when the victim is incapable of consent by reason of being physically helpless or mentally incapacitated;
> (3) when the victim is developmentally disabled and the perpetrator is a person who is not married to the victim and who has supervisory authority over the victim;
> (4) when the perpetrator is a health care provider, the victim is a client or patient, and the sexual intercourse occurs during a treatment session, consultation, interview, or examination; or
> (5) when the victim is a resident of a facility for mentally disordered or chemically dependent persons and the perpetrator is a person who is not married to the victim and has supervisory authority over the victim.

Rape in the second degree is a Class A felony.
(Washington Criminal Code 9A.44.050)

Third Degree Rape

A person is guilty of rape in the third degree when, under circumstances not constituting rape in the first or second degrees, the person engages in sexual intercourse with another person, not married to the perpetrator:

(1) where the victim did not consent to sexual intercourse with the perpetrator and such lack of consent was clearly expressed by the victim's words or conduct; or

(2) where there is threat of substantial unlawful harm to property rights of the victim.

Rape in the third degree is a Class C felony.
(Washington Criminal Code 9A.44.060)

Child Rape/Child Molestation

A person is guilty of rape of a child in the first degree when the person has sexual intercourse with another who is less than twelve years old and not married to the perpetrator and the perpetrator is at least twenty-four months older than the victim.

Rape of a child in the first degree is a Class A felony.

A person is guilty of rape of a child in the second degree when the person has sexual intercourse with another who is at least twelve years old but less than fourteen years old and not married to the perpetrator and the perpetrator is at least thirty-six months older than the victim. Rape of a child in the second degree is a Class A felony.

A person is guilty of rape of a child in the third degree when the person has sexual intercourse with another who is at least fourteen years old but less than sixteen years old and not married to the perpetrator and the perpetrator is at least forty-eight months older than the victim.

Rape of a child in the third degree is a Class C felony.

A person is guilty of child molestation in the first degree when the person has, or knowingly causes another person under the age of eighteen to have, sexual contact with another who is less than twelve years old and not married to the perpetrator and the perpetrator is at least thirty-six months older than the victim.

Child molestation in the first degree is a Class A felony.

A person is guilty of child molestation in the second degree when the person has, or knowingly causes another person under the age of eighteen to have, sexual contact with another who is at least twelve years old but less than fourteen years old and not married to the perpetrator and the perpetrator is at least thirty-six months older than the victim.

Child molestation in the second degree is a Class B felony.

A person is guilty of child molestation in the third degree when the person has, or knowingly causes another person under the age of eighteen to have, sexual contact with another who is at least fourteen years old but less than sixteen years old and not married to the perpetrator and the perpetrator is at least forty-eight months older than the victim.

Child molestation in the second degree is a Class C felony.

(Washington Criminal Code 9A.44.073/076/079/083/086/089)

Rape and Murder

A person is guilty of murder in the first degree when he commits or attempts to commit the crime of rape in the first or second degree and in the course of and in furtherance of such crime or in immediate flight therefrom he, or another participant, causes the death of a person.

Murder in the first degree is a Class A felony.

(Washington Criminal Code 9A.32.030)

The complete and unedited text of Washington's rape laws excerpted above can be found in The Revised Code of Washington, The Revised Code of Washington Annotated, *and* The Laws of Washington.

WEST VIRGINIA'S RAPE LAWS

Definitions

Forcible compulsion means:

(1) physical force that overcomes such earnest resistance as might reasonably be expected under the circumstances;

(2) threat or intimidation, expressed or implied, placing a person in fear of immediate death or bodily injury to himself or another person or in fear that he or another person will be kidnapped; or

(3) fear by a child under sixteen years of age caused by intimidation, expressed or implied, by another person four years older than the victim. **Resistance** includes physical resistance or any clear communication of the victim's lack of consent.

Married includes persons living together as husband and wife regardless of the legal status of their relationship.

Mentally defective means that a person suffers from a mental disease or defect which renders such person incapable of appraising the nature of his conduct.

Mentally incapacitated means that a person is rendered temporarily incapable of appraising or controlling his or her conduct as a result of the influence of a controlled or intoxicating substance administered to such person without his or her consent.

Physically helpless means that a person is unconscious or for any reason is physically unable to communicate unwillingness to an act.

Sexual contact means any intentional touching, either directly or through clothing, of the anus or any part of the sex organs of another person, or the breasts of a female or intentional touching of any part of another person's body by the actor's sex organs, where the victim is not married to the actor and the touching is done for the purpose of gratifying the sexual desire of either party.

Sexual intercourse means any act between persons not married to each other involving penetration, however slight, of the female sex organ by the male sex organ or involving contact between the sex organs of one person and the mouth or anus of another person.

Sexual intrusion means any act between persons not married to each other involving penetration, however slight, of the female sex organ or of the anus of any person by an object for the purpose of degrading or humiliating the person so penetrated or for gratifying the sexual desire of either party.

Bodily injury means substantial physical pain, illness or any impairment of physical condition.

Serious bodily injury means bodily injury which creates a substantial risk of death, which causes serious or prolonged disfigurement, prolonged impairment of health, or prolonged loss or impairment of function of any bodily organ.

Deadly weapon means any instrument, device or thing capable of inflicting death or serious bodily injury, and designed or specially adapted for use as a weapon, or possessed, carried or used as a weapon.

(West Virginia Criminal Code 61-8B-1)

Sexual Consent

Whether or not specifically stated, it is an element of every offense defined in this article that the sexual act was committed without the consent of the victim.

Lack of consent results from:

    (1) forcible compulsion;

    (2) incapacity to consent; or

    (3) if the offense charged is sexual abuse, any circumstances in addition to the forcible compulsion or incapacity to consent in which the victim does not expressly or impliedly acquiesce in the actor's conduct.

A person is deemed incapable of consent when such person is:

    (1) less than sixteen years old;

    (2) mentally defective;

    (3) mentally incapacitated; or

    (4) physically helpless.

(West Virginia Criminal Code 61-8B-2)

Sexual Assault

A person is guilty of sexual assault in the first degree when:

(1) such person engages in sexual intercourse or sexual intrusion with another person and, in so doing:

(a) inflicts serious bodily injury upon anyone; or

(b) employs a deadly weapon in the commission of the act; or

(2) such person, being fourteen years old or more, engages in sexual intercourse or sexual intrusion with another person who is eleven years old or less.

A person is guilty of sexual assault in the second degree when:

(1) such person engages in sexual intercourse or sexual intrusion with another person without the person's consent, and the lack of consent results from forcible compulsion; or

(2) such person engages in sexual intercourse or sexual intrusion with another person who is physically helpless.

A person is guilty of sexual assault in the third degree when:

(1) such person engages in sexual intercourse or sexual intrusion with another person who is mentally defective or mentally incapacitated; or

(2) such person, being sixteen years old or more, engages in sexual intercourse or sexual intrusion with another person who is less than sixteen years old and who is at least four years younger than the defendant.

Any person who violates the above provisions shall be guilty of a felony.

(West Virginia Criminal Code 61-8B-3/4/5)

Sexual Abuse

A person is guilty of sexual abuse in the first degree when:

(1) such person subjects another person to sexual contact without their consent, and the lack of consent results from forcible compulsion;

(2) such person subjects another person to sexual contact who is physically helpless; or

(3) such person, being fourteen years old or more, subjects another person to sexual contact who is eleven years old or less.

A person is guilty of sexual abuse in the second degree when such person subjects another person to sexual contact who is mentally defective or mentally incapacitated.

A person is guilty of sexual abuse in the third degree when such person subjects another person to sexual contact without the latter's consent, when such lack of consent is due to the victim's incapacity to consent by reason of being less than sixteen years old.

Any person who commits sexual abuse in the first degree shall be guilty of a felony. Any person who commits sexual abuse in the second or third degree shall be guilty of a misdemeanor. (West Virginia Criminal Code 61-8B-7/8/9)

Spousal Rape

A person is guilty of sexual assault of a spouse when such person engages in sexual penetration or sexual intrusion with his or her spouse without the consent of such spouse; and

(1) the lack of consent results from forcible compulsion;

(2) such person inflicts serious bodily injury upon anyone; or

(3) such person employs a deadly weapon in the commission of the offense.

Any person who violates this provision shall be guilty of a felony.
(West Virginia Criminal Code 61-8B-6)

Rape and Murder

Murder in the commission of or attempt to commit sexual assault is murder of the first degree. (West Virginia Criminal Code 61-2-1)

The complete and unedited text of West Virginia's rape laws excerpted above can be found in The West Virginia Code *and* The Acts of West Virginia.

WISCONSIN'S RAPE LAWS
Definitions

Sexual contact means any intentional touching by the complainant or defendant, either directly or through clothing by the use of any body part or object, of the complainant's or defendant's intimate parts if that intentional touching is either for the purpose of sexually degrading; or for the purpose of sexually humiliating the complainant or sexually arousing or gratifying the defendant.

Sexual intercourse includes vulvar penetration as well as cunnilingus, fellatio, anal intercourse, or any other intrusion, however slight, of any part of a person's body or of any object into the genital or anal opening of another, but emission of semen is not required.

(Wisconsin Criminal Code 939.22(36)/940.225(5))

Sexual Assault

Whoever does any of the following is guilty of first degree sexual assault, a Class B felony:

(1) has sexual contact or sexual intercourse with another person without consent of that person and causes pregnancy or great bodily harm to that person;

(2) has sexual contact or sexual intercourse with another person without consent of that person by use or threat of use of a dangerous weapon or any article used or fashioned in a manner to lead the victim reasonably to believe it to be a dangerous weapon; or

(3) is aided or abetted by one or more other persons and has sexual contact or sexual intercourse with another person without consent of that person.

Whoever does any of the following is guilty of second degree sexual assault, a Class C felony:

(1) has sexual contact or sexual intercourse with another person without consent of that person by use or threat of force or violence;

(2) has sexual contact or sexual intercourse with another person without consent of that person and causes injury, illness, disease or impairment of a sexual or reproductive organ or mental anguish requiring psychiatric care for the victim;

(3) has sexual contact or sexual intercourse with a person who suffers from a mental illness or deficiency which renders that person temporarily or permanently incapable of appraising the person's conduct, and the defendant knows of such condition; [or]
(4) has sexual contact or sexual intercourse with a person who the defendant knows is unconscious.

Whoever has sexual intercourse with a person without the consent of that person is guilty of third degree sexual assault, a Class D felony.

Whoever has sexual contact with a person without the consent of that person is guilty of fourth degree sexual assault, a Class A misdemeanor.

(Wisconsin Criminal Code 940.225(1-3))

Sexual Assault of a Child

Whoever has sexual contact or sexual intercourse with a person who has not attained the age of thirteen years is guilty of first degree sexual assault of a child, a Class B felony.

Whoever has sexual contact or sexual intercourse with a person who has not attained the age of sixteen years is guilty of second degree sexual assault of a child, a Class C felony.

A person responsible for the welfare of a child who has not attained the age of sixteen years is guilty of a Class C felony if that person has knowledge that another person intends to have, is having, or has had sexual intercourse or sexual contact with the child, is physically and emotionally capable of taking action which will prevent the intercourse or contact from taking place or being repeated, fails to take that action and the failure to act exposes the child to an unreasonable risk that intercourse or contact may occur between the child and the other person or facilitates the intercourse or contact that does occur between the child and the other person.

A defendant shall not be presumed to be incapable of violating this section because of marriage to the complainant.

This section applies whether a victim is dead or alive at the time of sexual contact or sexual intercourse.

(Wisconsin Criminal Code 948.02)

Sexual Consent

Consent means words or overt actions by a person who is competent to give informed consent indicating a freely given agreement to have sexual intercourse or sexual contact.

The following persons are presumed incapable of sexual consent:

(1) a person who is fifteen to seventeen years of age;

(2) a person suffering from a mental illness or defect which impairs capacity to appraise personal conduct; and

(3) a person who is unconscious or for any other reason is physically unable to communicate unwillingness to an act.

(Wisconsin Criminal Code 940.225(4))

Spousal Assault

No person may be prosecuted under these sexual assault provisions if the complainant is his or her legal spouse, unless the parties are living apart and one of them has filed for an annulment, legal separation, or divorce. (Wisconsin Criminal Code 940.225(6))

Rape and Murder

Whoever causes the death of another human being while committing or attempting to commit first degree sexual assault or second degree sexual assault may be imprisoned for not more than twenty years in excess of the maximum period of imprisonment provided by law for that crime or attempt. (Wisconsin Criminal Code 940.03)

The complete and unedited text of Wisconsin's rape laws excerpted above can be found in Wisconsin Statutes, Wisconsin Statutes Annotated, *and* The Laws of Wisconsin.

WYOMING'S RAPE LAWS

Definitions

Actor means the person accused of sexual assault.

Intimate parts means the external genitalia, perineum, anus or pubes of any person or the breast of a female person.

Physically helpless means unconscious, asleep or otherwise physically unable to communicate unwillingness to act.

Position of authority means that position occupied by a parent, guardian, relative, household member, teacher, employer, custodian or any other person who, by reason of his position, is able to exercise significant influence over a person.

Sexual assault means any act made criminal pursuant to the [sexual assault provisions that follow].

Sexual contact means touching, with the intention of sexual arousal, gratification or abuse, of the victim's intimate parts by the actor, or of the actor's intimate parts by the victim, or of the clothing covering the immediate area of the victim's or the actor's intimate parts.

Sexual intrusion means:

(1) any intrusion, however slight, by any object or any part of a person's body, except the mouth, tongue or penis, into the genital or anal opening of another person's body if that sexual intrusion can reasonably be construed as being for the purposes of sexual arousal, gratification or abuse; or

(2) sexual intercourse, cunnilingus, fellatio, analingus, or anal intercourse with or without emission.

Victim means the person alleged to have been subjected to sexual assault.

(Wyoming Criminal Code 6-2-301)

First Degree Sexual Assault

Any actor who inflicts sexual intrusion on a victim commits sexual assault in the first degree if:

(1) the actor causes submission of the victim through the actual application, reasonably calculated to cause submission of the victim, of physical force or forcible confinement;

(2) the actor causes submission of the victim by threat of death, serious bodily injury, extreme physical pain or kidnapping to be inflicted on anyone and the victim reasonably believes that the actor has the present ability to execute these threats;

(3) the victim is physically helpless, and the actor knows or reasonably should know that the victim is physically helpless and that the victim has not consented; or

(4) the actor knows or reasonably should know that the victim through a mental illness, mental defect, or developmental disability is incapable of appraising the nature of the victim's conduct.

(Wyoming Criminal Code 6-2-302)

Second Degree Sexual Assault

Any actor who inflicts sexual intrusion on a victim commits sexual assault in the second degree if, under circumstances not constituting sexual assault in the first degree:

(1) the actor causes submission of the victim by threatening to retaliate in the future against the victim or the victim's spouse, parents, brothers, sisters, or children, and the victim reasonably believes that the actor will execute this threat. **To retaliate** includes threats of kidnapping, death, serious bodily injury, or extreme physical pain;

(2) the actor causes submission of the victim by any means that would prevent resistance by a victim of ordinary resolution;

(3) the actor administers, or knows that someone else administered to the victim, without the prior knowledge or consent of the victim, any substance which substantially impairs the victim's power to appraise or control his conduct;

(4) the actor knows or reasonably should know that the victim submits erroneously believing the actor to be the victim's spouse;

(5) at the time of the commission of the act the victim is less than twelve years of age and the actor is at least four years older than the victim;

(6) the actor is in a position of authority over the victim and uses this position of authority to cause the victim to submit; or

(7) the actor inflicts sexual intrusion in treatment or examination of a victim for purposes or in a manner substantially inconsistent with reasonable medical practices.

A person is guilty of sexual assault in the second degree if he subjects another person to sexual contact and causes serious bodily injury to the victim under [certain] circumstances listed in first degree sexual assault.

A person is guilty of sexual assault in the second degree if he subjects a person between the age of twelve years through fifteen years to sexual contact and causes serious bodily injury to the victim.

(Wyoming Criminal Code 6-2-303)

Third Degree Sexual Assault

[A]n actor commits a sexual assault in the third degree if:

(1) the actor is at least four years older than the victim and inflicts sexual intrusion on a victim under the age of sixteen years; or

(2) the actor is an adult and subjects a victim under the age of twelve years to sexual contact without inflicting sexual intrusion on the victim and without causing serious bodily injury to the victim.

(Wyoming Criminal Code 6-2-304)

Fourth Degree Sexual Assault

[A]ny actor who subjects a victim to sexual contact under [certain] circumstances of the first or second degree sexual assault provisions without causing serious bodily injury to the victim commits sexual assault in the fourth degree. (Wyoming Criminal Code 6-2-305)

Crime and Punishment

An actor convicted of sexual assault shall be punished as follows:

> (1) sexual assault in the first degree is a felony punishable by imprisonment for not less than five years nor more than fifty years;
>
> (2) sexual assault in the second degree is a felony punishable by imprisonment for not more than twenty years;
>
> (3) sexual assault in the third degree is a felony punishable by imprisonment for not more than five years; and
>
> (4) sexual assault in the fourth degree is a misdemeanor punishable by imprisonment for not more than one year.

(Wyoming Criminal Code 6-2-306)

Spousal Rape

The fact that the actor and the victim are married to each other is not by itself a defense to a violation of first or second degree sexual assault. (Wyoming Criminal Code 6-2-307)

Rape and Murder

Whoever purposely and with premeditated malice, or in the perpetration of, or attempt to perpetrate, any sexual assault, kills any human being is guilty of murder in the first degree. A person convicted of murder in the first degree shall be punished by death or life imprisonment according to law. (Wyoming Criminal Code 6-2-101)

The complete and unedited text of Wyoming's rape laws excerpted above can be found in Wyoming Statutes *and* The Session Laws of Wyoming.

Rape Statistics For The 1990's

The stigma, intrusiveness and risk of retaliation that accompanies criminal charges have kept rape the most underreported major felony.

Deborah Rhode, **Justice and Gender**[1]

Chapter II: *Rape Statistics For The 1990's* is a comprehensive collection of up-to-date rape facts and figures drawn from the Federal Bureau of Investigation's *Uniform Crime Reports*, the single most authoritative criminal justice statistical source available.

Rape Statistics For The 1990's is broken down into three inter-related, mutually supporting geographic divisions - Regions, States, and Cities - and is presented in two forms: reported number of rapes and reported rape rates per each 100,000 persons.

In *Rape Statistics By Region*, you will find rape statistics for the first five years of the 1990's for each geographic region of the United States, broken down by *Reported Number Of Rapes* and *Reported Rape Rates*.

In *Rape Statistics By States*, you will find rape statistics for the first five years of the 1990's for all fifty U.S. States and the District of Columbia, broken down by *Reported Number Of Rapes* and *Reported Rape Rates*.

In *Rape Statistics By Cities*, you will find the *Reported Number Of Rapes* for the first five and one-half years of the 1990's for all 207 U.S. cities over 100,000 in population.

All of these rape statistics are drawn from *Uniform Crime Reports*, which is published annually, with semi-annual supplements, by the Federal Bureau of Investigation. *Uniform Crime Reports* uses this definition of rape:

> **Forcible Rape:** *The carnal knowledge of a female forcibly against her will. Assaults or attempts to commit rape by force or threat of force are also included; however, statutory rape (without force) and other sexual offenses are excluded.*

Rape And Statistics

Mark Twain is reported to have once said: "There are lies, damned lies, and damned statistical lies." While the numbers reported in *Rape Statistics For The 1990's* are the most authoritative available, many criminal justice experts and sexual violence advocates believe that the reported number of rapes and reported rape rates must be viewed not as the *true total* but as the *bare minimum*.

The following totals of *Reported Number Of Rapes* and *Reported Rape Rates* for the entire United States for the period January through December 1994 are drawn from the FBI's *Uniform Crime Reports:*

Reported Number Of Rapes
102,096

Reported Rape Rates
39.2

While these official numbers, gathered from victim reports of forcible rape to law enforcement, are the best statistics on rape available:

Rape is America's most underreported crime.

Many rape victims are reluctant in the extreme to report an act of sexual violence perpetrated against them. The social stigma, the intrusive nature of rape investigation, and the real fear of physical retaliation all serve to corrupt the collection of meaningful rape statistics.

It is variously estimated by reliable criminal justice sources that for every rape victim reporting an attack to the police there are anywhere from five[2] to twenty[3] rape victims who do not. The reported number rapes may need to be multiplied by as few as *five* to as many as *twenty* times to reach the *true* number of rapes.

This means that while the *reported* number of rapes in 1994 is officially **102,096** the *true* number of rape victims could be in fact be anywhere from **500,000** to **2,000,000**.

In addition, reported rape rates, which allows a statistical "level playing field" on which large and small states and cities may be equally compared and contrasted, are reported in the FBI's *Uniform Crime Reports* for each 100,000 "persons." As 51% of the population (and 99% of all rape victims) are female, many criminal statistics experts believe the reported rape rate should be *doubled* to reach the *actual* rape rate.

This means that, while the *reported* rape rate in 1994 is officially **39.2** per every 100,000 "persons," the *actual* rape rate could in fact be as high as **78.4** for every 100,000 females.

Lastly the *actual* reported rape rate is based on the reported number of rapes, which we have learned may in fact be five to twenty times greater than reported.

This means that, while the *actual* reported rape rate in 1994 may be **78.4** for every 100,000 females, the *true* rape rate could in fact be as high as **390** to **1,560** per every 100,000 females.

We have attempted to collect for *The Rape Reference* only the most reliable rape statistics available. We have neither multiplied the reported number of rapes nor doubled the reported rape rates. Mark Twain notwithstanding, we are offering these rape statistics unedited, but we remind and caution the reader that these statistics were gathered only from the victims of rape who were willing to come forward. The figures reported for all "persons" may represent only the tip of a massive sexual violence iceberg.

Footnotes To Rape Statistics For The 1990's

[1]Rhode, Deborah. *Justice and Gender.* Cambridge, MA:
  Harvard University Press, 1989.
[2]United States Senate. Judiciary Committee. *Violence
  Against Women.*
 University of South Carolina. National Victim Center. *Rape in
  America.*
[3]United States Senate. Judiciary Committee. *The Response to
  Rape.*

Reported Number Of Rapes By Region

Number of rapes reported for geographic regions from January 1990 - December 1994

United States

1990	102,555	1993	104,806
1991	106,593	1994	102,096
1992	109,062		

Northeast

1990	14,713	1993	14,567
1991	14,748	1994	13,606
1992	15,089		

New England (CT, MA, ME, NH, RI, VT)

1990	3,970	1993	4,149
1991	3,969	1994	3,789
1992	4,221		

Middle Atlantic (NJ, NY, PA)

1990	10,743	1993	10,418
1991	10,779	1994	9,817
1992	10,868		

Midwest

1990	25,393	1993	25,831
1991	27,373	1994	26,347
1992	27,639		

East North Central (IL, IN, MI, OH, WI)

1990	19,905	1993	19,733
1991	21,312	1994	19,102
1992	21,314		

West North Central (IA, KS, MN, MI, NE, ND, SD)

1990	5,488	1993	6,098
1991	6,061	1994	7,245
1992	6,325		

South

1990	**38,776**	1993	**40,387**
1991	**39,364**	1994	**39,393**
1992	**40,631**		

South Atlantic (DE, DC, FL, GA, MD, NC, SC, VA, WV)

1990	**19,811**	1993	**19,587**
1991	**19,419**	1994	**19,130**
1992	**20,379**		

East South Central (AL, KY, MS, TN)

1990	**5,936**	1993	**6,441**
1991	**6,268**	1994	**6,594**
1992	**6,456**		

West South Central (AK, LA, OK, TX)

1990	**13,029**	1993	**14,359**
1991	**13,677**	1994	**13,669**
1992	**13,796**		

West

1990	**23,673**	1993	**24,021**
1991	**25,108**	1994	**22,750**
1992	**25,703**		

Mountain (AZ, CO, ID, MT, NV, NM, UT, WY)

1990	**5,777**	1993	**6,421**
1991	**6,224**	1994	**6,246**
1992	**6,646**		

Pacific (AK, CA, HI, OR, WA)

1990	**17,896**	1993	**17,600**
1991	**18,884**	1994	**16,324**
1992	**19,057**		

Reported Rape Rates By Region
Rape rate for each 100,000 persons reported for geographic regions
from January 1990 - December 1994

United States

1990	41.2	1993	40.6
1991	42.3	1994	39.2
1992	42.8		

Northeast

1990	29.0	1993	28.4
1991	28.9	1994	26.5
1992	29.5		

New England (CT, MA, ME, NH, RI, VT)

1990	30.1	1993	31.4
1991	30.1	1994	28.6
1992	32.0		

Middle Atlantic (NJ, NY, PA)

1990	28.6	1993	27.3
1991	28.5	1994	25.7
1992	28.7		

Midwest

1990	42.6	1993	42.3
1991	45.5	1994	42.9
1992	45.5		

East North Central (IL, IN, MI, OH, WI)

1990	47.4	1993	45.9
1991	50.2	1994	44.2
1992	49.9		

West North Central (IA, KS, MN, MI, NE, ND, SD)

1990	31.1	1993	33.8
1991	34.0	1994	39.8
1992	35.2		

South

1990	45.4	1993	45.2
1991	45.3	1994	43.4
1992	46.1		

South Atlantic (DE, DC, FL, GA, MD, NC, SC, VA, WV)

1990	45.5	1993	42.8
1991	43.7	1994	41.2
1992	45.2		

East South Central (AL, KY, MS, TN)

1990	39.1	1993	41.0
1991	40.8	1994	41.5
1992	41.6		

West South Central (AK, LA, OK, TX)

1990	48.8	1993	51.3
1991	50.4	1994	48.1
1992	50.1		

West

1990	44.8	1993	42.9
1991	46.4	1994	40.0
1992	46.6		

Mountain (AZ, CO, ID, MT, NV, NM, UT, WY)

1990	42.3	1993	43.5
1991	44.3	1994	42.2
1992	46.2		

Pacific (AK, CA, HI, OR, WA)

1990	45.7	1993	42.6
1991	47.2	1994	39.2
1992	46.8		

Reported Number Of Rapes By State

Number of rapes reported by U.S. States
from January 1990 - December 1994

Alabama				Connecticut			
1990	1319	1993	1471	1990	918	1993	800
1991	1455	1994	1487	1991	960	1994	806
1992	1704			1992	884		

Alaska				Delaware			
1990	401	1993	502	1990	587	1993	539
1991	523	1994	418	1991	588	1994	534
1992	579			1992	591		

Arizona				District of Columbia			
1990	1500	1993	1488	1990	303	1993	324
1991	1590	1994	1465	1991	214	1994	249
1992	1647			1992	215		

Arkansas				Florida			
1990	1019	1993	1028	1990	6781	1993	7359
1991	1058	1994	1028	1991	6865	1994	7301
1992	990			1992	7310		

California				Georgia			
1990	12,688	1993	11,766	1990	3472	1993	2448
1991	12,896	1994	10,984	1991	2800	1994	2448
1992	12,761			1992	3057		

Colorado				Hawaii			
1990	1521	1993	1633	1990	360	1993	394
1991	1588	1994	1579	1991	375	1994	359
1992	1641			1992	440		

Idaho

1990	275	1993	388
1991	300	1994	316
1992	339		

Illinois

1990	4405	1993	4046
1991	4615	1994	3913
1992	4312		

Indiana

1990	2103	1993	2234
1991	2318	1994	2046
1992	2398		

Iowa

1990	510	1993	686
1991	583	1994	666
1992	528		

Kansas

1990	1002	1993	1016
1991	1118	1994	947
1992	1042		

Kentucky

1990	1068	1993	1301
1991	1315	1994	1350
1992	1209		

Louisiana

1990	1781	1993	1817
1991	1738	1994	1923
1992	1813		

Maine

1990	242	1993	329
1991	270	1994	318
1992	294		

Maryland

1990	2185	1993	2185
1991	2229	1994	2035
1992	2278		

Massachusetts

1990	2030	1993	2006
1991	1926	1994	1825
1992	2166		

Michigan

1990	7209	1993	6740
1991	7372	1994	6720
1992	7550		

Minnesota

1990	1487	1993	1588
1991	1762	1994	2725
1992	1840		

Mississippi

1990	1134	1993	1125
1991	1199	1994	1212
1992	1166		

Missouri

1990	1663	1993	1894
1991	1756	1994	1955
1992	1895		

Montana

1990	195	1993	234
1991	160	1994	233
1992	210		

Nebraska

1990	473	1993	447
1991	447	1994	500
1992	504		

Nevada

1990	748	1993	846
1991	848	1994	1001
1992	833		

New Hampshire

1990	386	1993	499
1991	330	1994	407
1992	424		

New Jersey

1990	2307	1993	2215
1991	2259	1994	1972
1992	2392		

New Mexico

1990	753	1993	842
1991	811	1994	866
1992	990		

New York

1990	5368	1993	5008
1991	5085	1994	4700
1992	5152		

North Carolina

1990	2272	1993	2379
1991	2331	1994	2334
1992	2455		

North Dakota

1990	114	1993	149
1991	116	1994	149
1992	148		

Ohio

1990	5075	1993	5444
1991	5748	1994	5231
1992	5739		

Oklahoma

1990	1479	1993	1592
1991	1615	1994	1616
1992	1556		

Oregon

1990	1332	1993	1554
1991	1561	1994	1333
1992	1580		

Pennsylvania

1990	3068	1993	3195
1991	3435	1994	3145
1992	3324		

Rhode Island

1990	248	1993	286
1991	310	1994	273
1992	311		

South Carolina

1990	1873	1993	1905
1991	2098	1994	1991
1992	2072		

South Dakota

1990	239	1993	318
1991	279	1994	303
1992	368		

Tennessee

1990	2415	1993	2544
1991	2299	1994	2545
1992	2377		

Texas

1990	8750	1993	9922
1991	9266	1994	9102
1992	9437		

Utah

1990	651	1993	829
1991	808	1994	806
1992	823		

Vermont

1990	146	1993	229
1991	173	1994	160
1992	142		

Virginia

1990	1915	1993	2083
1991	1879	1994	1868
1992	2008		

Washington

1990	3115	1993	338‹
1991	3529	1994	323(
1992	3697		

West Virginia

1990	423	1993	365
1991	415	1994	370
1992	393		

Wisconsin

1990	1013	1993	126‹
1991	1259	1994	119‹
1992	1315		

Wyoming

1990	134	1993	161
1991	119	1994	160
1992	163		

United States

1990	102,555
1991	106,593
1992	109,062
1993	104,806
1994	102,096

Reported Rape Rates By States

Rape rate for each 100,000 persons reported by U.S. States
from January 1990 - December 1994

Alabama

1990	**32.6**	1993	**35.1**
1991	**35.6**	1994	**35.2**
1992	**41.2**		

Alaska

1990	**72.9**	1993	**83.8**
1991	**91.8**	1994	**69.0**
1992	**98.6**		

Arizona

1990	**40.9**	1993	**37.8**
1991	**42.4**	1994	**36.0**
1992	**43.0**		

Arkansas

1990	**43.3**	1993	**42.4**
1991	**44.6**	1994	**41.9**
1992	**41.3**		

California

1990	**42.6**	1993	**37.7**
1991	**42.4**	1994	**34.9**
1992	**41.3**		

Colorado

1990	**46.2**	1993	**45.8**
1991	**47.0**	1994	**43.2**
1992	**47.3**		

Connecticut

1990	**27.9**	1993	**24.4**
1991	**29.2**	1994	**24.6**
1992	**26.9**		

Delaware

1990	**88.1**	1993	**77.0**
1991	**86.5**	1994	**75.6**
1992	**85.8**		

District of Columbia

1990	**49.9**	1993	**56.1**
1991	**35.8**	1994	**43.7**
1992	**36.5**		

Florida

1990	**52.4**	1993	**53.8**
1991	**51.7**	1994	**52.3**
1992	**54.2**		

Georgia

1990	**53.6**	1993	**35.4**
1991	**42.3**	1994	**34.7**
1992	**45.3**		

Hawaii

1990	**32.5**	1993	**33.6**
1991	**33.0**	1994	**30.4**
1992	**37.9**		

Idaho

1990	27.3	1993	35.3
1991	28.9	1994	27.9
1992	31.8		

Illinois

1990	39.4	1993	34.6
1991	40.0	1994	33.3
1992	37.1		

Indiana

1990	37.9	1993	39.1
1991	41.3	1994	35.6
1992	42.4		

Iowa

1990	18.4	1993	24.4
1991	20.9	1994	23.5
1992	18.8		

Kansas

1990	40.4	1993	40.1
1991	44.8	1994	37.1
1992	41.3		

Kentucky

1990	29.0	1993	34.3
1991	35.4	1994	35.3
1992	32.2		

Louisiana

1990	42.2	1993	42.3
1991	40.9	1994	44.6
1992	42.3		

Maine

1990	19.7	1993	26.6
1991	21.9	1994	25.6
1992	23.8		

Maryland

1990	45.7	1993	44.0
1991	45.9	1994	40.7
1992	46.4		

Massachusetts

1990	33.7	1993	33.4
1991	32.1	1994	30.2
1992	36.1		

Michigan

1990	77.6	1993	71.1
1991	78.7	1994	70.8
1992	80.0		

Minnesota

1990	34.0	1993	35.2
1991	39.8	1994	59.7
1992	41.1		

Mississippi

1990	44.1	1993	42.6
1991	46.3	1994	45.4
1992	44.6		

Missouri

1990	32.5	1993	36.2
1991	34.0	1994	37.0
1992	36.5		

Montana				North Carolina			
1990	24.4	1993	27.9	1990	34.3	1993	34.3
1991	19.8	1994	27.2	1991	34.6	1994	33.0
1992	25.5			1992	35.9		

Nebraska				North Dakota			
1990	30.0	1993	27.8	1990	17.8	1993	23.5
1991	28.1	1994	30.8	1991	18.3	1994	23.4
1992	31.4			1992	23.3		

Nevada				Ohio			
1990	62.2	1993	60.9	1990	46.8	1993	49.1
1991	66.0	1994	68.7	1991	52.5	1994	47.1
1992	62.8			1992	52.1		

New Hampshire				Oklahoma			
1990	34.8	1993	44.4	1990	47.0	1993	49.3
1991	29.9	1994	35.8	1991	50.9	1994	49.6
1992	38.2			1992	48.4		

New Jersey				Oregon			
1990	29.8	1993	28.1	1990	46.9	1993	51.3
1991	29.1	1994	24.9	1991	53.4	1994	43.2
1992	30.7			1992	53.1		

New Mexico				Pennsylvania			
1990	49.7	1993	52.1	1990	25.8	1993	26.5
1991	52.4	1994	52.4	1991	28.7	1994	26.1
1992	62.6			1992	27.7		

New York				Rhode Island			
1990	29.8	1993	27.5	1990	24.7	1993	28.6
1991	28.2	1994	25.9	1991	30.9	1994	27.4
1992	28.4			1992	30.9		

South Carolina

1990	53.7	1993	52.3
1991	58.9	1994	54.3
1992	57.5		

South Dakota

1990	34.3	1993	44.5
1991	39.7	1994	42.0
1992	51.8		

Tennessee

1990	49.5	1993	49.9
1991	46.4	1994	49.2
1992	47.3		

Texas

1990	51.5	1993	55.0
1991	53.4	1994	49.5
1992	53.4		

Utah

1990	37.8	1993	44.6
1991	45.6	1994	42.2
1992	45.4		

Vermont

1990	25.9	1993	39.8
1991	30.5	1994	27.6
1992	24.9		

Virginia

1990	31.0	1993	32.1
1991	29.9	1994	28.5
1992	31.5		

Washington

1990	64.0	1993	64.4
1991	70.3	1994	60.5
1992	72.0		

West Virginia

1990	23.6	1993	20.1
1991	23.0	1994	20.3
1992	21.7		

Wisconsin

1990	20.7	1993	25.2
1991	25.4	1994	23.5
1992	26.3		

Wyoming

1990	29.5	1993	34.3
1991	25.9	1994	33.6
1992	35.0		

United States

1990	41.2	1993	40.6
1991	42.3	1994	39.2
1993	42.8		

Number Of Rapes Reported By Cities

Number of rapes reported by U.S. cities over 100,000 in population - for four full years January 1990 - December 1994 and for one-half year January - June 1995

Abilene, Texas				Amarillo, Texas			
1990	92	1993	75	1990	75	1993	89
1991	64	1994	90	1991	80	1994	106
1992	89	1995	36	1992	103	1995	33

Akron, Ohio				Amherst Town, NY			
1990	193	1993	204	1990	8	1993	6
1991	223	1994	195	1991	11	1994	8
1992	204	1995	114	1992	11	1995	7

Albany, New York				Anaheim, California			
1990	82	1993	59	1990	94	1993	70
1991	71	1994	79	1991	111	1994	90
1992	77	1995	36	1992	90	1995	38

Albuquerque, NM				Anchorage, Alaska			
1990	222	1993	259	1990	203	1993	212
1991	261	1994	na	1991	264	1994	198
1992	294	1995	na	1992	253	1995	107

Alexandria, Virginia				Ann Arbor, Michigan			
1990	52	1993	33	1990	63	1993	na
1991	43	1994	37	1991	50	1994	42
1992	35	1995	13	1992	50	1995	23

Allentown, Pennsylvania				Arlington, Texas			
1990	22	1993	42	1990	139	1993	146
1991	14	1994	47	1991	166	1994	144
1992	21	1995	20	1992	146	1995	76

Arlington, Virginia

1990	44	1993	37
1991	36	1994	na
1992	39	1995	na

Atlanta, Georgia

1990	695	1993	492
1991	638	1994	422
1992	627	1995	202

Aurora, Colorado

1990	170	1993	166
1991	184	1994	147
1992	182	1995	56

Austin, Texas

1990	280	1993	271
1991	276	1994	249
1992	294	1995	na

Bakersfield, California

1990	65	1993	39
1991	71	1994	59
1992	51	1995	na

Baltimore, Maryland

1990	687	1993	668
1991	701	1994	637
1992	749	1995	331

Baton Rouge, Louisiana

1990	112	1993	177
1991	142	1994	180
1992	169	1995	80

Beaumont, Texas

1990	126	1993	200
1991	94	1994	219
1992	84	1995	96

Berkeley, California

1990	48	1993	35
1991	40	1994	36
1992	28	1995	19

Birmingham, Alabama

1990	267	1993	297
1991	279	1994	273
1992	362	1995	108

Boise, Idaho

1990	52	1993	72
1991	61	1994	60
1992	84	1995	21

Boston, Massachusetts

1990	539	1993	480
1991	486	1994	453
1992	537	1995	181

Bridgeport, Connecticut

1990	79	1993	72
1991	82	1994	59
1992	74	1995	17

Brownsville, Texas

1990	36	1993	28
1991	31	1994	31
1992	29	1995	14

ffalo, New York			
90	355	1993	295
91	319	1994	280
92	346	1995	121

dar Rapids, Iowa			
90	14	1993	na
91	na	1994	na
92	na	1995	na

andler, Arizona			
90	22	1993	27
91	23	1994	27
92	29	1995	12

arlotte, North Carolina			
90	384	1993	356
91	409	1994	350
92	361	1995	162

attanooga, Tennessee			
90	180	1993	154
91	163	1994	92
92	146	1995	10

esapeake, Virginia			
90	38	1993	61
91	68	1994	63
92	60	1995	37

icago, Illinois			
90	na	1993	na
91	na	1994	na
92	na	1995	na

Chula Vista, California			
1990	43	1993	37
1991	52	1994	53
1992	51	1995	22

Cincinnati, Ohio			
1990	388	1993	449
1991	478	1994	382
1992	486	1995	193

Clearwater, Florida			
1990	na	1993	70
1991	40	1994	48
1992	56	1995	25

Cleveland, Ohio			
1990	846	1993	834
1991	913	1994	749
1992	854	1995	308

Colorado Springs, CO			
1990	201	1993	265
1991	231	1994	228
1992	226	1995	115

Columbia, SC			
1990	103	1993	94
1991	119	1994	116
1992	105	1995	na

Columbus, Georgia			
1990	93	1993	49
1991	71	1994	37
1992	56	1995	17

Columbus, Ohio

1990	647	1993	658
1991	650	1994	679
1992	684	1995	312

Concord, California

1990	37	1993	44
1991	47	1994	45
1992	33	1995	24

Corpus Christi, Texas

1990	240	1993	194
1991	204	1994	178
1992	144	1995	96

Dallas, Texas

1990	1344	1993	1000
1991	1208	1994	957
1992	1096	1995	419

Dayton, Ohio

1990	321	1993	269
1991	316	1994	250
1992	298	1995	116

Denver, Colorado

1990	375	1993	393
1991	427	1994	366
1992	437	1995	139

Des Moines, Iowa

1990	96	1993	84
1991	na	1994	73
1992	93	1995	62

Detroit, Michigan

1990	1657	1993	na
1991	1427	1994	1116
1992	1225	1995	473

Durham, North Carolina

1990	79	1993	109
1991	98	1994	78
1992	111	1995	39

Elizabeth, New Jersey

1990	53	1993	42
1991	58	1994	41
1992	64	1995	23

El Monte, California

1990	47	1993	45
1991	51	1994	23
1992	53	1995	10

El Paso, Texas

1990	256	1993	281
1991	265	1994	233
1992	272	1995	120

Erie, Pennsylvania

1990	77	1993	59
1991	96	1994	63
1992	95	1995	23

Escondido, California

1990	44	1993	26
1991	30	1994	34
1992	38	1995	14

ıgene, Oregon

'90	76	1993	64
'91	59	1994	51
'92	57	1995	18

ansville, Indiana

'90	50	1993	43
'91	45	1994	50
'92	50	1995	11

int, Michigan

90	161	1993	na
'91	151	1994	202
'92	238	1995	105

ntana, California

'90	66	1993	79
'91	71	1994	67
'92	83	1995	25

ırt Lauderdale, Florida

'90	114	1993	76
'91	104	1994	94
'92	70	1995	54

ırt Wayne, Indiana

90	95	1993	130
'91	114	1994	100
'92	126	1995	41

ırt Worth, Texas

'90	432	1993	507
'91	442	1994	413
'92	525	1995	172

Fremont, California

1990	32	1993	39
1991	26	1994	42
1992	34	1995	13

Fresno, California

1990	258	1993	216
1991	282	1994	192
1992	203	1995	95

Fullerton, California

1990	52	1993	36
1991	46	1994	38
1992	31	1995	19

Garden Grove, California

1990	40	1993	33
1991	45	1994	41
1992	46	1995	23

Garland, Texas

1990	132	1993	114
1991	134	1994	93
1992	125	1995	49

Gary, Indiana

1990	150	1993	174
1991	182	1994	143
1992	173	1995	70

Glendale, Arizona

1990	83	1993	79
1991	65	1994	46
1992	75	1995	23

Glendale, California

1990	37	1993	30
1991	36	1994	15
1992	38	1995	13

Grand Prairie, Texas

1990	52	1993	54
1991	56	1994	39
1992	57	1995	20

Grand Rapids, Michigan

1990	378	1993	na
1991	370	1994	113
1992	413	1995	50

Green Bay, Wisconsin

1990	17	1993	62
1991	22	1994	46
1992	49	1995	37

Greensboro, NC

1990	114	1993	105
1991	114	1994	89
1992	106	1995	36

Hampton, Virginia

1990	44	1993	49
1991	71	1994	46
1992	51	1995	15

Hartford, Connecticut

1990	160	1993	99
1991	181	1994	97
1992	125	1995	68

Hayward, California

1990	30	1993	53
1991	41	1994	64
1992	46	1995	26

Hialeah, Florida

1990	68	1993	na
1991	43	1994	na
1992	na	1995	22

Hollywood, Florida

1990	48	1993	42
1991	39	1994	56
1992	40	1995	32

Honolulu, Hawaii

1990	278	1993	286
1991	275	1994	266
1992	326	1995	117

Houston, Texas

1990	1335	1993	1109
1991	1213	1994	931
1992	1169	1995	412

Huntington Beach, CA

1990	57	1993	38
1991	51	1994	39
1992	64	1995	22

Huntsville, Alabama

1990	83	1993	82
1991	na	1994	88
1992	73	1995	34

dependence, Missouri			
90	27	1993	51
91	23	1994	35
92	24	1995	12

dianapolis, Indiana			
90	541	1993	517
91	561	1994	483
92	541	1995	na

glewood, California			
90	103	1993	68
91	69	1994	47
92	67	1995	30

vine, California			
90	16	1993	12
91	15	1994	15
92	10	1995	7

ving, Texas			
90	90	1993	67
91	67	1994	60
92	53	1995	28

ckson, Mississippi			
90	184	1993	173
91	190	1994	207
92	210	1995	93

cksonville, Florida			
90	704	1993	699
91	798	1994	648
92	713	1995	329

Jersey City, New Jersey			
1990	114	1993	100
1991	97	1994	74
1992	93	1995	50

Kansas City, Kansas			
1990	167	1993	na
1991	182	1994	na
1992	178	1995	na

Kansas City, Missouri			
1990	517	1993	515
1991	477	1994	490
1992	564	1995	224

Knoxville, Tennessee			
1990	111	1993	102
1991	123	1994	109
1992	116	1995	61

Lakewood, Colorado			
1990	44	1993	31
1991	58	1994	53
1992	53	1995	28

Lancaster, California			
1990	52	1993	60
1991	53	1994	59
1992	55	1995	21

Lansing, Michigan			
1990	163	1993	na
1991	188	1994	156
1992	184	1995	71

Laredo, Texas

1990	17	1993	7
1991	14	1994	6
1992	14	1995	7

Las Vegas, Nevada

1990	371	1993	435
1991	443	1994	574
1992	393	1995	256

Lexington, Kentucky

1990	141	1993	139
1991	164	1994	116
1992	151	1995	64

Lincoln, Nebraska

1990	99	1993	83
1991	89	1994	109
1992	109	1995	42

Little Rock, Arkansas

1990	254	1993	215
1991	268	1994	191
1992	222	1995	76

Livonia, Michigan

1990	21	1993	na
1991	22	1994	18
1992	17	1995	12

Long Beach, California

1990	298	1993	200
1991	284	1994	167
1992	218	1995	76

Los Angeles, California

1990	2014	1993	1773
1991	1966	1994	1554
1992	1872	1995	735

Louisville, Kentucky

1990	122	1993	135
1991	157	1994	142
1992	120	1995	72

Lowell, Massachusetts

1990	na	1993	49
1991	na	1994	82
1992	na	1995	34

Lubbock, Texas

1990	160	1993	136
1991	137	1994	139
1992	158	1995	59

Macon, Georgia

1990	78	1993	102
1991	81	1994	96
1992	78	1995	38

Madison, Wisconsin

1990	62	1993	99
1991	93	1994	80
1992	81	1995	32

Memphis, Tennessee

1990	831	1993	725
1991	653	1994	695
1992	688	1995	356

Mesa, Arizona			
1990	95	1993	111
1991	156	1994	120
1992	119	1995	65

Mesquite, Texas			
1990	21	1993	33
1991	31	1994	17
1992	27	1995	10

Miami, Florida			
1990	299	1993	204
1991	253	1994	221
1992	272	1995	95

Milwaukee, Wisconsin			
1990	495	1993	424
1991	502	1994	429
1992	514	1995	177

Minneapolis, Minnesota			
1990	na	1993	518
1991	744	1994	578
1992	600	1995	na

Mobile, Alabama			
1990	146	1993	122
1991	151	1994	125
1992	172	1995	56

Modesto, California			
1990	65	1993	80
1991	69	1994	74
1992	74	1995	32

Montgomery, Alabama			
1990	102	1993	87
1991	160	1994	70
1992	120	1995	41

Moreno Valley, California			
1990	44	1993	58
1991	30	1994	49
1992	44	1995	19

Nashville, Tennessee			
1990	553	1993	577
1991	514	1994	508
1992	498	1995	262

Newark, New Jersey			
1990	326	1993	257
1991	244	1994	207
1992	313	1995	96

New Haven, Connecticut			
1990	168	1993	130
1991	118	1994	102
1992	131	1995	na

New Orleans, Louisiana			
1990	361	1993	298
1991	302	1994	436
1992	287	1995	310

Newport News, Virginia			
1990	99	1993	103
1991	107	1994	98
1992	115	1995	76

New York, New York

1990	3126	1993	2818
1991	2892	1994	2666
1992	2815	1995	1276

Norfolk, Virginia

1990	218	1993	204
1991	205	1994	157
1992	260	1995	89

Oakland, California

1990	517	1993	353
1991	460	1994	323
1992	418	1995	na

Oceanside, California

1990	95	1993	66
1991	89	1994	88
1992	76	1995	33

Oklahoma City, Oklahoma

1990	422	1993	515
1991	473	1994	546
1992	472	1995	236

Omaha, Nebraska

1990	217	1993	na
1991	207	1994	217
1992	na	1995	na

Ontario, California

1990	71	1993	66
1991	69	1994	53
1992	65	1995	42

Orange, California

1990	26	1993	30
1991	17	1994	32
1992	24	1995	9

Orlando, Florida

1990	181	1993	209
1991	na	1994	144
1992	140	1995	51

Overland Park, Kansas

1990	15	1993	na
1991	32	1994	na
1992	24	1995	na

Oxnard, California

1990	66	1993	55
1991	74	1994	29
1992	75	1995	31

Pasadena, California

1990	53	1993	44
1991	63	1994	36
1992	55	1995	28

Pasadena, Texas

1990	76	1993	106
1991	79	1994	101
1992	82	1995	29

Paterson, New Jersey

1990	75	1993	78
1991	68	1994	52
1992	84	1995	19

eoria, Illinois

990	na	1993	na
991	na	1994	na
992	na	1995	na

hiladelphia, Pennsylvania

990	734	1993	785
991	904	1994	721
992	817	1995	407

hoenix, Arizona

990	512	1993	444
991	480	1994	438
992	476	1995	210

ittsburgh, Pennsylvania

990	302	1993	226
991	300	1994	261
992	221	1995	110

lano, Texas

990	36	1993	32
991	39	1994	30
992	31	1995	11

omona, California

990	71	1993	81
991	86	1994	64
992	86	1995	28

ortland, Oregon

990	424	1993	479
991	464	1994	400
992	490	1995	208

Portsmouth, Virginia

1990	82	1993	56
1991	66	1994	65
1992	65	1995	38

Providence, Rhode Island

1990	97	1993	114
1991	107	1994	115
1992	116	1995	50

Pueblo, Colorado

1990	102	1993	87
1991	80	1994	84
1992	88	1995	22

Raleigh, North Carolina

1990	96	1993	94
1991	120	1994	89
1992	120	1995	54

Rancho Cucamonga, CA

1990	36	1993	31
1991	38	1994	19
1992	37	1995	14

Reno, Nevada

1990	143	1993	129
1991	167	1994	121
1992	130	1995	44

Richmond, Virginia

1990	180	1993	174
1991	150	1994	169
1992	178	1995	75

Riverside, California

1990	120	1993	131
1991	114	1994	134
1992	130	1995	51

Rochester, New York

1990	176	1993	159
1991	166	1994	145
1992	170	1995	70

Rockford, Illinois

1990	na	1993	na
1991	na	1994	na
1992	na	1995	na

Sacramento, California

1990	211	1993	167
1991	221	1994	174
1992	237	1995	na

St. Louis, Missouri

1990	331	1993	319
1991	342	1994	304
1992	349	1995	126

St. Paul, Minnesota

1990	269	1993	242
1991	286	1994	269
1992	237	1995	na

St. Petersburg, Florida

1990	175	1993	176
1991	184	1994	213
1992	195	1995	88

Salem, Oregon

1990	50	1993	67
1991	90	1994	63
1992	83	1995	30

Salinas, California

1990	50	1993	50
1991	42	1994	65
1992	54	1995	28

Salt Lake City, Utah

1990	167	1993	204
1991	182	1994	158
1992	187	1995	63

San Antonio, Texas

1990	430	1993	553
1991	698	1994	565
1992	616	1995	331

San Bernardino, California

1990	na	1993	129
1991	na	1994	163
1992	138	1995	42

San Diego, California

1990	439	1993	396
1991	472	1994	403
1992	485	1995	164

San Francisco, California

1990	419	1993	361
1991	400	1994	292
1992	395	1995	na

an Jose, California			
990	416	1993	391
991	445	1994	375
992	448	1995	183

anta Ana, California			
990	73	1993	77
991	76	1994	80
992	72	1995	36

anta Clarita, California			
990	20	1993	22
991	24	1994	31
992	25	1995	15

anta Rosa, California			
990	62	1993	102
991	84	1994	82
992	86	1995	26

avannah, Georgia			
990	102	1993	89
991	113	1994	75
992	79	1995	38

cottsdale, Arizona			
990	21	1993	29
991	26	1994	28
992	18	1995	12

eattle, Washington			
990	481	1993	356
991	398	1994	318
992	353	1995	120

Shreveport, Louisiana			
1990	133	1993	100
1991	120	1994	121
1992	136	1995	53

Simi Valley, California			
1990	16	1993	16
1991	13	1994	9
1992	11	1995	8

Sioux Falls, South Dakota			
1990	81	1993	103
1991	88	1994	70
1992	97	1995	32

South Bend, Indiana			
1990	na	1993	104
1991	na	1994	95
1992	130	1995	34

Spokane, Washington			
1990	98	1993	112
1991	98	1994	101
1992	92	1995	64

Springfield, Illinois			
1990	na	1993	na
1991	na	1994	na
1992	na	1995	na

Springfield, Massachusetts			
1990	132	1993	120
1991	146	1994	124
1992	161	1995	78

Springfield, Missouri

1990	58	1993	77
1991	54	1994	74
1992	61	1995	35

Stamford, Connecticut

1990	18	1993	22
1991	25	1994	15
1992	22	1995	7

Sterling Heights, Michigan

1990	38	1993	na
1991	41	1994	20
1992	31	1995	na

Stockton, California

1990	168	1993	157
1991	161	1994	121
1992	170	1995	58

Sunnyvale, California

1990	40	1993	21
1991	42	1994	27
1992	33	1995	15

Syracuse, New York

1990	118	1993	79
1991	86	1994	58
1992	85	1995	36

Tacoma, Washington

1990	245	1993	191
1991	277	1994	204
1992	309	1995	87

Tallahassee, Florida

1990	na	1993	137
1991	119	1994	114
1992	147	1995	67

Tampa, Florida

1990	343	1993	247
1991	347	1994	298
1992	303	1995	135

Tempe, Arizona

1990	69	1993	65
1991	70	1994	52
1992	73	1995	25

Thousand Oaks, California

1990	17	1993	22
1991	19	1994	18
1992	17	1995	9

Toledo, Ohio

1990	422	1993	357
1991	418	1994	356
1992	368	1995	136

Topeka, Kansas

1990	80	1993	na
1991	79	1994	na
1992	82	1995	na

Torrance, California

1990	31	1993	30
1991	23	1994	26
1992	27	1995	4

ucson, Arizona

990	290	1993	314
991	332	1994	289
992	386	1995	na

ulsa, Oklahoma

990	382	1993	339
991	414	1994	296
992	368	1995	126

allejo, California

990	52	1993	65
991	71	1994	54
992	76	1995	25

irginia Beach, Virginia

990	149	1993	181
991	127	1994	145
992	153	1995	48

Vaco, Texas

990	108	1993	141
991	105	1994	126
992	134	1995	70

Varren, Michigan

990	95	1993	na
991	113	1994	62
992	126	1995	23

Vashington, DC

990	303	1993	324
991	214	1994	249
992	215	1995	74

Waterbury, Connecticut

1990	32	1993	39
1991	32	1994	38
1992	61	1995	11

West Covina, California

1990	18	1993	33
1991	40	1994	26
1992	41	1995	11

Wichita, Kansas

1990	321	1993	265
1991	284	1994	224
1992	255	1995	93

Winston-Salem, NC

1990	169	1993	177
1991	148	1994	142
1992	144	1995	76

Worcester, Massachusetts

1990	na	1993	77
1991	na	1994	68
1992	112	1995	na

Yonkers, New York

1990	43	1993	34
1991	48	1994	41
1992	38	1995	15

Rape Readings

[R]ape is a sexual violation - a violation of the most personal, most intimate, and most offensive kind. Susan Estrich
Real Rape[1]

Rape Readings is a reading list for those most at risk. In the following pages the lay reader can find hundreds of well written and researched source materials on every aspect of rape and other forms of sexual violence.

Rape Readings is a "people's bibliography," designed specifically for the lay reader. We have purposely excluded all medical/legal and scholarly/technical works on rape. No legal texts. No police manuals. No medical treatises. No doctoral dissertations. All these works, while valuable, are characterized as being "expert-to-expert" writings on rape. We have searched and researched the available literature on rape and sexual violence for the very best "expert-to-lay person" writings. We asked this one important question about every single book we found: "Will it inform, educate, and assist a lay reader interested in but basically ignorant on the subject of rape?" *Rape Readings* contains the books on rape and sexual violence that fit this strict criteria. Their authors and editors, all acknowledged experts on rape and sexual violence, have, we believe, successfully crossed over the "expert-to-expert" barrier and have something of value to say to the non-expert lay reader. Most of the books we have included are available from your local public library. They can be found by Author (Brownmiller, Susan) or Title (Against Our Will) or Subject (Rape) in your library's card- or online catalog. Other books on rape and sexual violence can be found by looking up "Rape" or "Women - Crimes Against" in your library's subject card or online catalog. When in doubt ask a librarian.

Rape Readings is divided into these eleven sections beginning on the following pages:

This reader's resource was created to make you think, and re-think, what you thought you knew about the causes, prevention, treatment, and aftermath of rape. The best book in *Rape Readings* is the one that helps you.

[1]Estrich, Susan. *Real Rape.* Cambridge, MA: Harvard University Press, 1987.

Rape Readings

THE CRIME OF RAPE

Ageton, Suzanne S.
Facts About Sexual Assault.
Rockville, MD: U.S. Department of Health & Human
 Services, 1985.

Ageton, Suzanne S.
Sexual Assault Among Adolescents.
Lexington, MA: Lexington Books, 1983.

Allison, Julie A. & Lawrence S. Wrightman.
Rape: The Misunderstood Crime.
Thousand Oaks, CA: Sage Publications, 1993.

Barnes, Dorothy L.
Rape: A Bibliography.
Troy, NY: Whitston Publishing Co., 1991.

Bart, Pauline B. & Eileen G. Moran.
Violence Against Women.
Thousand Oaks, CA: Sage Publications, 1993.

Boston Women's Health Collective.
The New Our Bodies, Ourselves.
New York, NY: Simon & Schuster, 1984.

Botkin-Maher, Jennifer.
Nice Girls Don't Get Raped.
San Bernardino, CA: Here's Life Publishers, 1987.

Brownmiller, Susan.
Against Our Will: Men, Women, and Rape.
New York, NY: Simon & Schuster, 1975.

Burgess, Ann W.
Rape and Sexual Assault: A Research Handbook.
New York, NY: Garland Publishing, Inc., 1985.

Chappell, Duncan, Robley Geis & Gilbert Geis.
Forcible Rape: The Crime, The Victim, and The Offender.
New York, NY: Columbia University Press, 1977.

DeYoung, Mary.
Child Molestation: An Annotated Bibliography.
Jefferson, NC: McFarland, 1987.

DeYoung, Mary.
Incest: An Annotated Bibliography.
Jefferson, NC: McFarland, 1985.

Estrich, Susan.
Real Rape.
Cambridge, MA: Harvard University Press, 1987.

Faludi, Susan.
Backlash: The Undeclared War Against Women.
New York, NY: Crown Publishers, 1991.

Fiorenza, Elizabeth S. & M. Shawn Copeland.
Violence Against Women.
Maryknoll, NY: Orbis Books, 1994.

Fortune, Marie M.
Sexual Violence: The Unmentionable Sin.
New York, NY: Pilgrim Press, 1983.

Franck, Irene & David Brownstone.
The Women's Desk Reference.
New York: Viking Press, 1993.

Gager, Nancy & Cathleen Schurr.
Sexual Assault: Confronting Rape in America.
New York, NY: Grossett & Dunlap, 1976.

Goldsmith, Gloria.
Rape.
Beverly Hills, CA: Wollstonecraft, 1974.

Gordon, Margaret T. & Stephanie Riger.
The Female Fear.
New York, NY: Free Press, 1989.

Griffin, Susan.
Rape: The Power of Consciousness.
New York, NY: Harper & Row, 1979.

Guernsey, Jo Ann B.
The Facts About Rape.
New York, NY: Crestwood House, 1990.

Guernsey, Jo Ann B.
Rape.
New York, NY: Crestwood House, 1990.

Holmes, Ronald M.
Sex Crimes.
Thousand Oaks, CA: Sage Publications, 1991.

Jukes, Adam.
Why Men Hate Women.
London, England: Free Association Books, 1993.

Kemmer, Elizabeth J.
*Rape and Rape-Related Issues: An Annotated
Bibliography.*
New York, NY: Garland Publishing, Inc., 1977.

Koss, Mary P., et al.
No Safe Haven: Male Violence Against Women at Home,
at Work, and in the Community.
Washington, DC: American Psychological
Association, 1994.

London Rape Crisis Center.
Sexual Violence: The Reality for Women.
London, England: Women's Press, 1984.

Madanes, Cloe.
Sex, Love, and Violence.
New York, NY: Norton, 1990.

Medea, Andrea & Kathleen Thompson.
Against Rape.
New York, NY: Farrar, Straus & Giroux, 1974.

Nordquist, Joan.
Rape: A Bibliography.
Santa Cruz, CA: Reference & Research Services, 1990.

Rape.
Washington, DC: U.S. National Commission on the
Observance of International Women's Year, 1977.

Rape in America: A Report to the Nation.
Arlington, VA: National Victim Center, 1992.

Roberts, Cathy.
Women and Rape.
New York, NY: New York University Press, 1989.

Russell, Diana E.H.
Sexual Exploitation: Rape, Child Sexual Abuse and
Workplace Harassment.
Thousand Oaks, CA: Sage Publications, 1984.

Sanders, William B.
  Rape and Women's Identity.
  Thousand Oaks, CA: Sage Publications, 1980.

Scacco, Anthony M.
  Rape in Prison.
  Springfield, IL: C.C. Thomas, 1975.

Schwendinger, Julia R. & Herman Schwendinger.
  Rape and Inequality.
  Thousand Oaks, CA: Sage Publications, 1983.

Sobsey, Dick, et al.
  *Disability, Sexuality, and Abuse: An Annotated
    Bibliography.*
  Baltimore, MD: P.H. Brookes Publishing Co., 1991.

Swisher, Karin L., Carol Wekesser, & William Barbour.
  Violence Against Women.
  San Diego, CA: Greenhaven Press, 1994.

Tomaselli, Sylvana & Roy Porter.
  Rape.
  New York, NY: Blackwell, 1986.

U.S. Senate Committee on the Judiciary.
  *Violence Against Women: A Week in the Life of
    America.*
  Washington, DC: General Printing Office, 1992.

Ward, Sally K.
  *Acquaintance and Date Rape: An Annotated
    Bibliography.*
  Westport, CT: Greenwood Press, 1994.

Wilson, Carolyn F.
  Violence Against Women: An Annotated Bibliography.
  Boston, MA: G.K. Hall, 1981.

Wyre, Ray & Anthony Swift.
Women, Men, and Rape.
Kent, England: Hodder & Stoughton, 1990.

ACQUAINTANCE AND DATE RAPE

Adams, Caren & Jennifer Fay.
"Nobody Told Me It Was Rape": A Parent's Guide for Talking With Teenagers About Acquaintance Rape and Sexual Exploitation.
Santa Cruz, CA: Network Publications, 1984.

Bohmer, Carol & Andrea Parrot.
Sexual Assault on Campus: The Problem and the Solution.
New York, NY: Lexington Books, 1993.

Erhart, Julie K. & Bernice R. Sandler.
Campus Gang Rape: Party Games?
Washington, DC: Association of American Colleges, 1985.

Friedman, Joel, Marcia M. Boumil & Barbara E. Taylor.
Date Rape: What It Is, What It Isn't, What It Does To You, What You Can Do About It.
Deerfield Beach, FL: Health Communications, 1992.

Hughes, Jean D. & Bernice R. Sandler.
"Friends" Raping Friends: Could It Happen To You?
Washington, DC: Association of American Colleges, 1987.

Leone, Bruno.
Rape on Campus.
San Diego, CA: Greenhaven Press, 1995.

Levy, Barrie.
Dating Violence: Young Women in Danger.
Seattle, WA: Seal Press, 1991.

Mufson, Susan & Rachel Kranz.
Straight Talk About Date Rape.
New York, NY: Facts on File, 1993.

Parrot, Andrea.
Coping with Date Rape and Acquaintance Rape.
New York, NY: Rosen Publishing Group, 1988.

Parrot, Andrea & Laurie Bechhofer.
Acquaintance Rape: The Hidden Crime.
New York, NY: Wiley, 1991.

Pirog-Good, Maureen A. & Jan E. Stets.
Violence in Dating Relationships.
New York, NY: Praeger, 1989.

Rue, Nancy N.
Coping with Dating Violence.
New York, NY: Rosen Publishing Group, 1989.

Sanday, Peggy Reeves.
Fraternity Gang Rape: Sex, Brotherhood, and Privilege on Campus.
New York, NY: New York University Press, 1990.

Shuker-Haines, Frances.
Everything You Need to Know About Date Rape.
New York, NY: Rosen Publishing Group, 1990.

Warshaw, Robin.
I Never Called It Rape: The Ms. Report on Recognizing, Fighting, and Surviving Date and Acquaintance Rape.
New York, NY: Harper & Row, 1988.

MARITAL RAPE

Bayer, Edward J.
Rape Within Marriage.
Lanham, MD: University Press of America, 1985.

Finkelhor, David & Kersti Yllo.
License to Rape: Sexual Abuse of Wives.
New York, NY: Harper & Row, 1985.

Nordquist, Joan.
Domestic Violence: Spouse Abuse, Marital Rape.
Santa Cruz, CA: Reference & Research Services, 1986.

Russell, Diana E.H.
Rape in Marriage.
New York, NY: MacMillan, 1982.

AUTHORITY RAPE

Boyle, Patrick.
Scout's Honor: Sexual Abuse in America's Most Trusted Institution.
Rocklin, CA: Prima Publishing, 1994.

Burkett, Elinor & Frank Brani.
A Gospel of Shame: Children, Sexual Abuse, and the Catholic Church.
New York, NY: Viking, 1993.

Friedman, Joel & Marcia M. Boumil.
Betrayal of Trust: Sex and Power in Professional Relationships.
Westport, CT: Praeger, 1995.

Gonsiorale, John C.
Breach of Trust: Sexual Exploitation by Health Care Professionals and Clergy.
Thousand Oaks, CA: Sage Publications, 1995.

Rutter, Peter.
Sex in the Forbidden Zone: When Men in Power, Therapists, Doctors, Clergy, Teachers, and Others Betray Women's Trust.
Los Angeles, CA: J.P. Tarcher, 1989.

Trumpe, Pauline.
Doctors Who Rape.
Wakefield, NH: Longwood Academic, 1991.

Ward, Elizabeth.
Father-Daughter Rape.
New York, NY: Grove Press, 1985.

Waterman, Jill, et al.
Behind the Playground Walls: Sexual Abuse in Preschools.
New York, NY: Guilford Press, 1993.

SOCIETY AND RAPE

Beneke, Timothy.
Men on Rape.
New York, NY: St. Martin's Press, 1982.

Bourgue, Linda B.
Defining Rape.
Durham, NC: Duke University Press, 1989.

Buchwald, Emilie, Pamela R. Fletcher & Martha Roth.
Transforming a Rape Culture.
Minneapolis, MN: Milkweed Editions, 1993.

Davis, Angela Y.
*Violence Against Women and the Ongoing Challenge to
Racism.*
Latham, NY: Kitchen Table, 1985.

Haskell, Molly.
*From Reverence to Rape: The Treatment of Women in
the Movies.*
Chicago, IL: University of Chicago Press, 1987.

Horos, Carol.
Rape: The Private Crime, A Social Horror.
New Canaan, CT: Tobey Publishing Co., 1974.

Madigan, Lee & Nancy C. Gamble.
*The Second Rape: Society's Continued Betrayal of the
Victim.*
New York, NY: Lexington Books, 1991.

Pleck, Elizabeth H.
Rape and the Politics of Race, 1865-1910.
Wellesley, MA: Wellesley College, 1990.

Rodabaugh, Barbara J. & Melanie Austin.
Sexual Assault: A Guide for Community Action.
New York, NY: Garland Publishing, Inc., 1981.

Walters, Candace.
Invisible Wounds.
Portland, OR: Multnomah, 1987.

Weiss, Carl & David J. Frier.
*Terror in the Prisons: Homosexual Rape and Why
Society Condones It.*
Indiana, IN: Bobbs-Merrill, 1974.

Williams, Joyce E. & Karen A. Holmes.
The Second Assault: Rape and Public Attitudes.
Westport, CT: Greenwood Press, 1981.

RAPE AND THE LAW

Adler, Zsuzsanna.
Rape on Trial.
New York, NY: Rutledge & Kegan Paul, 1987.

Bailey, F. Lee & Henry B. Rothblatt.
Crimes of Violence: Rape and Other Sex Crimes.
Rochester, NY: Lawyers Co-operative Publishing Co., 1973.

Battelle Law & Justice Center.
Forcible Rape.
Washington, DC: Department of Justice, 1977.

Epstein, Joel & Stacia Langenbahn.
The Criminal Justice and Community Response to Rape.
Washington, DC: U.S. Department of Justice, 1994.

Eyman, Joy S.
How to Convict a Rapist.
New York, NY: Stein & Day, 1980.

Fairstein, Linda A.
Sexual Violence: Our War Against Rape.
New York, NY: Wm. Morrow & Co., 1993.

Feild, Hubert S. & Leigh B. Bienen.
Jurors and Rape: A Study in Psychology and Law.
Lexington, MA: Lexington Books, 1980.

Garrison, J. Gregory & Randy Roberts.
Heavy Justice: The State of Indiana v. Michael G. Tyson.
Reading, MA: Addison-Wesley Publishing Co., 1994.

Goodman, James E.
Stories of Scottsboro.
New York, NY: Pantheon Books, 1994.

Haskins, James.
The Scottsboro Boys.
New York, NY: H. Holt & Co., 1994.

Higgins, Lynn A. & Brenda R. Silver.
Rape and Representation.
New York, NY: Columbia University Press, 1991.

LaFree, Gary D.
Rape and Criminal Justice.
Belmont, CA: Wadsworth, 1989.

Ludwig, Frederick J.
Rape and the Law: The Crime and Its Proof.
New York, NY: Equal Justice Institute, 1977.

MacNamara, Donal E.J.
Sex, Crime and the Law.
New York, NY: The Free Press, 1977.

Rowland, Judith.
The Ultimate Violation.
Garden City, NY: Doubleday, 1985.

Schweber, Claudine & Clarice Feinman.
Criminal Justice, Politics, and Women: The Aftermath of Legally Mandated Change.
New York, NY: Haworth Press, 1985.

Sloan, Irving J.
Rape.
Dobbs Ferry, NY: Oceana Publications, 1992.

Spohn, Cassia & Julie Horney.
Rape Law Reform: A Grass Roots Revolution and Its Impact.
New York, NY: Plenum Press, 1992.

Sullivan, Timothy.
Unequal Verdicts: The Central Park Jogger Trials.
New York, NY: Simon & Schuster, 1992.

RAPISTS

Dean, Charles W. & Mary de Bruyn-Kops.
The Crime and Consequences of Rape.
Springfield, IL: C.C. Thomas, 1982.

Ellis, Albert & Ralph Brancak.
The Psychology of Sex Offenders.
Springfield, IL: C.C. Thomas, 1956.

Ellis, Lee.
Theories of Rape: Inquiries into the Causes of Sexual Aggression.
New York, NY: Hemisphere Publishing Corp., 1989.

Groth, A. Nicholas & H. Jean Birnbaum.
Men Who Rape: The Psychology of the Offender.
New York, NY: Plenum Press, 1979.

Holmes, Ronald M.
The Sex Offender and the Criminal Justice System.
Springfield, IL: C.C. Thomas, 1983.

MacDonald, John M.
Rape Offenders and Their Victims.
Springfield, IL: C.C. Thomas, 1971.

Miedzian, Myriam.
Boys Will Be Boys: Breaking the Link Between Masculinity and Violence.
Garden City, NY: Doubleday, 1988.

Morneau, Robert H. and Robert R. Rockwell.
Sex, Motivation, and the Criminal Offender.
Springfield, IL: C.C. Thomas, 1980.

O'Brien, Shirley J.
Why They Did It: Stories of Eight Convicted Child Molesters.
Springfield, IL: C.C. Thomas, 1986.

Poling, James N.
The Abuse of Power: A Theological Problem.
Nashville, TN: Abingdon Press, 1991.

Sanders, William B.
Gangbangs and Drive-Bys: Grounded Culture and Juvenile Gang Violence.
New York, NY: Aldine deGruyter, 1994.

Schuler, Margaret.
Freedom From Violence: A Study of Convicted Rapists.
Cambridge, MA: Unwin Hyman, Inc., 1990.

Scully, Diana.
Understanding Sexual Violence: A Study of Convicted Rapists.
Boston, MA: Unwin Hyman, 1990.

Vogelman, Lloyd.
The Sexual Face of Violence: Rapists on Rape.
Johannesburg, South Africa: Ravan Press, 1990.

Walker, Marcia J. & Stanley L. Brodsky.
Sexual Assault: The Victim and the Rapist.
Lexington, MA: Lexington Books, 1976.

ADULT VICTIMS

Bode, Janet.
The Voices of Rape.
New York, NY: Franklin Watts, Inc., 1990.

Burgess, Ann W. & Lynda Holmstrom.
Rape: Victims of Crisis.
Bowie, MD: Robert J. Brady, 1974.

Chapman, Jane R. & Margaret Gates.
The Victimization of Women.
Thousand Oaks, CA: Sage Publications, 1978.

Dean, Charles W. & Mary de Bruyn-Kops.
The Crime and Consequences of Rape.
Springfield, IL: C.C. Thomas, 1982.

Dowdeswell, Jane.
Women on Rape.
New York, NY: Thorsons Publishing Group, 1986.

Harlow, Caroline W.
Female Victims of Violent Crime.
Washington, DC: U.S. Department of Justice, 1991.

Hilberman, Elaine.
The Rape Victim.
New York, NY: Basic Books, 1976.

Hunter, Mic.
The Sexually Abused Male.
Lexington, MA: Lexington Books, 1990.

Hutchings, Nancy.
The Violent Family: Victimization of Women, Children, and Elders.
New York, NY: Human Sciences Press, 1988.

MacDonald, John M.
Rape Offenders and Their Victims.
Springfield, IL: C.C. Thomas, 1971.

McCombie, Sharon L.
The Rape Crisis Intervention Handbook: A Guide for Victim Care.
New York, NY: Plenum Press, 1980.

McMullen, Richie.
Male Rape: Breaking the Silence on the Last Taboo.
London, England: Gay Mens Press, 1990.

Mendel, Matthew P.
The Male Survivor: The Impact of Sexual Abuse.
Thousand Oaks, CA: Sage Publications, 1995.

Mezey, Gillian C. & Michael B. King.
Male Victims of Sexual Assault.
New York, NY: Oxford University Press, 1992.

Nass, Deanna R.
The Rape Victim.
Dubuque, IA: Kendall/Hunt Publishing Co., 1977.

Pekkanen, John.
Victims: An Account of Rape.
New York, NY: Dial Press, 1976.

Russell, Diana.
The Politics of Rape: The Victim's Perspective.
New York, NY: Stein & Day, 1974.

Ryan, William.
Blaming the Victim.
New York, NY: Pantheon, 1970.

Schultz, Le Roy G.
Rape Victimology.
Springfield, IL: C.C. Thomas, 1975.

Tormes, Yvonne.
Child Victims of Incest.
Denver, CO: The American Humane Association, 1968.

Walker, Marcia J. & Stanley L. Brodsky.
Sexual Assault: The Victim and the Rapist.
Lexington, MA: Lexington Books, 1976.

CHILD VICTIMS

Adams, Caren & Jennifer Fay.
No More Secrets: Protecting Your Child From Sexual Assault.
San Luis Obispo, CA: Impact Publishers, 1981.

Barker, Susan B.
About Sexual Abuse.
Springfield, IL: C.C. Thomas, 1989.

Boyle, Patrick.
Scout's Honor: Sexual Abuse in America's Most Trusted Institution.
Rocklin, CA: Prima Publishing, 1994.

Burgess, Ann W., et al.
Sexual Assault of Children and Adolescents.
Lexington, MA: Lexington Books, 1978.

Burgess, Ann W.
The Sexual Victimization of Adolescents.
Rockville, MD: U.S. Department of Health & Human Services, 1985.

Burkett, Elinor & Frank Brani.
A Gospel of Shame: Children, Sexual Abuse, and the Catholic Church.
New York, NY: Viking, 1993.

Ciba Foundation.
Child Sexual Abuse Within the Family.
New York, NY: Tavistock Publications, 1984.

Colao, Flora & Tamar Hosansky.
Your Children Should Know: Teach Your Children the Strategies that Will Keep Them Safe from Assault and Crime.
Indianapolis, IN: Bobbs-Merrill, 1983.

Crewdson, John.
By Silence Betrayed: Sexual Abuse of Children in America.
Boston, MA: Little Brown, 1988.

D'Arcy, Ann J.
When Your Son is Molested.
Cincinnati, OH: Pamphlet Publications, 1978.

Dayce, Frances S.
Private Zone: A Book Teaching Children Sexual Assault Prevention Tools.
New York, NY: Warner, 1984.

DeFrancis, Vincent.
Protecting the Child Victim of Sex Crimes Committed by Adults.
Denver, CO: The American Humane Association, 1965.

DeYoung, Mary.
The Sexual Victimization of Children.
Jefferson, NC: McFarland, 1982.

Ennew, Judith.
The Sexual Exploitation of Children.
New York, NY: St. Martin's Press, 1986.

Finkelhor, David, et al.
A Sourcebook on Child Sexual Abuse.
Thousand Oaks, CA: Sage Publications, 1986.

Finkelhor, David, Linda M. Williams & Nanci Burns.
Nursery Crimes: Sexual Abuse in Day Care.
Thousand Oaks, CA: Sage Publications, 1988.

Forward, Susan & Craig Buck.
Betrayal of Innocence: Incest and Its Devastation.
Los Angeles, CA: J.P. Tarcher, 1978.

Hagans, Kathryn B. & Joyce Case.
*When Your Child Has Been Molested: A Parent's Guide
to Healing and Recovery.*
Lexington, MA: Lexington Books, 1988.

Hart-Rossi, Janie.
*Protect Your Child From Sexual Abuse: A Parent's
Guide.*
Seattle, WA: Parenting Press, 1984.

Hillman, Donald & Janice Solek-Tefft.
*Spiders and Flies: Help for Parents and Teachers of
Sexually Abused Children.*
Lexington, MA: Lexington Books, 1988.

Justice, Blair.
The Broken Taboo: Sex in the Family.
New York, NY: Human Sciences Press, 1979.

Loontjens, Lois.
*Talking to Children/Talking to Parents About Sexual
Assault.*
Santa Cruz, CA: Network Publications, 1984.

Mrazek, Patricia B. & C. Heary Kempe.
Sexually Abused Children and Their Families.
New York, NY: Pergamon Press, 1981.

Nelson, Sarah.
Incest, Fact, and Myth.
Edinburgh, Scotland: Stramullion, 1987.

Newman, Susan.
Never Say Yes to a Stranger.
New York, NY: Putnam, 1985.

O'Brien, Shirley.
Child Abuse: A Crying Shame.
Provo, UT: Brigham Young University Press, 1980.

Rush, Florence.
The Best Kept Secret: Sexual Abuse of Children.
Englewood Cliffs, NJ: Prentice-Hall, 1980.

Sanford, Linda T.
*Come Tell Me Right Away: A Positive Approach to
   Warning Children About Sexual Abuse.*
Fayetteville, NY: Ed-U Press, 1982.

Sanford, Linda T.
*The Silent Children: A Book for Parents About the
   Prevention of Child Sexual Abuse.*
Garden City, NY: Doubleday, 1980.

Thorman, George.
Incestuous Families.
Springfield, IL: C.C. Thomas, 1983.

Waterman, Jill, et al.
*Behind the Playground Walls: Sexual Abuse in
   Preschools.*
New York, NY: Guilford Press, 1993.

Wexler, Richard.
Wounded Innocents.
Buffalo, NY: Prometheus Books, 1990.

Wyett, Gail E. & Gloria J. Powell.
Lasting Effects of Child Sexual Abuse.
Thousand Oaks, CA: Sage Publications, 1988.

RAPE RECOVERY

Bard, Morton & Dawn Sangrey.
The Crime Victim's Book.
New York, NY: Basic Books, 1979.

Benedict, Helen.
*Recovery: How to Survive Sexual Assault for Women,
Men, Teenagers, Their Friends and Families.*
Garden City, NY: Doubleday, 1985.

Bode, Janet.
*Fighting Back: How to Cope with the Medical,
Emotional, and Legal Consequences of Rape.*
New York, NY: MacMillan, 1978.

Braswell, Linda.
*Quest for Respect: A Guide to Healing for Survivors of
Rape.*
Ventura, CA: Pathfinder Publishing of California, 1989.

Ellis, Megan.
Surviving: Procedures After a Sexual Assault.
Vancouver, BC: Press Gang Publishers, 1986.

Gilmartin, Pat.
*Rape, Incest, and Child Sexual Abuse: Consequences and
Recovery.*
New York, NY: Garland Publishing, Inc., 1994.

Grossman, Rochel & Joan Sutherland.
Surviving Sexual Assault.
New York, NY: Congdon & Weed, 1983.

Johnson, Kathryn M.
If You Are Raped: What Every Woman Needs to Know.
Holmes Beach, FL: Learning Publications, 1985.

Katz, Judy H.
*No Fairy Godmothers, No Magic Wands: The Healing
Process After Rape.*
Saratoga, CA: R&E Publishers, 1984.

Kelly, Liz.
Surviving Sexual Violence.
Minneapolis, MN: University of Minnesota Press, 1988.

Ledray, Linda E.
Recovering from Rape.
New York, NY: Henry Holt, 1986.

McCahill, Thomas W., Linda C. Meyer, & Arthur M.
Fischman.
The Aftermath of Rape.
Lexington, MA: Lexington Books, 1979.

McCombie, Sharon L.
*The Rape Crisis Intervention Handbook: A Guide for
Victim Care.*
New York, NY: Plenum Press, 1980.

McEvoy, Alan W. & Jeff B. Brookings.
*If She Is Raped: A Book for Husbands, Fathers, and
Male Friends.*
Holmes Beach, FL: Learning Publications, 1984.

Mills, Patrick.
Rape Intervention Resource Manual.
Springfield, IL: C.C. Thomas, 1977.

Pellauer, Mary D., Barbara Chester & Jane A. Bogajian.
   Sexual Assault and Abuse: A Handbook for Clergy and
      Religious Professionals.
   San Francisco, CA: Harper & Row, 1987.

Quina, Kathryn & Nancy L. Carlson.
   Rape, Incest, and Sexual Harassment: A Guide for
      Helping Survivors.
   New York, NY: Praeger, 1989.

Stuart, Irving R. & Joanne C. Greer.
   Victims of Sexual Aggression: Treatment of Children,
      Women, and Men.
   New York, NY: Van Nostrand Reinhold, 1984.

RAPE PREVENTION

Adams, Aileen & Carl Abarbanel.
   Sexual Assault on Campus: What Colleges Can Do.
   Santa Monica, CA: Rape Treatment Center, Santa
      Monica Hospital Medical Center, 1988.

Adams, Caren, Jennifer Fay & Jan Loreen-Martin.
   No Is Not Enough: Helping Teenagers Avoid Sexual
      Assault.
   San Luis Obispo, CA: Impact Publishers, 1984.

Bart, Pauline B. & Patricia H. O'Brien.
   Stopping Rape: Successful Survival Strategies.
   New York, NY: Pergamon Press, 1985.

Bode, Janet.
   Rape: Preventing It, Coping with the Legal, Medical, and
      Emotional Aftermath.
   New York, NY: Franklin Watts, Inc., 1979.

Booher, Dianna D.
  Rape: What Would You Do If . . . ?
  New York, NY: J. Messner, 1981.

Brewer, James D.
  The Danger From Strangers: Confronting the Threat of Assault.
  New York, NY: Insight Books, 1994.

Csida, June B. & Joseph Csida.
  Rape: How to Avoid It and What to Do About It If You Can't.
  Chatsworth, CA: Books for Better Living, 1974.

Davis, Linda J. & Elaine M. Brody.
  Rape and Older Women: A Guide to Prevention and Protection.
  Rockville, MD: National Institute for Mental Health, 1979.

Fein, Judith.
  Are You a Target?: A Guide to Self-Protection and Personal Safety.
  Duncan Mills, CA: Torrance Publications, 1988.

Fein, Judith.
  Exploding the Myth of Self-Defense: A Survival Guide for Every Woman.
  Duncan Mills, CA: Torrance Publications, 1993.

Funk, Rus Ervin.
  Stopping Rape: A Challenge for Men.
  Philadelphia, PA: New Society, 1993.

Grauerholz, Elizabeth & Mary Koralewski.
  Sexual Coercion: A Sourcebook on Its Nature, Causes, and Prevention.
  Lexington, MA: Lexington Books, 1991.

Harman, Patricia.
   The Danger Zone: How You Can Protect Yourself from
   Rape, Robbery, and Assault.
   Park Ridge, IL: Parkside Publishing, 1992.

Keller, Daniel P.
   The Prevention of Rape and Sexual Assault on Campus.
   Goshen, KY: Campus Crime Prevention Programs, 1989.

Lindquist, Scott.
   Before He Takes You Out: The Safe Dating Guide for
   the '90's.
   Marietta, GA: Vigel, 1989.

Mauro-Cochrane, Jeanette.
   Self-Respect and Sexual Assault.
   Bradenton, FL: Human Services Institute, 1993.

McShane, Claudette.
   Warning! Dating May Be Hazardous to Your Health.
   Racine, WI: Mother Courage Press, 1988.

Molmen, Marcia E.M.
   Avoiding Rape Without Putting Yourself in Protective
   Custody.
   Grand Forks, ND: Athena Press, 1982.

Niehaus, Joseph.
   The Sixth Sense: Practical Tips for Everyday Safety.
   Tempe, AZ: Blue Bird Publishing, 1990.

Office of the California Attorney General.
   Sexual Assault Prevention Handbook.
   Sacramento, CA: Crime Prevention Center, 1989.

Offstein, Jerrold.
   Self-Defense for Women.
   Palo Alto, CA: National Press Books, 1972.

Parrot, Andrea.
*Acquaintance Rape and Sexual Assault Prevention
Manual.*
Holmes Beach, FL: LP Learning Publications, 1991.

Powell, Elizabeth.
Talking Back to Sexual Pressure.
Minneapolis, MN: CompCare Publishers, 1991.

Pritchard, Carol.
Avoiding Rape On and Off Campus.
Wenonah, NJ: State College Publishing Co., 1985.

Reimold, Cheryl.
The Woman's Guide to Staying Safe.
New York, NY: Monarch Press, 1985.

Reiss, Albert J., Jr. & Jeffrey A. Roth.
Understanding and Preventing Violence.
Washington, DC: National Academy Press, 1993.

Sanford, Linda T. & Ann Fetter.
*In Defense of Ourselves: A Rape Prevention Handbook
for Women.*
Garden City, NY: Doubleday, 1979.

Smith, Susan E.
*Fear or Freedom: A Woman's Options in Social Survival
and Physical Defense.*
Racine, WI: Mother Courage Press, 1986.

Storaska, Frederic.
How to Say No to a Rapist and Survive.
New York, NY: Random House, 1975.

Wiseman, Rosalind.
*Defending Ourselves: A Guide to Prevention, Self-
Defense, and Recovery from Rape.*
New York, NY: Noonday Press, 1995.

The Rape Glossary

Woman was and is condemned to a system under which the lawful rapes exceed the unlawful ones a million to one.

Margaret Sanger
Woman and the New Race[1]

The purpose of *The Rape Glossary* is to help the reader understand the technical-medical-legal jargon of rape. In the following pages you will find dozens of complete plain English definitions of the medical and legal words and phrases associated with rape.

A medical dictionary[2] defines "Rape" clinically:

> Heterosexual or homosexual intercourse against the will of the victim. Complete penetration of the vagina (or other body orifice) by the penis or emission of seminal fluid is not necessary to constitute rape.

A law dictionary[3] defines "Rape" legalistically:

> Unlawful sexual intercourse with a female without her consent. The unlawful carnal knowledge of a woman by a man forcibly and against her will. The act of sexual intercourse committed by a man with a woman not his wife and without her consent, committed when the woman's resistance is overcome by force or fear, or under other prohibitive conditions.

A home dictionary[4] defines "Rape" simplistically:

> Sexual intercourse with a woman by a man without her consent and chiefly by force or deception.

The Rape Glossary defines "Rape" in plain English:

> Any sexual penetration, however slight, of the oral, vaginal, or anal openings of a person committed against their will and without their consent by the use of force, fear, or violence.

The plain English definitions found in *The Rape Glossary* range from A: *Acquaintance Rape* to W: *Wife Rape* and include definitions of new crimes: *AIDS Rape*; old crimes: *Clergy*

Rape, new laws: *Sexual Predator Laws*, street slang: *Gangbang*, and "synonymous" crimes: *Anal intercourse = deviate sexual intercourse = sodomy.*

The definitions used in *The Rape Glossary* are our own, based on our reading and research. We hope that they will help assist the lay reader in understanding the technical-medical-legal jargon of rape.

[1]Sanger, Margaret. *Woman and the New Race.* New York, NY: Blue Ribbon Books, 1920.

[2]"Rape." Taber's Cyclopedic Medical Dictionary.

[3]"Rape." Black's Law Dictionary.

[4]"Rape." Webster's New Collegiate Dictionary.

The Rape Glossary

Acquaintance rape. An act of sexual penetration, however slight, of the oral, vaginal, or anal opening of a person committed against their will and without their consent by use of force, fear, or violence by a person previously known to the victim. A previous acquaintance does not constitute consent.

Age of consent. The age, set by state law, at which a female may legally consent to a sex act.

AIDS rape. An act of sexual penetration, however slight, of the oral, vaginal, or anal opening of a person committed against their will and without their consent by use of force, fear, or violence by a person aware of being infected with Acquired Immune Deficiency Syndrome (AIDS).

Aggravated rape. An act of sexual penetration, however slight, of the oral, vaginal, or anal opening of a person committed against their will and without their consent by use of force, fear, or violence by a perpetrator who inflicts upon a victim serious physical injury, uses threats of death or kidnapping, uses a deadly weapon, or is aided and abetted by one or more persons.

Anal rape. An act of sexual penetration, however slight, of the anal opening of a person by the penis of another committed against the will and without the consent of that person by use of force, fear, or violence. Ejaculation is not required to complete an act of anal rape.

Anal intercourse. Any penetration, however slight, of the anal opening of one person by the penis of another. Ejaculation is not required to complete an act of anal intercourse.

Analingus. An act of oral intercourse involving the mouth and/or tongue of one person and the anal opening of another.

Attempted rape. In rape statistics, a report by a person of an uncompleted act of sexual penetration, however slight, of the oral, vaginal, or anal opening of a person committed against their will and without their consent by use of force, fear, or violence.

Authority rape. An act of sexual penetration, however slight, of the oral, vaginal, or anal opening of a person committed against their will and without their consent by use of force, fear, or violence by a person threatening to use the authority of a public official to arrest, incarcerate, or deport the victim.

Buggery. An outdated synonym for **Sodomy**.

Campus rape. An act of sexual penetration, however slight, of the oral, vaginal, or anal opening of a person committed against their will and without their consent by use of force, fear, or violence committed on school grounds or a college campus.

Carnal abuse. See **Sexual contact**.

Carnal copulation. See **Sexual intercourse**.

Carnal knowledge. See **Sexual intercourse**.

Child. A legal minor.

Child molestation. An immoral or indecent act of sexual contact done upon the person or in the presence of a legal minor with the intent to either gratify the sexual desire of the molester or the for the purpose of degrading or humiliating the victim.

Child rape. An act of sexual penetration, however slight, of the oral, vaginal, or anal opening of a legal minor.

Clergy rape. An act of sexual penetration, however slight, of the oral, vaginal, or anal opening of a person committed against their will and without their consent by use of force, fear, or violence committed by a member of the clergy while engaged in the pastoral counseling of the person when the counseling relationship was used to facilitate the sexual contact.

Coitus. See **Sexual intercourse.**

Coercion. See **Force.**

Consensual sex. A sex act entered into freely between two persons over the legal age of consent.

Community notification laws. State laws enacted to notify residents of a community that a convicted sex offender is to be released or paroled into their neighborhood.

Completed rape. An act of sexual penetration, however slight, of the oral, vaginal, or anal opening of a person committed against their will and without their consent by use of force, fear, or violence.

Compulsion. See **Forcible compulsion.**

Condom rape. An act of sexual penetration, however slight, of the oral, vaginal, or anal opening of a person committed against their will and without their consent by use of force, fear, or violence by a person who agrees to a request by a victim to use a condom to prevent either pregnancy or disease. The victim's request for the use of a condom does not constitute consent.

Consent. Positive cooperation by an adult in a sexual act pursuant to an exercise of free will. Actual words or conduct indicating freely given agreement to have sexual intercourse or sexual contact. The persons involved in a sexual act must do so freely and voluntarily and have knowledge of the nature of the act involved.

Copulation. See **Sexual intercourse.**

Corruption of a minor. See **Child rape.**

Crime against nature. See **Anal intercourse** and **Sodomy.**

Criminal sexual penetration. See **Rape.**

Crisis intervention. Post-rape assistance and counseling given to sexual violence victims to counter the physical, emotional, and psychological after-effects of rape, including: short-term crisis counseling; peer group support; liaison with police, prosecutors, and court personnel; and referrals to medical and legal services.

Cunnilingus. An act of oral intercourse involving the mouth and/or tongue of one person and the vagina of a female.

Custody rape. An act of sexual penetration, however slight, of the oral, vaginal, or anal opening of a person committed against their will and without their consent by use of force, fear, or violence by a person who has assumed the position of parent to a minor victim, or a person having custody, supervisory, or disciplinary authority of a victim of any age acting as an employee or agent of any private, charitable, or governmental institution, including hospitals and prisons.

DNA testing. "Genetic fingerprinting" of bodily fluids used in rape investigations and prosecutions.

Date rape. An act of sexual penetration, however slight, of the oral, vaginal, or anal opening of a person committed against their will and without their consent by use of force, fear, or violence by a person who is in a current dating relationship with the victim. A current dating relationship does not does not constitute sexual consent.

Day care rape. See **Child rape.**

Deadly force. In rape, the use of deadly force is justifiable by a rape victim only when that person believes that such force is immediately necessary for the purpose of protecting themselves against death, serious bodily injury, kidnapping, or sexual intercourse compelled by force or threat.

Deadly weapon. In rape, the use of any instrument or device designed primarily for use in inflicting death or injury upon a human being or anything capable of inflicting death or injury upon a human being. Deadly weapons include, but are not limited to, handguns, loaded or unloaded, electronic weapons, stun guns and tasers, chemical weapons, mace and pepper spray, and knives.

Deceitful rape. An act of sexual penetration, however slight, of the oral, vaginal, or anal opening of a person committed against their will and without their consent by use of force, fear, or violence by a person who intentionally deceives another as to the nature of the act, or who leads the victim to erroneously believe that the person is the victim's spouse. Deceit does not constitute sexual consent.

Deviate oral copulation. See **Analingus** and **Sodomy**.

Deviate sexual intercourse. An act of sexual gratification involving the sex organs of one person and the mouth or anal opening of another.

Disability rape. An act of sexual penetration, however slight, of the oral, vaginal, or anal opening of a person committed against their will and without their consent by use of force, fear, or violence committed against a person with a physical or mental disability.

Domestic rape. An act of sexual penetration, however slight, of the oral, vaginal, or anal opening of a person committed against their will and without their consent by use of force, fear, or violence by one family or household member against another. Family or household members include spouses, former spouses, adults related by blood or marriage, adults residing together, or persons having a child in common whether they are living together or not.

Duress. Direct or implied threats of force, violence, danger, or retaliation sufficient to coerce a person to perform an act which they otherwise would not consent to.

Ejaculation. Release of semen. Ejaculation is not necessary to complete an act of vaginal, oral, or anal rape.

Elder rape. See **Senior rape.**

Emission. See **Ejaculation.**

Exchange of bodily fluids. In rape, transmission, by sexual penetration, of the bodily fluids of one person to another.

Family rape. An act of sexual penetration, however slight, of the oral, vaginal, or anal opening of a person committed against their will and without their consent by use of force, fear, or violence by a family member, including natural or adoptive parents, siblings, or grandparents. Family members also include anyone who has resided in the victim's household continually for at least one year.

Fellatio. An act of oral intercourse involving the mouth and/or tongue of one person and the penis of a male.

Female sex organs. Vagina, Vulva, Labia Major, Labia Minora.

Finger rape. An act of sexual penetration, however slight, of the oral, vaginal, or anal opening of a person committed against their will and without their consent by use of force, fear, or violence by a person with either a finger or any other part of the human body except the mouth, tongue, or penis.

First degree murder. See **Rape and murder.**

First degree forcible sodomy. See **Aggravated rape.**

First degree rape. See **Aggravated rape.**

Felony. A serious criminal offense punishable by either death or imprisonment. The crimes of rape and forcible sodomy are, in all jurisdictions, felonies.

Felonious sexual assault. See **Rape.**

"Female of previously chaste character." The legal assumption that a rape victim is chaste and in no way responsible for being sexually assaulted.

Force. An overcoming of resistance causing submission by the exertion of greater physical size, strength, weight, or power or by physical restraint or physical confinement.

Forcibly ravish. See **Rape.**

Forcible compulsion. In rape, use of physical force or threat of force, or any combination thereof, expressed or implied, that either overcomes earnest resistance or places a person in fear of immediate death or serious physical injury or kidnapping to themselves or others.

Forcible sodomy. See **Anal rape.**

"Friend" rape. See **Acquaintance rape.**

Gangbang. See **Gang rape.**

Gang rape. An act of sexual penetration, however slight, of the oral, vaginal, or anal opening of a person committed against their will and without their consent by use of force, fear, or violence by multiple attackers.

Genital intercourse. See **Sexual intercourse** and **Vaginal sexual intercourse.**

Genitals. See **Female sex organs** and **Male sex organs.**

Guardian rape. An act of sexual penetration, however slight, of the oral, vaginal, or anal opening of a person committed against their will and without their consent by use of force, fear, or violence by a natural or adoptive parent, stepparent, legal guardian, legal custodian, foster parent, or anyone who, by virtue of a living arrangement, is placed in a position of authority or trust over a minor.

"Granny" rape. See **Senior rape.**

Great mental anguish. In rape, psychological or emotional damage that requires psychiatric or psychological treatment or care.

Gross sexual assault. See **Rape.**

Gross sexual imposition. See **Rape.**

HIV rape. An act of sexual penetration, however slight, of the oral, vaginal, or anal opening of a person committed against their will and without their consent by use of force, fear, or violence by a person aware of being infected with Human Immunodeficiency Virus (HIV).

Handicap rape. See **Disability rape.**

Health care rape. An act of sexual penetration, however slight, of the oral, vaginal, or anal opening of a person committed against their will and without their consent by use of force, fear, or violence committed by a health care practitioner, including physicians, psychologists, nurses, counselors, therapists, technicians, social workers, and other health care providers engaged in the treatment of illness, symptoms, or conditions, when the treatment or counseling relationship was used to facilitate the sexual contact.

Heterosexual rape. An act of sexual penetration, however slight, of the oral, vaginal, or anal opening of a person committed against their will and without their consent by use of force, fear, or violence perpetrated by a person of a different sex.

Homosexual rape. An act of sexual penetration, however slight, of the oral, vaginal, or anal opening of a person committed against their will and without their consent by use of force, fear, or violence perpetrated by a person of the same sex.

"Ignorance of age is no defense." A legal maxim that, in cases of statutory rape, neither belief by the perpetrator nor misrepresentation by the under-age victim as to the victim's true age is a defense in a criminal proceeding.

Inability to rape. A presumption in law, usually no longer in force, that a male under the age of fourteen years is physically incapable of committing rape or engaging in sexual intercourse.

Incapable of consent. In rape, a person who is physically helpless, mentally incapacitated, mentally defective, or under the age of consent.

Incest. An act of sexual penetration, however slight, of the oral, vaginal, or anal opening of a person committed against their will and without their consent by use of force, fear, or violence by a person who knows he is related either by blood or marriage as follows: father and daughter or stepdaughter, mother and son or stepson, brother and sister of the whole or half blood, grandparent and grandchild, aunt and nephew, or uncle and niece.

Infamous crime against nature. See **Anal intercourse, Analingus, Cunnilingus**, and **Fellatio**.

Intimate sexual contact. Contact of the intimate parts of one person to the intimate parts of another.

Intimate parts. The primary genital area, pubic region, sexual organs, anus, groin, inner thigh, buttocks, or breasts.

Indecent assault. See **Rape** and **Anal rape**.

Indecent liberties with a child. Any lewd fondling or touching of a child, or by a child, with the intent to arouse or to satisfy the sexual desire of either the child or the offender.

Kidnapping. The act of forcible abduction.

Lack of consent. Inability of consenting to a sexual act if one is under the age of consent, mentally defective, mentally incapacitated, or physically helpless.

Lewd or lascivious acts with a child. Any sexual contact with a child with the intent of arousing or gratifying the sexual desires of the perpetrator or the child.

Live-in rape. An act of sexual penetration, however slight, of the oral, vaginal, or anal opening of a person committed against their will and without their consent by use of force, fear, or violence by a person not legally married to but cohabiting with the victim.

Lust murder. Outmoded synonym for **Rape and murder.**

Male rape. An act of sexual penetration, however slight, of the oral or anal opening of a male committed by another against his will and without his consent by another male by use of force, fear, or violence for the purposes of sexual arousal, gratification, or abuse.

Male sex organ. The penis.

Marital rape. See **Spousal rape.**

Menace. Any threat by a rapist which shows an intention to inflict extreme pain, serious bodily harm, or death.

Mentally defective. In rape, a person suffering from a mental disease or defect which renders him or her substantially incapable of understanding the nature of his or her conduct or of resisting an act of sexual intercourse or of communicating an unwillingness to submit to the act. A person who is mentally defective is incapable of consent.

Mentally incapacitated. In rape, a person rendered temporarily incapable of understanding or controlling his or her conduct due to the influence of a narcotic or intoxicating substance administered to him or her without his or her consent and made incapable of resisting an act of sexual intercourse or of communicating an unwillingness to submit to the act. A person who is mentally incapacitated is incapable of consent.

Minor. A child under a stated statutory age.

Multiple attackers. See **Gang rape.**

Non-stranger rape. An act of sexual penetration, however slight, of the oral, vaginal, or anal opening of a person committed against their will and without their consent by use of force, fear, or violence by a person previously known to the victim.

Object rape. An act of sexual penetration, however slight, of the oral, vaginal, or anal opening of a person committed against their will and without their consent by use of force, fear, or violence by a person manipulating an inanimate object.

Oral copulation. Oral contact with the mouth and/or tongue of one person and the penis of another.

Oral sex. Oral contact with the mouth and/or tongue of one person and the penis, vagina, or anus of another person.

Personal injury. Bodily injury, mental anguish, chronic pain, pregnancy, disease, or loss or impairment of a sexual organ.

Physically helpless. In rape, a person who is, for any reason, physically unable to communicate unwillingness to act or physically to resist or flee. A person who is physically helpless is incapable of consent.

Playground rape. See **Child rape.**

Police rape. See **Authority rape.**

Preschool rape. See **Child rape.**

Prior sexual conduct. In rape prosecutions, opinion and reputation evidence on the specific prior sexual conduct of the rape victim before the rape, either with the accused or another, including use of contraceptives, living arrangement and life style, are generally irrelevant and inadmissible and no reference can be made to this prior sexual conduct in the presence of the jury.

Prison rape. An act of sexual penetration, however slight, of the oral, vaginal, or anal opening of a person committed against their will and without their consent by use of force, fear, or violence committed while incarcerated in a jail, prison, or penitentiary.

Psychotherapy rape. An act of sexual penetration, however slight, of the oral, vaginal, or anal opening of a person committed against their will and without their consent by use of force, fear, or violence by a practitioner engaged in the treatment or counseling of a mental or emotional illness, symptom, or condition, when the treatment or counseling relationship was used to facilitate the sexual contact.

Rape. An act of sexual penetration, however slight, of the oral, vaginal, or anal opening of a person committed against their will and without their consent by use of force, fear, or violence. Ejaculation is not required to complete an act of rape.

Rape and murder. A person commits murder in the first degree if, in the perpetration of any sexual assault, the victim is killed. First degree murder is punishable by life imprisonment with or without the possibility of parole or death.

Rape rates. In rape statistics, reported attempted and completed rapes for each 1,000 or 100,000 persons.

Rape recovery. The healing process from the emotional and psychological after-effects of rape.

Rape shield law. Law enacted to protect victims of rape from harassment, intimidation, psychological trauma, and/or unwarranted invasions of their privacy by prohibiting the disclosure of their identities to the public.

Rape trauma syndrome. Emotional and psychological after-effects of a rape.

Rapist. A person who commits an act of sexual penetration, however slight, of the oral, anal, or vaginal opening of a person committed against their will by use of force and violence, or by threats of immediate and great bodily harm, or threats of retaliation for the purpose of their own sexual arousal or gratification. Also called the accused, actor, attacker, offender, or perpetrator.

Ravish. See **Rape.**

Reported rape. In rape statistics, a report by a person of an attempted or completed act of sexual penetration, however slight, of the oral, vaginal, or anal opening of a person committed against their will and without their consent by use of force, fear, or violence.

Resistance. In rape prosecutions, resistance is any clear physical or verbal communication of lack of consent. Modern rape laws do not require that the victim physically resist force or threats of force to the utmost, or to resist if resistance would be futile or foolhardy. The victim need resist only to the extent that it is reasonably necessary to make the victim's refusal to consent known to the defendant. Force, fear, or threat alone is sufficient to show lack of consent.

Retaliation. Threats made by a rapist to kidnap, or inflict extreme pain, serious bodily injury, or death on either the victim or another.

"Second rape." Term used by rape victims to describe insensitive, unsympathetic, and/or hostile treatment by members of the law enforcement or criminal justice system.

Seduction by a teacher. See **Teacher rape.**

Senior rape. An act of sexual penetration, however slight, of the oral, vaginal, or anal opening of a person committed against their will and without their consent by use of force, fear, or violence when the victim is a person sixty-five years of age or older.

Senior sexual assault. See **Senior rape.**

Self-defense. See **Resistance.**

Serial rapist. See **Sexual predator.**

Serious physical injury. In rape, threats of, or use of, or attempts to use, great bodily harm or pain, permanent disability, or permanent disfigurement, to force submission.

Sex act. In rape, any sexual contact or act of sexual penetration between two persons, involving either the insertion of the penis into the vagina or anus, or contact between the genitals of one person and the genitals or anus of another person, or contact between the finger or hand of one person and the genitals or anus of another, or an artificial sexual organ or substitute object and the genitals or anus of another.

Sexual abuse. See **Sexual contact.**

Sexual assault. See **Rape.**

Sexual battery. See **Rape.**

Sexual contact. Any touching or fondling, either directly or indirectly, of the sexual or other intimate parts, done for the purpose of either gratifying the sexual desire of either party or for the purpose of degrading or humiliating the victim.

Sexual intercourse. Any penetration, however slight, of the vaginal opening by the penis. Emission of semen is not required to complete sexual intercourse.

Sexual intrusion. See **Object rape.**

Sexual misconduct. See **Rape.**

Sexual penetration. In rape, the forcible entry of the penis or finger or any object into the vagina, anus, or mouth of another. Any penetration, however slight, constitutes penetration. The depth of insertion is not relevant.

Sexual predator. A person committing more than one unlawful sexual offense upon the same or different victims.

Sexual violence. See **Rape.**

Sexually transmitted disease rape. See **STD Rape.**

Sodomy. Any penetration, however slight, into the anus of one person by the penis of another, or any oral/genital or oral/anal contact between persons. Emission of semen is not required to complete an act of sodomy.

Spouse. A person legally married to and living with another.

Spousal rape. An act of sexual penetration, however slight, of the oral, vaginal, or anal opening of a person committed against their will and without their consent by use of force, fear, or violence by a person legally married to and living with the victim.

Statutory age. See **Age of consent.**

Statutory rape. An act of sexual penetration, however slight, of the oral, vaginal, or anal opening of a person under the age of consent.

Statutory seduction. See **Statutory rape.**

STD rape. An act of sexual penetration, however slight, of the oral, vaginal, or anal opening of a person committed against their will and without their consent by use of force, fear, or violence by a person known to have a sexually transmitted venereal disease including, but not limited to, syphilis, gonorrhea, and genital herpes, or genital warts.

Stranger rape. An act of sexual penetration, however slight, of the oral, vaginal, or anal opening of a person committed against their will and without their consent by use of force, fear, or violence by a person unknown to the victim.

Subsequent sexual conduct. In rape prosecutions, opinion and reputation evidence on the specific subsequent sexual conduct of the rape victim after the rape, either with the accused or another, including use of contraceptives, living arrangement and life style, are generally irrelevant and inadmissible. No reference can be made to this subsequent sexual conduct in the presence of the jury.

Subsequent sexual offenses. A person convicted of second or third sexual offenses in the same or different states may be sentenced to increased penalties.

Teacher rape. An act of sexual penetration, however slight, of the oral, vaginal, or anal opening of a person committed against their will and without their consent by use of force, fear, or violence committed by a teacher, administrator, coach, or other person in authority, who uses the student/teacher relationship to facilitate the sexual contact.

Therapeutic exception. Any sexual penetration performed by a health care professional for medically recognized treatment or diagnostic purposes is excepted from the definitions of rape.

Threats. Use of intimidation and menace that force submission of a person to any sex act by causing fear of imminent death, kidnapping, suffocation, strangulation, disfigurement, extortion, retaliation, or serious physical injury to themselves or to another.

Under-age rapists. See **Inability to rape.**

Unlawful sexual intercourse. See **Rape.**

Unlawful sexual intercourse with a child. See **Child rape** and **Statutory rape.**

Unnatural sexual intercourse. See **Anal intercourse, Deviate sexual intercourse,** and **Sodomy.**

Use of force. Use of a dangerous instrument, actual physical force or violence, or superior physical strength against a victim.

Use of threats. Use against a victim of the threat, expressed or implied, of imminent death, serious bodily injury, extreme pain, or kidnapping.

Vaginal sexual intercourse. Any penetration, however slight, of the vagina by the penis. Emission of semen is not required to complete an act of vaginal sexual intercourse.

Victim. A person who is the object of a sexual crime of any degree. Also called complainant, or survivor.

Violation of a minor. See **Child rape.**

Violence. See **Force.**

Wheelchair rape. See **Disability rape**.

Wife rape. See **Spousal rape**.

Without consent. An act of sexual penetration where a person, with or without resisting, is coerced by the immediate use or threatened use of force against that person, or an act of sexual penetration where a person is incapable of consent by reason of mental disorder, drugs, alcohol, sleep, or any other similar impairment of understanding.

Workplace rape. An act of sexual penetration, however slight, of the oral, vaginal, or anal opening of a person committed against their will and without their consent by use of force, fear, or violence committed in the workplace.

America's Rape Hot Lines

Whatever they may be in public life, whatever their relations with men, in their relations with women, all men are rapists and that's all they are. They rape us with their eyes, their laws, and their codes.

Marilyn French
The Women's Room [1]

Between 110,000 and 140,000 rape attacks are *reported* in America every year.[2] As few as 625,000[3] to as many as 2,000,000[4] rape attacks may go *unreported* every year. Nice girls do get raped. So do their mothers, sisters, brothers, and friends. Where can the survivors of rape find help? A post-rape call to a police emergency "911" line is a very personal decision. A post-rape call to a -7273 (RAPE) or -4377 (HELP) crisis line is an equally personal decision.

America's Rape Hot Lines is a listing of the rape counseling and crisis intervention telephone hot lines serving nearly three hundred cities and towns - urban, suburban, and rural - in every state throughout the nation. Rape hot lines offer their services to adult rape and child sexual assault and incest victims, battered women, and their concerned families and friends. These services can include short-term crisis counseling, long-term peer group support, liaison with police, prosecutors, and court personnel, and referrals to needed medical/legal services. Their assistance can be life-saving.

Rape hot lines offering emergency and counseling services for rape survivors are almost always under-funded and mostly personned by community-based volunteers whose training and experience may vary. The publication of these numbers is not intended as an endorsement of their services. Every effort has been made to provide up-to-date telephone listings for *America's Rape Hot Lines*. (No addresses are provided to protect the privacy and security of rape victims and counselors alike.)

Telephone numbers are always changing. If any of these numbers do not answer or if your city or town is not listed, check your local Yellow Pages under "Rape" or "Sexual Assault Counseling and Prevention Services," or "Crisis Intervention Services," or call Directory Assistance: "411." You can also call your local public library's reference desk, your local hospital's emergency room or ob/gyn department, or your Police Department's Rape and Sex Crimes Unit.

America's Rape Hot Lines is an assistance and information resource for rape survivors and their families. Rape, incest, child molestation, or other sexual violence survivor organizations may exist in your community. Your local hot line will know. In the pages that follow you will find the telephone numbers for nearly three hundred rape crisis hot lines. Help is out there. *America's Rape Hot Lines* can help you find it.

[1]Marilyn French. *The Women's Room.* New York, NY: Summit Books, 1977.
[2]United States Justice Department. Bureau of Justice Statistics. *National Crime Victimization Survey.*
Federal Bureau of Investigation. *Population-at-Risk.*
Federal Bureau of Investigation. *Crime in America.*
[3]United States Senate. Judiciary Committee. *Violence Against Women.*
University of South Carolina. National Victim Center. *Rape in America.*
[4]United States Senate. Judiciary Committee. *The Response to Rape.*

America's Rape Hot Lines

NATIONAL DOMESTIC VIOLENCE HOTLINE:
800-799-SAFE

Akron, Ohio	(216)434-7273
Albany, New York	(518)447-7100
Albuquerque, New Mexico	(505)266-7711
Amarillo, Texas	(806)373-8022
Anaheim, California	(213)778-1000
Anchorage, Alaska	(907)276-7273
Antioch, California	(510)754-7273
Appleton, Wisconsin	(414)733-8119
Arlington, Texas	(817)927-5544
Asheville, North Carolina	(704)255-7576
Athens, Georgia	(706)353-1912
Atlanta, Georgia	(404)616-4861
Austin, Texas	(512)440-7273
Bakersfield, California	(805)398-1800
Baltimore, Maryland	(410)366-7273
Barre, Vermont	(802)223-7755
Baton Rouge, Louisiana	(504)383-7273
Beaufort, South Carolina	(803)525-6699
Beaumont, Texas	(409)835-3355
Bel Air, Maryland	(410)836-8430
Bellingham, Washington	(360)671-5714
Beloit, Wisconsin	(608)365-4440
Billings, Montana	(406)259-6506
Birmingham, Alabama	(205)323-7273
Bismarck, North Dakota	(701)222-8782
Boston, Massachusetts	(617)492-7273
Boulder, Colorado	(303)443-7300
Bowling Green, Kentucky	(502)782-5014
Branson, Missouri	(417)334-0149

Breckenridge, Minnesota	(218)643-6110
Bristol, Virginia	(703)466-2312
Brookings, South Dakota	(605)692-7233
Buffalo, New York	(716)834-3131
Carlisle, Pennsylvania	(717)258-4324
Cedar Rapids, Iowa	(319)363-5490
Charleston, Illinois	(217)348-7666
Charlotte, North Carolina	(704)375-9900
Charlottesville, Virginia	(804)295-7273
Cheyenne, Wyoming	(307)637-7233
Chicago, Illinois	(312)644-4357
Chico, California	(916)342-7273
Cincinnati, Ohio	(513)381-5610
Claremont, California	(909)626-4357
Clarksville, Tennessee	(615)647-3632
Cleveland, Ohio	(216)391-4357
Cocoa Beach, Florida	(407)784-4357
Coeur D'Alene, Idaho	(208)661-2522
Colorado Springs, Colorado	(719)444-7000
Columbus, Georgia	(706)327-3238
Columbus, Ohio	(614)221-4447
Corpus Christi, Texas	(800)886-7273
Dallas, Texas	(214)653-8740
Davenport, Iowa	(319)326-9191
Davis, California	(916)758-8400
Dayton, Ohio	(513)276-8400
Defiance, Ohio	(419)782-4906
Denver, Colorado	(303)329-9922
Des Moines, Iowa	(515)822-5752
Detroit, Michigan	(313)596-1950
Downers Grove, Illinois	(708)971-3927
Durham, North Carolina	(919)286-4546
East Lansing, Michigan	(517)337-1717

Eau Claire, Wisconsin	(715)838-7273
El Centro, California	(619)352-7273
Ellwood City, Pennsylvania	(412)752-2423
El Paso, Texas	(915)779-7130
Erie, Pennsylvania	(814)455-9414
Eureka, California	(707)445-2881
Evansville, Indiana	(812)424-7273
Fairfield, California	(707)422-7273
Fargo, North Dakota	(701)293-7273
Fayetteville, Arkansas	(501)443-2000
Fayetteville, North Carolina	(910)485-7273
Flint, Michigan	(810)766-7178
Fort Pierce, Florida	(407)465-1814
Fort Wayne, Indiana	(219)426-7273
Fort Worth, Texas	(817)927-2737
Fremont, California	(510)845-7273
Fresno, California	(209)222-7273
Garland, Texas	(800)886-7273
Geneva, New York	(315)781-2110
Glendale, California	(818)793-3385
Grafton, West Virginia	(304)265-6534
Grand Rapids, Michigan	(616)776-7273
Green Bay, Wisconsin	(414)436-8899
Greensboro, North Carolina	(919)273-7273
Hamilton, Ohio	(513)856-8618
Hampton, Virginia	(804)851-6333
Hartford, Connecticut	(203)522-6666
Hattiesburg, Mississippi	(601)264-7777
Hickory, North Carolina	(704)322-6011
Hillsboro, Oregon	(503)640-5311
Hilo, Hawaii	(808)935-0677
Honolulu, Hawaii	(808)524-7273
Houston, Texas	(800)886-7273

Huntington Beach, California	(714)831-9110
Huntsville, Alabama	(205)539-6161
Hutchinson, Kansas	(316)663-2522
Idaho Falls, Idaho	(208)522-7016
Indianapolis, Indiana	(317)632-7575
Indio, California	(619)568-9071
Iowa City, Iowa	(319)335-6001
Ithaca, New York	(607)273-5589
Jackson, Mississippi	(601)982-7273
Jacksonville, Florida	(904)355-7273
Jersey City, New Jersey	(201)451-7278
Johnson City, Tennessee	(615)928-6583
Kalamazoo, Michigan	(616)345-3036
Kansas City, Missouri	(816)531-0233
Kingwood, West Virginia	(304)329-1687
Kissimmee, Florida	(407)846-7255
Knoxville, Tennessee	(615)558-9040
Lafayette, Louisiana	(318)233-7273
Lancaster, California	(805)723-7273
Lancaster, Pennsylvania	(717)392-7273
Laredo, Texas	(210)724-1919
Las Vegas, Nevada	(702)366-1640
Las Cruces, New Mexico	(505)526-3437
Lawrence, Kansas	(913)841-2345
Lebanon, Pennsylvania	(717)272-5308
Lewiston, Maine	(207)784-5272
Lexington, Kentucky	(606)253-2511
Lincoln, Nebraska	(402)475-7273
Little Rock, Arkansas	(501)663-3334
Long Beach, California	(310)545-1230
Los Angeles, California	(310)392-8381
Louisville, Kentucky	(502)581-7273
Lowell, Massachusetts	(508)452-7721

Lubbock, Texas	(806)763-7273
Ludington, Minnesota	(616)845-5808
Lumberton, North Carolina	(910)739-6278
Madera, California	(209)661-7787
Madison, Wisconsin	(608)251-7273
Manitowoc, Wisconsin	(414)682-8869
Marietta, Ohio	(614)374-3111
Mattoon, Illinois	(217)234-6405
McAllen, Texas	(210)630-4878
Memphis, Tennessee	(901)528-2161
Meriden, Connecticut	(203)235-4444
Meridian, Mississippi	(601)482-2828
Mesa, Arizona	(602)784-1500
Metairie, Louisiana	(504)456-1734
Miami, Florida	(305)549-7273
Middletown, Connecticut	(203)346-7233
Milford, Connecticut	(203)878-1212
Milwaukee, Wisconsin	(414)937-5555
Minneapolis, Minnesota	(612)347-3161
Mobile, Alabama	(205)661-3001
Moline, Illinois	(309)797-1777
Monterey, California	(408)373-3955
Montgomery, Alabama	(205)279-7837
Morgantown, West Virginia	(304)292-5100
Moscow, Idaho	(208)885-6616
Myrtle Beach, South Carolina	(803)448-7273
Napa, California	(707)258-8000
Nashua, New Hampshire	(603)883-0377
Nashville, Tennessee	(615)259-9055
Newark, New Jersey	(201)733-7273
New Bern, North Carolina	(919)638-5995
New Britain, Connecticut	(203)223-1787
New Castle, Delaware	(302)577-2599

New Haven, Connecticut	(203)624-2273
New London, Connecticut	(203)442-4357
New Orleans, Louisiana	(504)888-8888
Newport News, Virginia	(804)245-0041
New York, New York	(212)577-7777
Norfolk, Virginia	(804)622-4300
Norristown, Pennsylvania	(610)277-5200
North Adams, Massachusetts	(413)664-6610
Norway, Maine	(207)743-9777
Oakland, California	(510)845-7273
Ocala, Florida	(904)622-8495
Oil City, Pennsylvania	(814)677-7273
Oklahoma City, Oklahoma	(405)943-7273
Omaha, Nebraska	(402)345-7273
Orange County, California	(714)957-2737
Orlando, Florida	(407)740-5408
Owensboro, Kentucky	(502)926-7273
Oxford, Mississippi	(601)234-9929
Paducah, Kentucky	(502)442-7273
Pasadena, California	(818)793-3385
Penn Yan, New York	(315)536-9654
Philadelphia, Pennsylvania	(215)985-3333
Phoenix, Arizona	(602)391-5055
Pine Bluff, Arkansas	(501)535-6770
Pittsburg, California	(510)439-7273
Pittsburgh, Pennsylvania	(412)765-2731
Pittsfield, Massachusetts	(413)442-6708
Pleasant Hill, California	(510)798-7273
Pocatello, Idaho	(208)232-9169
Portland, Maine	(207)774-3613
Portland, Oregon	(503)235-5333
Portsmouth, New Hampshire	(603)436-4107
Pottsville, Pennsylvania	(717)628-2965

Provo, Utah	(801)377-5500
Raleigh, North Carolina	(919)733-7974
Reading, Pennsylvania	(610)372-4065
Redlands, California	(909)335-8777
Richland, Washington	(509)946-2377
Richmond, Virginia	(804)643-0888
Ridgecrest, California	(619)375-0745
Riverside, California	(909)686-7273
Rochester, New York	(716)546-2777
Roswell, New Mexico	(505)623-1480
Sacramento, California	(916)371-1907
Saginaw, Michigan	(517)755-6565
Saint Cloud, Minnesota	(612)251-4357
St. Louis, Missouri	(314)531-2003
St. Paul, Minnesota	(617)777-1117
St. Petersburg, Florida	(813)530-7273
Salamanca, New York	(716)945-3970
Salem, North Carolina	(910)722-4457
Salisbury, North Carolina	(704)636-4718
Salt Lake City, Utah	(801)467-7273
San Antonio, Texas	(210)349-7273
San Diego, California	(619)233-3088
Sanford, Florida	(407)321-7273
San Francisco, California	(415)647-7273
San Jose, California	(408)287-3000
San Luis Obispo, California	(805)545-8888
San Marcos, Texas	(512)396-4357
San Pablo, California	(510)236-7273
Santa Ana, California	(714)836-7400
Santa Barbara, California	(805)963-6832
Santa Monica, California	(310)392-8381
Savannah, Georgia	(912)233-7273
Searcy, Arkansas	(501)268-1955

Seattle, Washington	(206)632-7273
Schenectady, New York	(518)374-5353
Shreveport, Louisiana	(318)222-0556
Slidell, Louisiana	(504)643-4259
Somerville, New Jersey	(908)526-8005
South Lake Tahoe, California	(916)544-4444
Spartanburg, South Carolina	(803)585-9569
Spokane, Washington	(509)624-7273
Springfield, Illinois	(217)744-2560
Springfield, Ohio	(513)325-3707
Stamford, Connecticut	(203)329-2929
Statesville, North Carolina	(704)872-3403
Stockton, California	(209)465-4997
Sumter, South Carolina	(803)773-4357
Syracuse, New York	(315)422-7273
Tacoma, Washington	(206)474-7273
Tampa, Florida	(813)238-7273
Toledo, Ohio	(419)241-7273
Torrington, Connecticut	(203)482-7133
Trenton, New Jersey	(609)588-7508
Tucson, Arizona	(602)372-7273
Tulsa, Oklahoma	(918)744-7273
Uniontown, Pennsylvania	(412)437-3737
Utica, New York	(315)733-0665
Vallejo, California	(707)644-7273
Valparaiso, Indiana	(219)465-3408
Vandalia, Illinois	(618)283-1414
Vero Beach, Florida	(407)569-0209
Virginia Beach, Virginia	(804)622-4300
Visalia, California	(209)732-7273
Wailuku, Hawaii	(808)242-4335
Warren, Ohio	(216)394-4060
Washington, DC	(202)333-7273

Waterbury, Connecticut	(203)753-3613
Waterloo, Iowa	(319)233-8484
Waterville, Maine	(207)872-0601
Wenatchee, Washington	(509)663-7446
Westminster, Maryland	(410)857-0900
Westport, Connecticut	(203)221-1616
Wheeling, West Virginia	(304)234-8519
Wichita, Kansas	(316)263-3002
Wilmington, Delaware	(302)761-9100
Wilmington, North Carolina	(910)392-7460
Woodbridge, Virginia	(703)680-7799
Worcester, Massachusetts	(508)791-9546
Yonkers, New York	(914)684-9877
Youngstown, Ohio	(216)782-3936
Zanesville, Ohio	(800)234-0038

THE MURDER REFERENCE
Everything You Never Wanted To Know About Murder In America

25,000 Americans were murdered in 1995. Every year since 1965 at least 10,000 Americans have been murdered. Almost every year since 1975 at least 20,000 Americans have been murdered. In only the first 5 years of this decade more than twice as many Americans were murdered than died in the entire Vietnam War.

The Murder Reference contains the actual laws, authoritative statistics, true crime studies, and headline murders of the twentieth century. **The Murder Reference** is the only all-in-one comprehensive resource for the study of murder in America. Library readers, writers, and researchers will find in **The Murder Reference**:

America's Murder Laws. Selected excerpts from current criminal murder laws of all fifty states carefully edited into <u>plain non-legal English</u> for the general adult reader.

Murder Statistics: The real "who, what, when, where" facts and figures of murder in America drawn from up-to-date and authoritative federal and state law enforcement sources.

Murder Ink: An annotated bibliography of hundreds of outstanding non-fiction "true crime" books including: Truman Capote's <u>In Cold Blood,</u> Vincent Bugliosi's <u>Helter Skelter,</u> and Norman Mailer's <u>Executioner's Song.</u>

A Century Of Murder: A complete chronology of headline murders from 1906's "Girl In The Red Velvet Swing" to 1994's Simpson/Goldman Murders.

EXCELLENT BOOKS ORDER FORM

(Please xerox this form so it will be available to other readers.)

Please send

Copy(ies)

_____ of THE RAPE REFERENCE @ $16.95 each

_____ of THE MURDER REFERENCE @ $16.95 each

_____ of LANDMARK DECISIONS @ $14.95 each

_____ of LANDMARK DECISIONS II @ $15.95 each

_____ of LANDMARK DECISIONS III @ $15.95 each

_____ of LANDMARK DECISIONS IV @ $15.95 each

_____ of LANDMARK DECISIONS V @ $16.95 each

_____ of ABORTION DECISIONS: THE 1970's @ $15.95 each

_____ of ABORTION DECISIONS: THE 1980's @ $15.95 each

_____ of ABORTION DECISIONS: THE 1990's @ $15.95 each

_____ of CIVIL RIGHTS DECISIONS: 19th CENTURY @ $16.95 ea.

_____ of CIVIL RIGHTS DECISIONS: 20th CENTURY @ $16.95 ea.

_____ of FREEDOM OF SPEECH DECISIONS @ $16.95 each

_____ of FREEDOM OF THE PRESS DECISIONS @ $16.95 each

_____ of FREEDOM OF RELIGION DECISIONS @ $16.95 each

_____ of THE ADA HANDBOOK @ $15.95 each

Name: _____

Address: _____

City: _____ **State:** _____ **Zip:** _____

Add $1 per book for shipping and handling

California residents add sales tax

OUR GUARANTEE: Any Excellent Book may be returned at any time for any reason and a full refund will be made.

Mail your check or money order to: Excellent Books, Post Office Box 927105, San Diego, California 92192-7105 or call/fax (619) 457-4895